DATE			

© THE BAKER & TAYLOR CO.

Administrator's Guide to an Individualized Performance Results Curriculum

WILLIAM E. STRADLEY

The Center for Applied Research in Education, Inc.

521 Fifth Avenue, New York, N.Y. 10017

Dedicated to
My Parents

© 1973 *BY*

The Center for Applied
Research in Education, Inc.

New York

Library of Congress Cataloging in Publication Data

Stradley, William E
    Administrator's guide to an individualized performance results curriculum.

    1. School management and organization--Handbooks, manuals, etc. 2. Curriculum planning. 3. Individualized instruction. 4. Educational innovations. I. Title.
LB2805.S77   371.2   73-7325
ISBN 0-87628-146-3

Printed in the United States of America

ABOUT THE AUTHOR

William E. Stradley has been an educator for 25 years. During this time, he has served as a teacher and an administrator at the elementary, middle, and senior high levels, and as an instructor of college graduate courses for teachers. Over the past seven years, he has been principal of Goddard Middle School, Littleton, Colorado, and also the supervising principal responsible for opening two new middle schools and developing their programs.

Mr. Stradley has written articles for a number of professional publications, including *Teacher, Instructor, Clearing House,* and the *California Teachers Journal.* He is also the author of two previous books, *Supervising Student Teachers* (Danville, Ill.: Interstate, 1968) and *A Practical Guide to the Middle School* (New York: Center for Applied Research in Education, Inc., 1971).

BUILDING A RESPONSIVE
EDUCATIONAL PROGRAM

Change must be accepted as a way of life in education. Though this idea has been accepted in philosophy by educators, it has not been consistently reflected in actual practice. Now, however, social and value forces are making it imperative that educators put into action the ideas they profess. This poses a problem because many traditional classroom and building instructional structures are not conducive to implementing the newer and different approaches demanded by constantly evolving social and value demands. Further, many staff members do not possess the singular skills needed to work within the new and different learning-oriented frameworks.

This book was written in the belief that demands on schools such as relevancy, accountability, performance results, and priorities identification are valid and, consequently, educators must develop and implement programming and functioning practices that are responsive to these valid demands. The book has been developed on the basis that educators must take a more active role in designing and managing programs. Thus, it describes ways they can assume more leadership in initiating programming and functioning change forces that will make learning experiences of more use to each student as he functions in a changing society.

In order to achieve a more responsive educational program, educators must start by looking at themselves and answering questions such as the following:

1. What are the characteristics of educational changes? How can we determine specific change effectiveness?
2. What new skills must teachers master in order to function within a change framework?
3. What are the necessary characteristics of the different learning frameworks needed by schools?
4. How can school staffs develop learner-oriented curricular structures?
5. How can teachers learn to initiate and manage directional forces?
6. How can the individual teacher prove how effective he is?

This book discusses these questions from the application standpoint, through the performance results curricular structure approach:

A performance results curriculum is a program structure that stresses the identification of specific learning needs and related instructional demands, and the development of individualized teacher and student operational emphases and patterns in terms of those needs and demands. Functioning success is determined by the performance levels an individual attains as he progresses through the identified curricular objectives. Subject matter is an instructional tool, not the primary basis for program structuring.

Administrator's Guide to an Individualized Performance Results Curriculum is written to help practicing school personnel answer questions such as the preceding ones, for themselves and for their patrons. The book has evolved as a result of my own experience in working with school staffs and serving as a consultant in the areas of performance results, individualized programming, differentiated staffing, open-ended program development, and staff development. Consequently, it stresses the practical approach.

Discussed in detail are major new demands and forces which call for:

- increasing staff and program accountability;
- organizing priorities in terms of transitory change situations;
- initiating and managing learning forces;
- developing operational structures and functioning patterns in terms of observable performance results;

The performance results curriculum uses the need-objective-performance-result sequence as the basic operational unit or module. A module is an identified instructional/learning stage, *not* a predetermined, arbitrary time unit. Each stage is developed in terms of learning needs and objectives, performance demands, and selected subject matter organized on the short course basis. Appendix 1 (p. 247) illustrates this basic module approach in a middle school social studies program.

- designing and re-designing learning programs that are action-oriented;
- developing assessment procedures that are consistent with new situations.

Serious consideration must be given to these new demands because the traditional structuring of the program of studies is no longer viable enough to incorporate curricular aspects pertaining to present and future learner needs and demands. In its place there must be an open-ended program structure that provides carefully identified "starting places" for the learners, that provides optional alternatives selection, that provides expanded progress routes with no arbitrarily imposed "end of program point," and that provides for student performance application.

I have found that educators, as they attempt to develop and implement such change characteristics as these in their total program structures, often tend to utilize traditional closed practices and procedures to develop open-ended programs. Because of the attendant conflicts and frustrations, they either abandon their efforts or modify the basic program idea until it assumes the characteristics that are consistent with the existing skill patterns possessed by the staff members involved. The result is merely an exercise in futility.

This book offers practical suggestions for developing and implementing open program structure aspects that incorporate continuous change characteristics as demanded by desired teacher-learner effectiveness. It describes specific techniques and methods for analyzing present staff practices and for developing consequent procedures and processes that will facilitate open-ended instructional planning and design, at both the building and classroom levels.

New situations bring about a need for consequent new skills and differing ways of functioning. Traditional skills, use levels, and performance patterns generally are not consistent with new forces and demands. Still, many school staffs attempt to implement new program structures without identifying the differences between present performance patterns and new performance demands. Building faculties can no longer expect to pacify the learners and the public simply by professing an interest in someone's idea, or by making an attempt to change some minor aspect of an existing program, and, at the same time, going about their daily activities in the same traditional way. The time is past when staff members can merely rework or retitle an existing aspect of the school program, and with change of name then forget about emerging new educational directions.

This book will help educators in their learning to identify trends and forces behind these new directions and in their development of new program frameworks that are consistent with the new situations evolving as a result of changing forces. It shows school personnel how to become initiators and managers of new ideas, as well as program unit modifiers. Processes are presented that will help teachers to:

- develop new skills, or activate their latent ones;
- work effectively in terms of recognizing and organizing priorities;
- develop and manage facilitating forces;
- design new program structures;
- identify and implement performance results objectives;
- develop methods that will enable staff members to determine accurately staff, learner, and program effectiveness.

The book provides detailed guidelines for school personnel to demonstrate their effectiveness. These guidelines show staff members how to become more concerned with teacher and learner performance within a continuing action framework in which the primary emphasis is on people, not on content and teacher-imposed classroom moves. Staff members are shown how to reassess their roles and responsibilities, their planning bases, and their own operational demands in terms of an action-framework that stresses revealed performance results by both teacher and learners.

Innovative program implementation attempts fail less because the basic idea is poor than because the involved staff members do not have, or were not given the opportunities to gain, the necessary operational skills to bring the program to fruition and to maintain performance effectiveness within the program functioning pattern demands. Innovation not only involves changes in programming; it also demands changes in staff functioning skills and patterns.

At the same time, these changes are providing demands and opportunities for school staffs to develop and implement new and different individual structures and operational patterns. Unless they recognize these new demands and take advantage of the expanding opportunities, the lack of paralleling change will result in instructional structures and staff functioning patterns being out of phase with learner needs and demands.

This book will help educators avoid such a situation because it details procedures they can use to become adept at generating, developing, and implementing ideas consistent with identified specific learning needs. It will help staff members learn how to plan and function in terms of performance results, how to recognize needed functioning levels related to differing framework performance patterns, and how to identify the singular methods, skills, and techniques demanded by the particular functioning framework they devise to use.

In addition, the book describes in detail new concepts related to program development, staff assignment and utilization, student scheduling, and teacher-student program evaluation techniques. These concepts are discussed from the implementation standpoint so that building staffs can readily see possible applications relating to existing building program frameworks. They are also discussed from the practical standpoints of teacher-student operational procedures and functioning patterns, using case examples drawn from my own experiences and experiences of other educators across the country.

Administrator's Guide to an Individualized Performance Results Curriculum was written by a school principal who has had 15 year's experience in developing and implementing innovative concepts within his own school assignments and within his experience as a consultant, author, and instructor of college graduate courses for educators. It is a result of his working with various groups of educators to develop ways and means of making teachers, students, and programs more effective.

William E. Stradley

CONTENTS

1. **Designing a Performance Results Curriculum . 21**

   Structuring the curricular framework . Identifying specific objectives . Shifting to a personal interaction emphasis . Using a module structure . Individual need scheduling . Programming advantages . Student scheduling in the modular curriculum . Developing broad course frameworks . Creating sequential module courses . Establishing individual objectives . Instructional programming

2. **Time Utilization and Student Performance . 45**

   Class scheduling . Staff scheduling . Determining teacher-need time . Flexible use of time . Planning time allotments . Time and management effectiveness . Example – Time management analysis . Developing an individualized progress chart . Example

3. **Structuring a Results-Oriented Program . 59**

   Identifying bases for individualized results . Setting transitional objectives . Determining performance results level . Procedures for evaluating performance level attainment . Developing the evaluative criteria framework . Determining instructional stopping points . How to modify the closed program structure . Example of open-ended programming methods . How to extend the results approach beyond the building level . Utilizing student appraisal options . How to staff for improved effectiveness

4. **Developing a Performance-oriented Staffing Framework . 92**

   Developing open staff roles and responsibilities . Staffing according to program functioning demands . Examples of support personnel utilization . How to improve administrative skills through open staffing . How to begin developing total staff performance objectives . Devising in-service activities for development of staff objectives . Developing teacher per-

4. Developing a Performance-oriented Staffing Framework *(Cont.)*

formance patterns according to program demands . Defining basic aspects of effective performance patterns . Factors affecting teacher delineation of action areas . Developing a program organizational chart

5. Teaching Emphasis for Performance Results . 122

Establishing an action strategy framework . Formulating action techniques . Changing the teacher role in parent-student conferencing . Improving teacher organizational efficiency . Establishing a performance data file . Increasing effectiveness through flexible staffing practices . Organizing for learning performance . Developing the basic learning structure . Utilizing performance contracting . Developing of student and teacher schedules . Student scheduling and class size . Improving the curriculum through student scheduling . Developing a progress appraisal system

6. Instructional Planning for Performance Results . 153

Using the learner as a basis for planning . Developing the teacher's management role . Design according to objectives and performance . Using teacher self-appraisal as a design determinant . Designing a classroom performance framework . How to use the flexible structure approach . Implementing the performance plan . Evaluation aspects of the instructional design . Using student progress as the basic appraisal criterion

7. Planning Bases for Performance Monitoring . 174

Identifying underlying forces affecting appraisal accuracy . Recognizing change as an appraisal factor . Developing continuous criteria . Identifying program functioning patterns and demands . Appraising and changing school's basic educational assumptions . Effective assessment and program functioning demands . Bases for developing success appraisal criteria . Bases for teacher performance monitoring . Developing a performance self-appraisal form . Individualizing performance assessment . Developing a staff appraisal system

8. Teacher Functioning in a Performance Results Program . 203

Resolving teacher-learner conflicts . Behavioral basis for instructional planning . Promoting a positive behavior of learning . Developing positive motivating forces . Curriculum development and student behavior . Keying change to observed behavior . Changing behavior expectations . Setting specific behavioral objectives . Managing a flexible learning environment . The teacher as a catalyst . Basing curriculum on behavior performance . Instructional structuring for results . Setting individual performance

8. Teacher Functioning in a Performance Results Program *(Cont.)*

goals . Personalized measurement and self-evaluation . Opportunities, alternatives, and decision-making . An example . Decision-making opportunities . Determining instructional management objectives . Personalizing education . Developing a team relationship

9. Performance Contracting and Performance Results . 231

Defining the role of commercial support firms . Identifying the contractual performance level . Staff responsibilities in performance contracting . Developing contractual objectives . Dovetailing staff and support agency functions . Examples of functioning area coordination . Determining operational effectiveness . Common contractual unit assessment criteria areas . Developing new teacher operational skills . Examples of departmental performance contracting . Specific examples of contract utilization . Performance contracting and curriculum improvement

Appendix I . 247

Appendix II . 254

Index . 262

1

DESIGNING A PERFORMANCE RESULTS CURRICULUM

An urgent problem facing educators today is that of developing programs that emphasize as end results the students' successful application of what they learn. To deal successfully with this problem, staff efforts must be directed toward applied learning usage, programming that provides for new courses and deletion of old courses according to changing student needs, individualized learning design, and curriculum development based on staff and learner-induced continuously changing learning conditions. This necessitates the development of new program design approaches.

One of the continuing problems inherent in many existing curricular structures is their structural inconsistency with what research says about human learning characteristics. The result of this inconsistency is never-ending concern about articulation and coordination of the various program aspects. Difficulties here cannot be realistically reduced, or solved, until efforts to articulate and coordinate the program are expanded to include student learning patterns. To facilitate this, the program structure itself must emphasize learning and curricular relationships. It cannot depend primarily on teacher functioning patterns and instructional stresses.

A school program should be developed in terms of the specifically identified reasons why the institution exists in a given community and in terms of what the school is expected to accomplish as learning results.

Identified reasons and expectations for Goddard Middle School in Littleton, Colorado, serve as a case in point.

Reasons	Expectations
1. To provide adequate opportunities for each student to learn how to function positively in the existing social structure	1. To have each student become proficient in interacting positively with differing groups of peers and adults
2. To help each student to learn how to become self-sufficient	2. To have each student become progressively more responsible for his own decision-making related to his performance in the school program
3. To provide each student directed guidance in his learning basic content and skills deemed important by the community	3. To provide each student opportunities to use in practical situations the skills and knowledge he has learned in his classes

From these reasons and expectations, the school philosophy and performance objectives can be identified and reduced to writing. The philosophy and performance emphases, then, determine the type of curricular structure used.

CLOSED TRADITIONAL STRUCTURE	OPEN-ENDED STRUCTURE
1. Student exposure to pre-determined teacher-selected content	1. Staff and student development and use of self-appraisal
2. Cognitive-based, teacher-oriented performance demand structure	2. Identification of satisfactory performance levels by both staff and learners

3. Standardized appraisal system concerned primarily with student's cognitive functioning levels

4. Student conformity to teacher functioning demands

3. Involvement of students in selection of learning activities

4. Implementation of a learner-oriented personalized classroom structure

STRUCTURING THE CURRICULAR FRAMEWORK

Basically, the program of instruction under any type of curricular structure must be developed in terms of the learner, if it is to be effective, though this is virtually impossible with a closed or rigid traditional structure. In the last analysis, it is the learner who determines this effectiveness. He continually accepts and rejects various aspects of instruction. His patterns of acceptance and rejection are going to affect greatly his patterns of learning. Learner functioning patterns, then, need to be developed in terms of the learner's priority needs and values as they relate to societal needs and values.

As an example, one teacher with whom the author worked was experiencing difficulty in his "low" math class because ten of his students felt that he "preached at them just like a parent, he was moody, and he spent too much time repeating the same thing over and over in class." They could also "get good grades just like anybody else." Because of these feelings, the students decided not to hand in homework. They also took turns coming to his class late.

Before this conflict could be resolved, the teacher had to re-establish personal interaction with the group, adjust his instruction to their stated feelings of capability, and become more aware of how the students defined a "good" teacher. From this, evolved a pattern of classroom demands both teacher and students accepted.

IDENTIFYING SPECIFIC OBJECTIVES

Program and individual teacher-learner objectives must be developed within these conceptual frameworks. This involves careful consideration of the types of courses included in the curriculum as well as the types of expected performance behavior.

The selection, inclusion, and consequent development of course content is determined by the identification and priority classification of those commonly quoted, but less often consciously implemented, concepts of cognitive, affective, and psycho-motor domains and "education of the whole child," physically, mentally, emotionally, and socially. If the total program and sub-program objectives are geared to these bases, it is only consistent to develop overall curricular and specific teacher-learner performance objectives in terms of specific, changing needs. Course selection and development, then, must be done in terms of these stated program objectives.

Some examples of these teacher-learner performance objectives are:

1. Identification of present learner functioning levels on the content and program continua and anticipated functioning levels the student ' will attain at end of a given period of time
2. Identification of the specific new learning skills and functioning patterns the student will master in order to attain his desired continua positions
3. Determination of levels of emphases the teacher-learner team will place on each of the learning domains
4. Determination of the expected changes in learning demands of the student as he progresses through continua phases
5. Identification of the progressively high functioning demands expected as the student progresses through an identified learning module
6. Identification of specific areas in which the teacher will be less needed by the student

Course leveling and sequencing, consequently, must be done with the personal, content, program, and change continua in mind. These continua are separate, yet interacting, in terms of the learning effectiveness that takes place. As a result, course development, leveling, and sequencing must also be done with this in mind. Generally, course development dovetailing the program and content continua poses no real problem in curriculum development. It is the development and dovetailing of the personal learner and change continua that pose problems for the staff, and, as a result, are often ignored by the teachers, but not by the students. Herein, conflict evolves.

Typical Continua Characteristics

Learner	*Change*
Functioning patterns	Identified student change vs. actual student change
Attitude changes due to maturation stages	Identified expected performance pattern changes in program structure
Personal objectives and values	Variations in teacher reactions to student actions
Interest conflicts	Changes emphases in cognitive and affective domains

SHIFTING TO A PERSONAL INTERACTION EMPHASIS

Identifying, dovetailing, and integrating these various levels of continua in the learning program demand a change of emphasis in the functioning patterns of the school staff—from a content structure-oriented emphasis to a personal interaction emphasis. It necessitates not only the addition of special need courses but also teachers and counselors who know courses, course sequences, and individual student special needs well enough to plug in courses according to evolving student need. The types of courses that could be particularly adaptive here are the skills courses considered as prerequisites to content classes, special courses such as group guidance, social interaction, individual adjustment, career counseling, and independent study. Students in this structured framework could schedule classes more according to needs change rather than in terms of traditional time allotments.

Examples of these special need courses are:

Basic math skills
Group guidance
Science laboratory skill development
Spelling/vocabulary
Study skills
Orientation to work program assignments
Classes pertaining to:
  peer interaction
  personal/social changes
  development of effective learning patterns

This approach emphasizes the flexibility needed in terms of changing student need; it is a dovetailing of the personal and change continua within the broader framework of the program continuum. It also works within the content continuum because of the scope and sequence satellite areas that affect the level of student performance within the content area. This emphasis on flexibility and need also provide an instructional framework that enables, and even forces, the staff member to function in a parallel fashion. The traditional inflexible teacher cannot be effective in this program structure; but, then, he is not effective, from the learner's relevancy standpoint, in other frameworks either.

USING A MODULE STRUCTURE

The module curricular concept stresses the short course unit as the basis for curriculum structure. It involves the breaking down of traditional course divisions and content into varying numbers of sub-units that, taken as a whole, extend beyond the typical subject matter frameworks. These sub-units are developed at various levels of student performance expectation and progress paces. They are also developed in sequence so that there are close parallels between skill level courses and the content courses, and between the differing skills courses and the various content courses.

Goddard Middle School in Colorado uses the short course unit structure as a basis of its program. Because individualization and personalization of instruction are important aspects of the program, the module curricular concept is considered essential. Such schedules as the following are developed within this school's framework of instruction.

Sample Student Module Course Schedules for Two Quarters

Session I

Student A	Student B
Period 1—Science Lab Skills Development	Period 1—Independent Science Lab
2—Basic Math Fundamentals	2—Basketball Fundamentals
3—Minor Sports	3—Readings in Epic Poetry
4—Small Appliance Repair	4—Community Value Structure
5—Local Government Structure	5—Computer Programs
6—Reading the Newspaper	6—Career Education

Session II

Period 1—Introduction to
   Fundamentals
   of Electricity
   2—Math/Woodshop Inter-
   /3 disciplinary Class
   4—Wrestling

   5—Group Guidance

   6—Reading the Magazine

Period 1—Independent Science
   Lab Study

   2—Computer Programming
   3—Basketball Team Play
   4—Writing the Research
      Paper
   5—Personal and Social
      Change
   6—Participation in
      School-City-Library
      Program

INDIVIDUAL NEED SCHEDULING

The modular unit structure facilitates individual student personal need scheduling by providing a wider selection of leveled course selections from which the teacher and student can select in terms of the specific present and anticipated needs of the learner. Selected course units can be completed at individual student pace and others added according to need. Because of the short, concentrated course emphasis, specific units can be developed and utilized according to changes in learner need and interest emphasis. In this way, time is used as a variable rather than as one constant unit factor against which, supposedly, achievement is measured.

Examples of the flexibility of this structure is evident when it is compared to a traditional programing approach. Arapahoe County School District Number Six, in suburban Denver, uses the variable scheduling framework in its three high schools. These schools' course offerings provide teacher-learner flexibility such as the following examples.

Since the learning opportunity structure is developed in terms of learner need, student progress appraisal can more easily be determined in terms of performance. When each course is based, sequentially, on specific objective achievement, progress can be appraised on actual applied performance rather than on arbitrarily identified and subjectively interpreted assumptive criteria. The emphasis here is on appraisal of revealed performance of the learner, and indirectly of the teacher, because it is revealed as

SAMPLE MODULAR UNIT SCHEDULE

(Changed as needed)

American History

1. Major Battles of World War II
2. U.S. Constitution
3. Social Science Study Skills
4. Study of American History through Literary Selections
5. Independent Study
6. Geographical Influences
7. Personal Value Changes

American Literature

1. Study Skills
2. Political Influences
3. History through Magazines
4. The Future as Seen in Literature
5. Short Course in Grammar
6. Readings for Special Purposes

Flexibility

1. Selection of units according to performance levels
2. Time allotment according to needs
3. Selectivity for basic requirements
4. Student involved in course content determination
5. Selections made according to specific teacher/learner objectives

SAMPLE TRADITIONAL SCHEDULE

(Full year)

American History
American Literature
Physical Education
Biology
Woodshop
General Math

Standardization

1. Time demands predetermined
2. Teacher selection of unit topics and order of learning
3. Arbitrary content coverage
4. Little or no student input relative to learning demands
5. District-set objectives of primary importance

opposed to vague traditional appraisal criteria such as conduct, working to capacity, turning in homework assignments, ad infinitum.

The individual courses can be developed more in tune with learner demands because performance objectives are developed sequentially in terms of shorter units of time and in terms of shorter, more specific learning demand spans. A satellite value here is that the course time units correspond more closely with the time limits within which students can be expected to maintain high levels of interest and concentration relative to a given subject emphasis.

An argument can be advanced that this parallels the traditional unit approach to a year's time spent in a given class. The major differences, however, are that in the short course approach, the more vague "yearly objectives" are broken down into more specific sub-objectives, student interest can be more easily maintained over a shorter period of time, and a change in short course emphasis, topics, and approaches offers variation in both teacher and learner patterns.

PROGRAMMING ADVANTAGES

Goddard Middle School's program structure facilitates scheduling to student needs, since the modular framework provides for the inclusion of various levels of courses that will enable the teacher to concentrate on student weaknesses by working through his strengths. This can be done, for example, by structuring specific courses that concentrate on the singular skills a student is lacking but will need when he begins study in a particular content area. The advantages here are that the student, once he has gained the necessary skills, can approach the content study in a more positive manner; emphasis can be placed on content study rather than diluted emphases on skill need and content demand at the same time, and student schedules can be changed more readily as learner progress is made.

The modular curriculum also facilitates the cycling of courses and learning opportunities. Students vary in their time requirements for learning given skills and for content. Pupils also vary in the extent to which they can retain this learning. Within the traditional structure, there is little, or no, opportunity for individual students to gain reinforcing instruction as needed. Modular structuring enables the school staff to recycle a student through individual skill or content classes or a series of sequential skill classes, for example, as his skill-use levels reveal the need. There is no resulting failure here, but instead, a reestablishment of projected time allotments according to objectives and degrees of accomplishment.

Open personal needs classes can also be scheduled for individuals and groups of individuals in the same manner. These

Student Needs	Student Strengths	Courses/Techniques
1. Improve reading skills	1. Good listener	1. Elementary electronics
2. Improve interest in reading	2. Interest in working with hands	2. Following directions in building a code practice set
	3. Amateur-radio-hobby	3. Draw a diagram of a self-selected circuit and write complete directions for constructing

II.

1. Improve skills in working with fractions	1. Likes to work with wood	1. Woodshop/math team application
	2. Revealed some skill in drawing	2. Apply identified math skills in shop
		3. Use woodshop terminology, and examples in math class
		4. Math special help class
		5. Hand skill oriented objectives

open-need classes very easily could be considered as "required" courses, through the guidance and counseling approach, for students having problems that affect their functioning within the school demands and are within the help capabilities of the staff members. Personalized, individualized scheduling, through this approach, becomes an established mode of operation, rather than an exception.

The open personal needs classes at Goddard Middle School relate to such areas as:

Emotional problems
Chronic behavior and failure situations

Need for short-term tutoring help

Room and change of pace for students' having common adjustment problems

Individual and small group value conflicts

Other areas in which a given student, or group of students feel a need to "talk things over" with staff members or support personnel

STUDENT SCHEDULING IN THE MODULAR CURRICULUM

Generally speaking, school programs are developed in terms of requireds and electives. Students then, are expected to adapt their needs and interests to them. Following these adaptations, students are expected to develop self-satisfying learning schedules. A primary problem here is that the curricular structure is developed in terms of specialized courses as identified by clearly divided subject matter lines that are not akin to the broader personal factors affecting learner needs and demands. Yet, school people, elementary through university, persist in perpetuating this dichotomy.

The following situation with which the author had to deal is a typical case in point.

Student: a boy sixteen years old who was not considered a "good student," who had a serious reading problem, had few friends, possessed a quietly resistive attitude toward formal classroom demands, liked to work with his hands.

Original Class Schedule	*Revised Class Schedule*
English	Reading Skill
U.S. History	Physical Education
Physical Education	Special Math Skills
General Math	U.S. History
General Business	A-V Student Assistant
Earth Science	Shop

Primary Activities	*Primary Activities*
Traditional Academic	Reading and Math geared to specific functioning levels and problems in electronics
	Shop and Student Assistant geared to his primary interests, and skills, in electronics

Outcome: Because of change in learning-functioning demands and the interest of the A-V coordinator, this boy assumed a major responsibility for repairing A-V equipment, providing maintenance for the stage audio unit, and designing some individual earphone hookups for the language classes. These activities served as resource and reinforcement areas for his work.

This boy went on to the high school with passing grades.

DEVELOPING BROAD COURSE FRAMEWORKS

Whenever an individual desires to bring about change in a structure, he must devote time and energy to overcoming the varying degrees and various areas of inertia inherent in the organization. Students face this same dilemma when they attempt to develop their class schedules within the conflict framework of sterile program requireds and electives. To avoid this result and to concentrate on learner needs and relevancy, broader course frameworks should be developed so that specific student needs and interests can be built into course offerings. These needs and interest aspects should dovetail with content emphases. Of consequence, would be the building into the course such aspects as relevancy, learner accountability, and interest motivation. There should, also, be built in controversial topics, topics beyond the existing singular skills and interests of individual teachers, for this can also be a motivating device for them.

Once the broader instructional-learning divisions of the curriculum framework are identified and reduced to written details, then the broader objectives relating directly to these divisions can be developed. These, of course, should pertain to what the learners will be expected to learn, how they will function, and what they will be able to do with the knowledge and skills they have gained as a result of participating in the identified educational endeavors. By extension, these objectives will, in a way, describe singular characteristics of the students completing the self-prescribed and staff-prescribed programs of study.

The following example, though certainly not intended to be complete, gives the reader a good idea of a procedure for developing a broader instructional learning framework within which the school staff can develop more specific course offerings and outlines.

Broad Instructional-Learning

1. Common learnings—academic areas judged basic by the local community
2. Vocational—talent development, learning of job skills, working with others
3. Personal interest—self-improvement, avocational pursuits, widening of experiences
4. Social/emotional development—values, decision-making self-direction
5. Recreational—leisure time pursuits, health, safety, and self-preservation

Objectives	*Courses and experiences-related to*
Expected to learn	
1. (a) Fluent in use of native language	1. Reading, writing, speaking skills
(b) Function in terms of his society in social and value system	2. Development of modes of functioning in, and understanding of, local, national, global social structures
(c) Mastery of basic computational and science skills fundamental to his participation in a technological society	3. Learning and applying technological skills and knowledge
(d) Positive social interaction	4. Group participation, human relations
2. (a) Capability of successfully using native ability	1. Career education
(b) Becoming self-sufficient	2. Independent and group directed areas of endeavor
(c) Contributing to group	3. Development of specialty skills—art, music, linguistics
(d) Recognizing areas of potential economic success	4. Exploration and work experiences

3. (a) Broadening scope of   1. Personal care and hygiene
        intellectual interests
   (b) Development of   2. Cultural arts
        social graces
   (c) Development of   3. Sociological foundations
        self-satisfying pat-
        terns of living
   (d) Improvement of life   4. Avocational interests
        style

4. (a) Development of   1. Group guidance
        socially acceptable
        modes of behavior
   (b) Deal satisfactorily   2. Value structure development
        with conflicts
   (c) Adjust to changing   3. Assumption of responsibility decision-mak-
        situations   ing, and self-direction
   (d) Responsible for
        own actions

5. (a) Capability for man-   1. Independent study projects
        aging own time
   (b) Care of mental and   2. Individual and team sports
        physical health for
        longer life
   (c) Development of   3. Social and physical development
        hobbies and second-
        ary vocations
   (d) Organization of per-
        sonal life

   These broader objectives must be developed in the same manner
as are the instructional-learning divisions. That is, if there is an
overlapping of division emphases, if there is a sequential, prerequisite division structure, if there is a leveling of divisions
according to varying student groupings, then these should be
reflected in the division objectives. These objectives of each
division should, also, be open-ended enough to facilitate the
adding to them, without major changes, the varied objectives of
the individual students working within the demands of a particular
division.

CREATING SEQUENTIAL MODULE COURSES

Following this, then, the staff can devote its attention and efforts to the development of sequential module courses within the division frameworks. These courses should be written from the basic standpoints of inter-division and intra-division sequences, by levels and areas of need-emphases in terms of skills, content, and the various support levels needed within the confines of each particular school-need situation. In addition, these module courses will need to be developed with the specific characteristics and needs of the student, change, content, and overall program continua in mind.

Within the various sub-units of content and skills, courses must be so developed that various learning approaches and learner achievement levels are identified. Courses must also be developed in terms of sequential progress toward the division and total program results objectives. With these requirements in mind, inter-disciplinary courses with rather similar performance goals can be developed from such specific aspects as the various domain levels, social and emotional emphases, and the overlapping, reinforcing needs aspects common to the various divisions.

The following brief outline of a sample middle level science series, paralleling those developed at Goddard Middle School, illustrates the needed continuity pertaining to content, learning approaches, and performance expectations.

Level I–Development of Laboratory Skills

Learning approach:

1. The student will become familiar with the techniques and procedures of working in the science laboratory.
2. He will be able to identify and become familiar with the uses of elementary equipment related to electricity.

Achievement level:

Every student will, by the end of the course, be able to use this equipment in circuitry testing at least five times without instructor assistance. Every student will demonstrate that he is ready to enroll in Elementary Electricity by

    a. his accuracy in use of equipment

b. his basic knowledge of test equipment

c. his application of rules regarding personal safety and care of equipment.

Level II—Elementary Electricity

Learning approach:

The student will spend most of his time working with equipment, in building and testing elementary circuits. The teacher will devote most of his time to individual help and demonstration. Emphasis will be on following directions to attain specified results.

Achievement level:

Every student will demonstrate his knowledge of electricity by constructing correctly four out of five circuits.

Application:

Every student will select from the following minimum list or develop his own equivalent projects.

1. Electric magnet
2. Relay circuit
3. Code practice oscillator
4. A series and a parallel light circuit
5. Build a battery and prove its energy through it lighting a bulb

Level III—Electricity and Communications

Learning approach:

The students will explore the use of electricity in communications and the construction of the radio transmitter, the television receiver, the teletype, and the computer. They will visit a radio/TV station, and a business concern possessing a computer.

Achievement Level and Application:

1. Every student will build an elementary radio circuit, explain orally, or in writing how a TV and teletype work with 80 percent accuracy, and discuss orally, or in writing, the basic functioning of a computer of his choice, with 60 percent accuracy.
2. In small group work, each group will meet with two persons from the electronics industry to discuss two of the four types of communicators.

Along with the development of the module units of learning, the school staff should develop corresponding diagnostic methods and instruments that will identify specific areas oɪ student weaknesses and strengths. These tools should, to be useful to both teacher and student, pertain to such specifics as content, skills, possible program continuum placement, and student self-evaluation in terms of his personal objective expectations and possibilities of satisfactory sub-unit completion.

These diagnostic methods must be developed in terms of the specific course demands. For the above course, Electricity and Communications, for example, diagnostic emphases include

1. Understanding of, and working with, abstractions
2. Skills in group interaction involving both peers and adults
3. Capabilities of building a completed working model from a schematic
4. Problem solving

ESTABLISHING INDIVIDUAL OBJECTIVES

Once this learner-oriented structure is established, students can then analyze their own needs and interests, and from this analysis, begin to formulate their individual educational and personal objectives. In effect, the only real limitations imposed on the student, other than those he imposes on himself, are the limitations evolving as a result of staff talents, individual and collective, experiences, and motivation, the limitations of facilities, materials, and equipment, and overall program balance. Program balance here means the extent to which the curriculum reflects the general needs of the entire student body and community values. Financing plays an important role here, of course.

The author has found from personal experience with open-ended programming that reduction of unnecessary teacher end program restrictions placed on the student results in an improvement in student functioning. Evidence of improvement has been observed in the specific areas of attitude, assumption of responsibility, desire to apply in practical situations skills and knowledge learned, and identification of learner purposes.

Following are examples of student objectives written by students in ninth-grade mathematics and social studies classes.

Mathematics:

1. To use multiplication, division, subtraction, and addition well enough to hold my job in the drug store
2. To know how to budget expenses and manage my money because I will be spending the summer away from home and I will be responsible for making my monthly allowances last. I don't want to be broke the last two weeks of the month
3. I plan to go into engineering. I know that I will have to learn everything I can in algebra this year
4. I'm tired of being in a low math class. I want to pass these tests so I can move into a higher level and learn something different
5. I want to take this algebra course because I want to take Computer I and I have to have algebra first

Social Studies:

1. Since the course is required, my main purpose is to get good grades to please my parents
2. Our family travels during the summer. In social studies, I like to study about the countries we are planning to visit
3. I can vote when I am 18. I feel I need to know more about public issues and to learn how to look at all sides of a question. I need to start learning how to do that now
4. I want to know more about why people in other countries live and act the way they do. In social studies, we discuss these reasons

Student objectives are developed not only on the bases of personal desires for the future, but also on the bases of present curricular strengths and deficits as revealed by self-evaluation and diagnostic testing. Once these areas and aspects have been identified as realistic for each student, he can work closely with his assigned counselor and faculty advisor to implement a sequential program of study that insures a dovetailing of objectives and study endeavors.

Ideally, parents should also be involved in the regularly scheduled student-counselor-advisor conferences (see Figure 1-1). From the practical standpoint, however, most parents do not make the effort to be actively involved over an extended period of time.

The student-counselor-parent-advisor team approach is mentioned here because this author has utilized it and found that it does greatly facilitate personalization of instruction and, at the same time, plays an important role in public relations. However,

Figure 1-1

Goddard Middle School

A Student-Counselor-Parent-Advisor
Team Structure

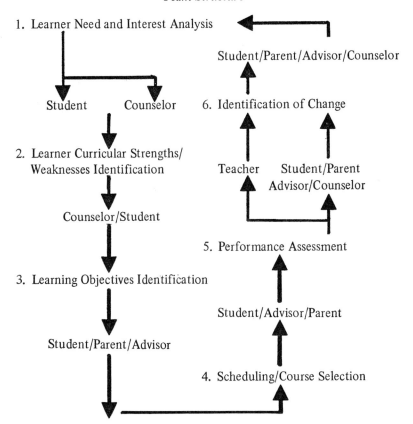

1. Learner Need and Interest Analysis

Student/Parent/Advisor/Counselor

Student   Counselor   6. Identification of Change

2. Learner Curricular Strengths/
   Weaknesses Identification   Teacher   Student/Parent
                                                     Advisor/Counselor

Counselor/Student

                                        5. Performance Assessment

3. Learning Objectives Identification

                                        Student/Advisor/Parent

Student/Parent/Advisor

                                        4. Scheduling/Course Selection

whether or not a school staff uses this approach or some other approach is immaterial. The important thing is that staff functioning procedures within the module structure are consistent with the objectives of the total program.

A specific case in which the author was involved pertains to a ninth-grade student who transferred to the school from another state. He had failing grades on his transcript, was mature in terms of his new peers, and did not want to continue his schooling. Following is a summary of the steps taken.

I. Learner Needs/Interests Strengths/Weaknesses (Student-Counselor)	1. Wanted to be with students his own size and age 2. Did not want to repeat the grade 3. Needed remedial work in math and English 4. Could function in practical arts areas
II. Learning Objectives (Student-Parent-Advisor)	1. To get a job as a carpenter's helper 2. To learn to read building plans 3. To use math needed "to build things" 4. To go to the high school rather than the middle school

III. Scheduling
(Student-Parent-Advisor)
	1. Placed on a half-day schedule
	    Remedial Reading
	    Business Math
	    Shop
	    Physical Education
	
	2. Made arrangements for the student to be transferred to the high school at the semester, pending satisfactory performance

IV. Performance and Change Assessment
 	
(Student-Parent-Teachers-Counselor-Advisor)
	1. In terms of desire to transfer to the high school, his efforts revealed
	
	    1. reading at eighth-grade level
	    2. evidence of math use related to shop project figuring
	    3. could not function successfully with less mature students

V. Decision (Student-Parent-Teachers-Counselor-Advisor)	Transferred the student to the high school at the end of the first semester

Once both student objectives, and consequent teacher objectives, have been developed, the learner and his instructional advisors can sit down together to analyze his needs, and, then, to look at course offerings in terms of these needs. Within the wide variety of courses offered, this team can match the specific emphasis courses with student need and interest. Depending upon the identified learning priorities, the student course selection can be flexible enough to schedule for a given student mostly skill level courses, mostly content level courses, or any combination of these.

This approach is particularly adaptable to specific short term student needs because of the length of module courses, and because of the consequent course unit adaptability to changing learner need emphases. Since learning unit selection is made in terms of identified needs, and written learning objectives, progress along the various continua can be kept at the primary emphasis level and content/skills emphases do not tend to become ends in themselves. Organizational framework, in this respect, tends to be a deterrent to this attrition effect.

Emphasis on learner progress necessitates both the teacher's and the learner's planning beyond the implementing of a program based on present need and interest demands. Consequently, the instructor-learner team needs to project student functioning demands and patterns in terms of continua phases and the related sequenced performance objectives. An emphasis on continuity here requires a corresponding emphasis on learning unit articulation. These units can be developed in terms of continuity and articulation, but if they are not scheduled for, and with the student, in the same manner, the traditional learning gaps still exist.

It is essential that both teacher and learner, as well as parents, spend some time programming for the immediate future. They must develop the skills necessary for relatively accurate forecasts of the learner's next program needs and continua stage locations. As they do this, both the teacher and the learner must select module course units in terms of probable blocks; that is, they need to identify sequential modules in series of three to four units. This procedure also helps learner and instructor plan along lines consistent with the identified broader goals and objectives and to plan more consistent appraisal techniques. This also helps maintain continuity and articulation between course units and between major subject matter divisions.

INSTRUCTIONAL PROGRAMMING

At the instructional level, the utilization of module series encourages departmental and individual teacher objectives planning and course development interaction. Because of short-term need emphasis, consequent module unit changes, and over-lapping discipline skill needs, it is necessary for teachers in differing content areas to be involved in the identifying of the learner's module series. An important consequent result here is the breaking down, or at least the narrowing, of subject matter divisions. Multiple curricular resources and teacher talents are unified for the development of a common program for an individual student. There is, then, the tendency for staff members to view staff offerings as selective tools to be used as learner needs and demands materialize. Instead of an emphasis on isolated curricular parts, there is more of a tendency on the parts of both teacher and student to view curriculum as a single support entity.

Student Needs	Teaching Areas	Module Courses
I. Improving self-confidence and group participation.	1. Speech and Drama 2. Gymnastics 3. Choir	1. Public speaking 2. Folk Singing 3. Writing for publication 4. Physical conditioning
II. Improving capability of working with fractions.	1. Industrial Arts 2. Auto Mechanics 3. Mathematics 4. Home Economics	1. Special Math help 2. Beginning Drawing 3. Engine Knowledge 4. Boy's Cooking

The utilization of unit series also facilitates the mechanical functioning of the modular curriculum. Because of the planning of sequence and series according to expected learner change, flexibility is built in, lessening the need for a constant shuffling of a student's total schedule to facilitate one identified need change.

The design of the performance results curriculum must stress effective functioning of the individual student and the individual staff member. The structure is developed in terms of short time units to maintain the curricular flexibility that is necessary to keep the overall school program structure responsive to the changing functioning needs and levels of the learners. The performance results curriculum is an ongoing structural process because it must be continuously changed as the students progress from one need/demand level to another.

Some Action Guidelines

Program:

1. The performance results curriculum emphasizes programming for student learning application. It also emphasizes programming for effective teacher functioning. Consequently, the program demands must be developed in terms of continuously changing teaching conditions as well as learning conditions. Static instructional demands will result in unchanging learning demands.
2. Course selection and development will determine the overall program emphasis. Courses, then, must always be developed in terms of the basic program objectives. Progressive courses should reveal increasing student functioning responsibility and lessening teacher dominance.
3. The program structure should stress teacher progress as well as learner progress. Continuous staff training, related to new staff skill, and functioning demands, evolving from student need change, should be scheduled as an integral part of the total program.

Personnel:

1. Just as students accept and reject various aspects of instruction, staff members accept and reject various demands made on them by the program structure. It is essential, then, that teachers whose basic dominant operational traits are in conflict with the basic program demands not be assigned to function within the performance curricular structure.
2. Courses must be developed in terms of differing teacher functioning levels as well as differing student functioning levels. Little learning can occur if there are gaps between the levels of functioning effectiveness of the student and the instructor. Scheduling must be done in terms of course demands on the teacher as well as on the student.
3. Staff scheduling should involve more than subject area specialties as assignment bases. Because the teacher is involved, in the performance results structure and in continuous course development, he needs to identify his functioning strengths in terms of total program demands rather than only in terms of a subject to be taught.

Performance:

1. As learner needs change, teacher objectives must change accordingly. These new objectives often demand differing teacher functioning emphases. Many times, teachers will recognize the necessity for changing objectives, but insist on maintaining an unchanging operational pattern.

2. Student needs and paralleling teacher objectives vary in time demands. Learning effectiveness is often limited because teachers let time, rather than student needs and progress, become the primary point of emphasis.

3. Teacher effectiveness should be viewed in terms of the extent his efforts expand student learning and program effectiveness beyond the curricular framework. Satisfactory performance in terms of the identified guidelines should be considered only as a basic functioning level.

2

TIME UTILIZATION AND
STUDENT PERFORMANCE

Many school programs being implemented are relatively innovative in design, methodology, or staffing. They do not, however, vary to any appreciable extent from traditional programming in terms of time utilization. Effective learner programming can not be accomplished unless time usage is considered as an individualized learner need. The module curricular structure facilitates student scheduling in terms of both time and performance.

CLASS SCHEDULING

The development of the student's actual class schedule becomes a relatively simple matter since the previously described decision areas actually are progressive steps toward the making of his program of study. Before the mechanics of arranging a learner's course units according to a time schedule are followed, another decision-making step needs to be taken. According to the new available information related to the student's present situation and anticipated stages, decisions must be made relative to areas of emphasis his class schedule will reflect.

According to the learner's priority listing of needs at any given time and stage along the various continua, primary scheduling emphasis can be given to skill level series, content level series, special emphasis in a single subject matter area, or various combinations of these. Specifically desired support courses, such as typing, where concentrated effort and extended time units may be desired, can also be easily scheduled within this curricular framework.

Since the emphasis here is on the individualization and personalization of educational programming, within this module curricular structure, special attention can be given to meeting the singular needs of the differing categories of learner levels. Students tend to seek out their own levels within the curricular structure. Staff members working within the modular curricular structure can more easily recognize this tendency and use it to advantage. Once a student feels within himself that he has been placed in a level consistent with his personal need and desire levels, there is much less conflict between him and what appears to be imposed on him. A consequent feeling of comfort on his part is essential to the motivation process.

STAFF SCHEDULING

The advantages mentioned here, relative to student scheduling, reveal parallel advantages in instructor scheduling. In addition to the obvious scheduling to teacher strengths and interests, there is the advantage of built-in variations available to the teachers that will help to discourage the consequent feelings of boredom, of endless instructional repetition, and of a "locking in" that results from static traditional methods of developing teaching assignments. In the modular curricular structure, given teacher assignments can be varied according to skill and content levels, single discipline or inter-discipline schedules, or other combinations. An important point here is that faculty members can have input relative to their assignments and can make changes in them that parallel changes in student schedules. Teachers will also seek their own levels.

Following is an example of the flexibility in teaching assignments that is possible in the short course team scheduling approach.

TEACHER ASSIGNMENT

SESSION I

1. Introduction to the computer
2. Basic Math Help
3. Basic Math Help
4. Personal Budgeting
5. Technology and careers math

SESSION II

1. Computer Programming
2. Algebra Help
3. Math/Shop Resource Team
4. Geometry (3 sessions)
5. Geometry (3 sessions)

DETERMINING TEACHER-NEED TIME

Not too often, does one hear teachers complain about content or other specifics related to their particular areas of specialization. One does, however, hear them complain about student skill levels, about the increased demand on them by students, and about a "lack of time." Fortunately, aspects such as these are ones individual teachers can do something about. Since a primary function of teachers is to make themselves progressively less needed, it could be assumed that a low function level here provides a basis for the complaints. This assumption, however would not be entirely valid. At least part of the problem, though, is caused by teachers not utilizing time and talent as effectively as they should in terms of their stated objectives. Of consequent importance, then, is the need for teachers to do self-studies related to time and effort.

FLEXIBLE USE OF TIME

There is no question that there are increasing demands being placed on all educators, not just those assigned to the classroom. The primary problem, perhaps, is their tendency to accept these added responsibilities without taking the time and effort to determine what the new demands and responsibilities can replace. Classroom teachers, particularly, do not maintain an ongoing program related to the phasing out of material, methods, and procedures in connection with the phasing in of new concepts and programs. Changing needs and new situations demand consequent changes in methodology and teacher functioning patterns if educational effectiveness is to be maintained. Planning additions should be accompanied by a parallel planning of selected deletions within the teacher functioning framework.

Status Quo Conditions	New Conditions	Possible Changes
1. Arbitrarily developed staff evaluative criteria	1. Performance objectives approach	1. Replacement of standardized teacher evaluation form
2. Traditional daily bell schedule	2. Emphasis on individual differences	2. Individualized student time allotments
3. Self-contained classrooms	3. Continuous progress	3. Interdisciplinary teaming
4. Program development based on subject matter emphasis	4. Involvement of parents and students in student scheduling	4. Personalized open-ended programming

It is essential then that teachers view their roles and responsibilities in terms of time as well as in terms of subject matter and numbers of students. In contrast to content and K-12 guidelines which, relatively speaking, remain more consistently constant, time must be considered as a planning and operational variable. Staff members can become locked in by their attitudes toward time utilization as much as they can be hampered by other attitudinal factors. They become more concerned with a "lack of time" than with more efficient use of time.

The teacher must be just as concerned about the way his students use time as he is with his own methods of time utilization. Therefore, as he analyzes his priorities and functioning patterns, he must work to identify, for example, specific reasons for his providing teacher-initiated help and why there are student-initiated requests for help. This analysis should also include the amount of time the teacher is really needed by students and the amount of time the teacher is not needed but imposes himself on the learner's time. This involves out-of-class time relative to homework, special study, and so on. In many cases, the teacher will be surprised how much of his time is desired by the student, but not really needed. In many cases, the teacher will be surprised how much time is saved by his not engaging in classroom endeavors that are so unimportant that no adverse effects arise as a result of his not doing them.

Many teachers allow themselves to be victims of chronometry and demand, so to speak, rather than being initiating managers of time. This is partly because they tend to plan, implement, and evaluate in terms of the identified units of the curriculum instead of seeing them as sequential steps of the total continua. Time is determined by content, as an example, instead of by learner progress and related need of the teacher. Related to this same problem is the tendency of teachers to view student needs, concerns, and difficulties as probable conflict areas. Therefore, the result is their concentrating on continua plateau problems rather than sequential progress development of the learner. Defensive teaching wastes time.

PLANNING TIME ALLOTMENTS

Within the module curriculum framework, planning both teacher and student time allotments is essential. The accuracy with which a teacher can plan and commit time is affected by his methods of operations and how he identifies them. This, again, involves the self-diagnostic approach that enables the teacher to analyze his own patterns of functioning, his priorities, his use of or dependence on, particular methods and techniques. He needs to rate these findings in terms of difficulty of student handling, of teacher skill use levels, and in terms of the gaps between his extent of their dominance of use and the extent to which he is forcing the continued reliance of student on the teacher. The practice of maintaining excess student dependence is an excessive consumer of teacher time.

If the teacher really expects to gain time through implementing the teacher-need time concept, he must expect to make changes in his functioning pattern framework. The planned need-time structure will determine the types of techniques used, student progress expectations, delegation of activities to staff support personnel, and the general classroom operational methods.

The determination of operational methods and expectations will be influenced by the teacher's:

1. Organizational management
2. Awareness of the congruity between program priorities and his functioning patterns
3. Recognition of learner's ability to utilize time
4. Identification of his own role and responsibilities toward program objectives attainment

5. Appraisal of his performance level capabilities
6. Methods of decision-making and performance attainment
7. System of operational tool selection and rejection

Though in his day-to-day operation the average teacher is not aware of it, the gapping between lesson planning and time expenditure relative to student learning progress creates uncontrolled time demands on him. In effect, this reduces itself to a gapping between assumed teacher expectancy related to student progress and actual student achievement during a given time space. Since there is, by extension, little or no student progress and a consequent lack of teacher effectiveness related to this gapping, it is incumbent on the teacher to plan and schedule both his and the students' time carefully. Accuracy here has a direct effect on teaching-learning effectiveness.

Another less obvious aspect that influences the extent of teacher-need time is individual course difficulty. Identification here is not particularly difficult for the teacher, especially if he utilizes the individualized, personalized approach to learning. The problem is related to the teacher's distribution of his time in relation to the various individual student achievement levels within a class. Because of the many variables, solutions here must be worked out by each teacher. However, he needs to keep in mind that (1) he does not have enough time available to allot time to every student every day, (2) not every student needs teacher time daily, (3) there are times he is not needed by given students, so why attempt to allot unneeded time?

In determining teacher-need time, the teacher also must look beyond his own classroom activities. He has support people available to help him, if he knows how to use them, if he knows how and when to delegate responsibility. This, again, involves a change in the teacher's functioning patterns because delegation means involvement of other people. As a result, the classroom does not remain a traditionally isolated instructional facility. Also, the teacher becomes a member of a number of instructional teams, through his delegation of responsibility.

Some support staff members are professional staff and district people such as the librarian, counselors, and special services personnel. Other support people can be recruited by the individual teacher/administrator team. These include volunteer lay aids, tutors, and student assistants. An often overlooked group of support personnel are the students themselves. Effective, relevant learning occurs when students are given opportunities and responsibilities, in line with individual capabilities, for directing some of their own learning activities. Students are the primary determiners of staff time allotment. Since they are consumers of staff time, teachers will find it advantageous, when it is within student capabilities, to utilize students as support personnel.

Teacher-need time can also be affected by the extent to which a staff member develops his instructional activities. Most teachers devote time and energy to planning lessons centered around the first level of activity—what is written down in the plan book for primary student action. The teacher needs also to engage in planning at the second level, that of developing individual support programs of study that supplement an individual student's regular course of study. These support programs are the short-term units that are geared to provide the student with reinforcement activities, review skill work, and points of concentration related to foreseeable areas of possible pupil difficulty as he progresses through a module unit or series of units, of study. Through planning, the student can automatically phase these sub-units in at the point of immediate need. The teacher does not need to take time to develop these on a "crisis-level" basis. It is true these take time to develop on a continuing basis, but the teacher is selecting and managing the time spans he devotes to this development.

TIME AND MANAGEMENT EFFECTIVENESS

The staff member who is an effective manager of time does not just let the teaching-learning sequences evolve; he schedules them, but does allow flexibility for the unforeseen. The way he manages time should be related to the way he organizes and manages the other aspects of the teaching-learning endeavors. These ways and methods reflect his patterns of functioning and how he sees his role and responsibilities. The manner in which he evaluates processes, methods, and material, his listing of priorities, his methods of instructional additions and deletions, and his utilization of time as an instructional element can also reveal if the teacher is results-oriented, if he is a change agent, if he is an innovator, if he is student-oriented, or if he is just a subject matter middleman, functioning between the textbook and the class.

The staff member who is an effective manager of time is a person able to identify the various demand forces with which he must deal and, then, classify them according to priority, not only in terms of learner need but also in terms of the anticipated learner objective attainment rate. This is not easy for many teachers to do.

The time analysis sheet in Figure 2-1 can be of value to staff members who are concerned about improving effectiveness through time management.

Figure 2-1.
Time Management Analysis

Student Time Demands	*What Was Actually Accomplished*
Period_____	_____
Anticipated Teacher-Need Time:	
_____	_____
Objective (s)_____	_____
_____	Revised Anticipated Teacher-
_____	Need Time_____
Activities *Minutes*	What Was Effective?
_____ _____	_____
_____ _____	_____
_____ _____	_____
Dominant Teacher Role	*What Was Ineffective?*
_____	_____
_____	_____
Methods/Techniques Used	*Changes to Be Made In*
_____	*Teacher Operational Methods*
_____	_____
_____	_____
Minutes Demanded by Students	_____
_____	_____
_____	_____

APPRAISING STUDENT PROGRESS

Student progress appraisal cannot be done with any real degree of satisfaction in isolation from the program in which the pupil is expected to show progress. Consequently, any student evaluation, or staff evaluation for that matter, is also an evaluation of the program structure in terms of the individual. In too many cases, an overlooked factor affecting student progress is the varying degree of conflict between the program structure demands and the individual student performance patterns. Whichever is the dominant force, in effect, determines the extent of learner progress.

The overall program framework inhibits or facilitates student progress according to the extent it correlates with the learning role and responsibilities of the student. As a result, student progress appraisal must include an analysis of any student functioning problems caused by structure. In effect, this is combining diagnostic and evaluative methods, the result of which can give the teacher an indication of present and future needed changes in programming that will more readily facilitate learning. It will help to eliminate conflicts, often beyond student control, that tend seriously to limit a given student's functioning, and consequent appraisal, level. The module curriculum, because of its flexible structure, because of its emphasis on learner needs, and because of its "plug-in" characteristic, lends itself readily to variation according to learner-need change.

Progress appraisal should also be done in terms of what the student contributes to his own program of learning. His contributions, however, are going to be governed by how much the functioning demands are keyed to his strengths. An overemphasis on his weaknesses alone tends to result in a negative approach to learning. The consequent development, or maintenance, of a negative attitude on his part will limit his contributions to his own learning. He will have difficulty developing his own specific learning methods, techniques, and objectives. Also, he will tend, as will the teacher, to concentrate on the cognitive aspects almost entirely.

DEVELOPING AN INDIVIDUALIZED PROGRESS CHART

Regardless of the methods of appraisal used by the teacher, the overall evaluative process needs to be individualized just as the student's learning program should be individualized. Individualized learning should not be appraised through the use of categorical concepts and methods. It is essential, then, that the teacher develop an individualized progress chart (Figure 2-2) for each

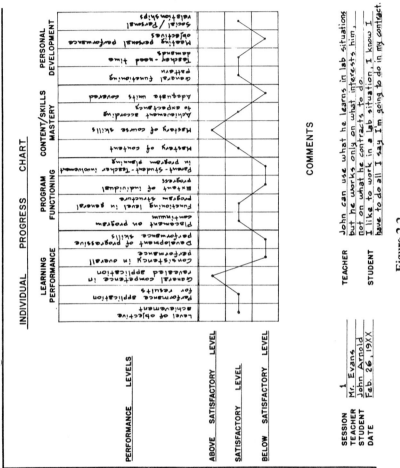

Figure 2-2

student. This means going beyond the traditional grading methods, check lists, and anecdotal records. It means that the teacher is going to have to go so far as to determine the type of learner each student is, whether he is a person who can initiate his actions and follow through with them, whether he views the teacher as a dominant parental image, or whether he is simply a follower. Each type of learner demands a different mode of operation by the instructor, and a consequent different appraisal approach. Effective appraisal, as well as effective instruction begins "where the student is." "Where he is" is affected by what he is.

The charting of individualized progress also means that the instructor must take into definite consideration each student's rate and extent of movement along each continuum line. When this is done, the charting can assume characteristics of a performance graph with such lines of progress being noted as a progress line for content/skills, a line for personal aspects, a line for total program functioning, and a line for change in functioning patterns for increased performance. Of course, these graphs can be developed in various ways and use various criteria. The important idea, however, is that a detailed appraisal picture has been developed that can be easily read and understood by both student and parent so that they understand the learner's total progress and his performance according to individual learner/program priorities.

With this approach, both appraisal and diagnostic needs are met. Not only can performance be delineated according to real and expected levels, specific identification can also be made of learning tasks that must be done as compared to those the pupil would prefer to do.

Since, in the module curriculum, the parent can easily and consistently be involved in the setting of learning objectives and the developing of learning schedules, he can also be involved in the appraisal procedures. Input from student, from parent, and from teacher during the appraisal conference can be used for the cooperative development of a performance graph. When this is done in terms of the previously teacher-student-parent-developed learning objectives, there is much less chance of misinterpretation, misunderstanding, and consequent disagreement among the principals involved. Since each was involved from the beginning, each is also appraising his own previous input and own previous decisions.

Performance results curriculum design requires that the school staff place its operational emphasis on the individual teacher and learner functioning patterns and performance levels. This approach necessitates the staff's development of a transitional program structure based on continuous change conditions that evolve from revealed teaching-learning effectiveness. This development involves paralleling student-teacher functioning, flexible programming, effective staff time and talent management, and continuous performance level appraisal.

The performance results curriculum is a learner-oriented program that stresses the programming of module courses according to student needs. It is a program developed on the basis of identified teacher-learner objectives, with time, resources, and teacher talent allotted according to individual student demand. Programming is a continuing activity geared to the individual progress and performance of each student, with the teacher serving in a primary design-management role.

Some Action Guidelines

Program:

1. A basis of performance curriculum development is the identification of learner priority needs through the staff use of questionnaires, interviews, diagnostic tests, and observation of daily student functioning
2. The program goals and objectives are developed from these priority needs
3. The learner functioning structure is developed from the needs and objectives. Developmental guidelines are identified according to such basic aspects as
   —a comparison of present structure to the needed framework indicated by the priority needs listing
   —revealed student performance levels and functioning patterns identification of present staff functioning pattern levels, and skills
   —domain level emphasis of objectives
   —levels and types of performance skills students are to have when they have completed the program
   —anticipated changes in functioning needs, and effectiveness levels of both staff and students

4. Course development needs to be geared to specific present and anticipated student needs. Various courses must be developed in terms of
—specific learner application
—singular program objective(s)
—differing learner functioning levels
—correlation to learner progress
—changing student needs
—social, academic, and maturation emphases
—specific program continua stages
—demands for individualization and continuous progress
—identified specific course purpose

Personnel:

1. In the development of the performance results curriculum, staff members are "teachers" only in the narrow sense of the word. They are also, and primarily, managers and designers. These skills do not come automatically with a "teaching certificate."
The staff can often benefit from in-service training in the specific program aspects of
curriculum design
program organization
performance assessment
time management
2. Support people should be involved in the program because of their areas of expertise and because they will be participants in program implementation
3. As the program structure is being developed, staff members must identify and define their roles, responsibilities, and authority at each progressive stage
4. Staff members, at each stage of development, should participate in actual programming activities so that their skills are developed as development progresses
—identifying areas necessitating staff
—assignment changes
—developing individual student schedules according to different need criteria
—coordinating student/teacher objectives
—changing program objectives to teaching/learning action
5. Staff members must devote time to the delineation of parent roles and responsibilities. Parents must also be provided opportunities to

participate in program development at all stages; participate in orientation activities designed to help them be more proficient in their team roles

6. At all stages of program development, staff members need to define the learning demands and student functioning patterns. They need, then, to define the consequent teacher modes of functioning

Performance:

1. Staff performance relative to the development of the performance results curriculum should be assessed in terms of the stated program objectives and priority needs. The extent of satisfactory performance during the developmental stages is indicative of the success functioning levels of the staff members within the totally implemented program structure

2. Proof of performance effectiveness can be gained through pilot implementation of the various program stages as they are developed. Consequent needed changes can be made at the time of pilot completion. These improvements will be more reliable bases for the following stage development

3. Revealed student performance in the pilot stages will also be indicative of the success functioning levels of the learners within the totally implemented program structure

3

STRUCTURING A RESULTS-
ORIENTED PROGRAM

Keys to learning achievement are the staff and program emphases on individualized student performance. Emphasis on individualized performance requires staff development of a transitional program structure in which both teacher and learner performance demands are progressive, sequential, and changing in direct relationship to the changes occurring in the student as a result of his learning experiences. This results-oriented program is developed around the individual student's functioning in terms of his setting and attaining objectives, his involvement in determining the scope and direction of his learning endeavors, and his participation in his performance assessment.

Emphasis has not been on this approach in the past. The learner consequently has had his progress evaluated on the basis of an incomplete structure. An obvious question here is, how can the teacher tell whether an individual is a "good" student or a "bad" student when the appropriate learning program has not been developed for him? The result is the student's being criticized for not functioning in an instructional environment which is not designed for him.

In this case, as in many others, it is the designer, the teacher, and often the total program structure that are at fault. The learner should be evaluated in a program of demands that coordinates his needs, forces, patterns, skill, and achievement levels with the corresponding characteristics of the instructor and the program.

The author worked with a teacher and a counselor who were concerned about a 15-year-old girl who attended school only because of the state's compulsory attendance law. The girl was mature for her age; instead of a dress, she always wore overalls, carried a surplus army knapsack, and had twice run away from home. She was originally enrolled in the traditional school academic program.

Naturally, conflicts arose because she did not conform to school-community dress expectations, and because she was more interested in self-expression, and in "being treated as a mature individual." She functioned satisfactorily with peers and teachers outside the classroom demands, but resisted classroom routine. Consequently, her teachers looked upon her as "sloppy, antagonistic, not interested in improving herself, and will quit school as soon as she is 16."

Conferences with the girl revealed that her primary need was a program of studies that would take into account her desires for recognition and her feelings related to her maturity. Consequently, the following program was developed for her, and with her.

Course Areas	Objectives
Journalism	Provide an outlet for creative efforts and peer recognition
Home Economics	Personal dress needs
Speech and Drama	Personal recognition and opportunity for self-expression
Physical Education	Physical poise and interaction with other girls in informal situations
Student Assistant	Opportunities to work with adults

The teacher-student-counselor team continued to focus on these objectives and related course needs until the above desires had ceased to be the only bases for the girl's actions.

IDENTIFYING BASES FOR INDIVIDUALIZED RESULTS

In order for a learning program to be effective for the teacher and meaningful to the student, it must be patterned in terms of the learner's singular characteristics. Also, it must be a pattern that is consistent with the structure of the overall instructional program. It follows, then, that the overall program structure must be flexible enough to meet changing individual needs. In other words, it really is nothing more than a framework that will insure some consistency, articulation, and coordination for the learning subprograms developed within it.

Consequently, the overall program must be developed in terms of a continuum of learning and human development without the traditional emphasis on grade or age levels. It must be structured so that an individual student can be plugged into it at any place his needs and achievement levels dictate. It should be developed in terms of a progress time line of sequential objectives and check points for student progress rather than units of content.

This involves a departure from the traditional structuring of programs of instruction, as revealed by schools in Atlanta, Georgia, and Littleton, Colorado. Time, for example, is determined by the learner, but influenced by the teacher. The order of content prerequisites, common learnings, and so forth, is determined by each individual learner's experiences, background, interests, needs, and achievement performance. This, of course, is based on both the teacher's and student's understanding the realistic learning capabilities of the student.

Another consequent outgrowth of this program approach is the breakdown of the division between traditional requireds and electives, per se. Every course, and the level of that course, is selected in terms of identified and desired student performance and objectives. A given course could be a necessary area of study for one student while, at the same time, it could simply be an option for another student. "Requireds" and "electives" should vary with individual students.

	"Required"	"Elective"
Student A	Reading for special Purpose	Algebra
	Politics and Military Tactics	Introduction to the Novel
	Health Education	Introduction to Science Lab Skills
	Pre-algebra	U.S. Constitutional History
Student B	Algebra	Reading for Special Purposes
	Introduction to the Novel	History Through Major Battles
	U.S. Consitution	First Aid
	Biology	Health Education

SETTING TRANSITIONAL OBJECTIVES

Student-teacher-parent set objectives beyond mere subject matter memory work determine an individual's requirements for a given course. His evaluation of achievement would be in terms of these objectives and in terms of his progress through the recognized continuum of learning as developed for the individual learner. All this relates directly to the premise that the student who possesses rote learning but cannot, or does not, have the opportunity to apply it is in reality no better off than the student who does not possess the knowledge. Neither can use it.

Change necessitates change. Since students are continually maturing, they are constantly changing. The individualized performance-oriented learning structure must reflect corresponding change. This poses a problem for many staff members because they have difficulty maintaining a change-oriented approach once they have initiated it. They have a tendency to want to revert back to the easier, subject matter-oriented structure because they do not know how to plan for, initiate, and evaluate change.

The author was involved in working with a group of teachers selected to staff a middle school. As program development progressed during the first few months, change began to be stifled by habit.

1. The staff wanted to develop and implement the variable grouping and continuous progress concepts, but they lacked experience needed to develop the structure.
2. Teachers wanted class assignments according to elementary and secondary divisions rather than according to student needs and desired program structure.
3. Teachers tended to plan and function as they did in their previous schools.

Fortunately, through administrative and departmental chairman leadership, such problems as these were resolved through effective in-service programs.

There must be individuals on the staff, led by the administrators, who see themselves as staff-change agents and who can work with the more reticent and less sure staff members in maintaining an effective change procedure. Staff members, for example, have to be shown how to develop a learning time line, how to anticipate and recognize learner change, and how to update a time line up and down the learning continuum.

Learning skills such as this are important if the teacher, who must be a reacting change agent himself, is to remain in close enough contact with the learner so that gaps do not occur between teacher-student objectives and between teacher and student expectations. Concerns such as this also help the instructor to be constantly aware of the way the student sees him and how the student feels the learning structure can be most effective for him.

A primary problem a staff member faces in maintaining the change approach is avoiding the gapping between planning and implementing. This gapping can be caused by such factors as the following:

1. Lack of adequate teacher skill in performance curriculum design
2. Lack of teacher skills in translating planning to action
3. Rigidity of program structural demands
4. Inadequate administrative leadership
5. Inconsistency between program functioning demands and assessment criteria emphases

An example of the "created" gapping here is the following "plan" given the author by a teacher.

Objective:

The purpose of this unit is to help students make a first hand study of selected insects.

Instruction:

1. Instructional methods will be selected in terms of an individual student's needs as they are recognized by the student and the instructor. We will use
   a. structured class activities
   b. structured small group activities
   c. individualized activities
2. Each student will be encouraged to function at his highest level

Primary results:

1. Students will make observations based on direct experiences
2. Students will draw conclusions from simple observations
3. Students will research the development and life habits of one insect, using the library and direct observation
4. Students will develop a laboratory experiment on the insect's effect on man

Evaluation:

Tests and written reports

An analysis of this "plan" will reveal the areas of gapping between the planning level and the implementation level.

1. Planning by teacher	Implementation by student
2. Teacher-set objectives	No learner input
3. Teacher-determined functioning patterns	No concern for most effective learner patterns
4. Teacher assessment	No student self-appraisal
5. Closed program emphasis	Open student curiosity
6. Group process demands	Individual student needs
7. Teacher selection of learning activities	Limited student use of optional choices
8. Teacher-implied need for instructing	No student-identified purpose for learning

The indication here is that this individual has made some attempt to incorporate in his planning certain performance results aspects but he has not made any effort to reduce them to the implementation level. This can be a result of his not possessing the necessary functioning skills or because he has little interest in changing from the traditional teaching-emphasis position to a position concerned with articulation and continuity of teaching and learning performance.

There is also indication that the teacher has given little consideration to such basic performance concerns as identification of learner functioning levels, development of specific performance appraisal criteria, or flexibility for unexpected learner need changes.

DETERMINING PERFORMANCE RESULTS LEVELS

The student, again, in the last analysis, determines his own performance level. There are, however, various ways, directly or indirectly, a teacher can determine how and to what extent the student determines his performance level. Both the instructor and student must develop the philosophy that they are a learning team and that performance levels evolve as a result of a number of factors.

TEACHER DETERMINATION METHODS	STUDENT DETERMINATION FACTORS
1. Identification of student motivational factors	1. Level of self-image
2. Influence of program and teacher performance demands on student	2. Parental influence
3. Identification of student growth and development patterns	3. Peer pressure and values
4. Understanding of student value system	4. Desire for self-satisfaction
5. Identification of student functioning levels	5. Extent of feeling of freedom to set levels
	6. Capability of developing functioning role

The traditional approaches to checking student progress such as unit tests, class discussion, and standardized achievement tests are not adequate for a number of reasons that are familiar to most educators. They have their place, of course, if they are not used alone and as end results. They should be considered as only a few of many indicators both the teacher and student should use.

The determination of performance levels must be done jointly by the teacher and the student. As they are being worked out, the teacher, as the team leader, must be constantly aware of the human factors involved. This goes beyond the typical approaches of diagnostic testing, post tests, and the checking of other assorted written endeavors of the student. The teacher must also take time to schedule regular individual interviews with each student to ascertain such things as attitude, the changes in learning difficulties, changes in student-teacher relationships, analysis of instructional emphases, and varying teaching-learning conditions. These are, of course, related to the content areas but, more importantly, they deal with the human aspects of learning—those that will determine the actual efforts and degrees of learning.

The setting of performance levels for the student by the student and the teacher involves their analysis of the total present situation and how they project the future. This is not a primary reliance on paperwork simply because it is, alone, unreliable and subjective. It is only as good as the teacher is able to make it—and many times this "checking on the past" reveals only surface checks of isolated areas.

The following dialogue between a teacher and five students in a basic skills class is a case in point.

PROBLEM: The students were acting out and becoming discipline problems in class. The teacher was upset as homework assignments were not being turned in. A counselor served as mediator between the teacher and students. After a declaration of "non-war," problem discussions began. The interaction conversation below indicates how the conflict resolution came about.

Student: "The grading—we're confused because we don't know how we're doing, so I don't turn in my homework."

Teacher: "I gave you a handout at the first of the year so you could keep track of yourself."

Student: "All teachers do this. It doesn't work. Teachers should first find out what capabilities students have, then work out what is expected."

Teacher: "You want another system of record keeping?"

Student: "Yeah—a chart—so we can see how we're doing."

Teacher: "Will you turn assignments in if the record is there—posted on the wall?"

Student: "Yeah."

Teacher: "OK—I'll make an open chart of grades and homework so you can see your current grades."

SUMMARY: The students' needs were to have an open "on the spot" report on how they were doing. The teacher's need was to get the homework in. Once both needs were cleared up, a solution to meet both their needs was easily found.

The result of this was an increase in homework turned in and a better relationship between students and teacher.

The determination of performance levels actually involves more personalized, human emphasis and aspects than content stress. Once the human side of the learning environment has been adequately considered, the more formalized content endeavors will fall into place. This goes for the teacher and for the student because the team members cannot work in isolation from each other. This team approach implies a cooperative involvement in decision-making, in responsibility assumption, and in personal reciprocal respect in the demands the team members make on each other.

Both the teacher and the student must re-orient their thinking and their actions away from the more narrow concept of content emphasis to the broader concerns of the "how's" and "why's" of learning and the ways content can serve as a learning vehicle. Failure to master and maintain this philosophical and practical learning approach will result in a deterioration of performance emphasis and consequent lower results levels. This, then, evolves into a more negative approach to learning by the student, and to the student by the teacher, because both have placed blocking factors in their learning plans.

A typical human tendency is to put the blame on someone else. The setting of performance levels by and for both the teacher and the student in terms of their realistic capabilities and in terms of the objectives of the team, and the consequent adherence to these can much more clearly delineate the functioning patterns of both pupil and instructor. Each, then, has a clearer idea of the modes of behavior expected of him by the other person and by the cooperatively self-set demands.

PROCEDURES FOR EVALUATING PERFORMANCE LEVEL ATTAINMENT

This different approach brings with it a need for the teacher, and school, to develop correspondingly different approaches to determining student levels of achievement and paces of progress. Less attention should be given to such mechanical procedures as giving "pop" quizzes and group oral reviews. More emphasis must be given to formal and informal observation of the student's daily functioning, his variations in performance levels, his reactions to different types of activities and instructional techniques, and the singular demands of the teacher's evaluative procedures.

Since evaluation must be a continuing process, these procedures and techniques must be built into the learning activities as integral parts, not specially designed procedures above and beyond the regular classroom activities and responsibilities, not something composed and imposed on the pupil.

Keys to the development of evaluation criteria, of course, are (1) the functions the student is expected to master, (2) the performance level he is expected, and expects, to reveal, (3) his beginning place on the learning continuum and (4) his anticipated location as a result of his learning experiences.

In a course related to small appliance repair, for example, such criteria as the following would be apropos.

1. The variety of small appliances the student can repair
2. The extent of the learner's understanding of the basic components and wiring circuits of small appliances
3. The learner's capability for using test equipment
4. The number of successful repairs the student makes in relation to the number of jobs attempted
5. Identification of the specific skills and knowledge the student has mastered since he started the course

This involves the teacher's and student's developing progress criteria in terms of the learner and the instructor as well as in terms of subject and performance levels. The criteria must be developed with such things in mind as learner's and instructor's functioning patterns, cooperative and individual techniques used, relationships of performance and need, relationships of learning activities and objectives to the overall educational program of the individual student, and the extent the learning techniques and emphases change as the student reveals progress as he works to attain a given results objective.

It is essential, then, that the evaluative process and techniques be built in as integral parts of the progressive learning tasks and demands as learning devices themselves. This cannot be done, however, until the teacher-learner team comes to a realistic agreement about the definition of satisfactory performance. Some point on the individual's learning continuum must be designated by the teacher and the student as the "satisfaction point"—the level of performance the student could normally be expected to achieve in terms of his background, achievement, desire, and so forth, in terms of learning conditions, in terms of teacher capability, and in terms of subject matter.

DEVELOPING THE EVALUATIVE CRITERIA FRAMEWORK

The evaluative criteria framework, like the learning program, must be an open structure. As the student progresses along the continuum from objective to objective, and from one learning endeavor to another, the satisfaction points will be raised or lowered according to the student's part and expected performance. The criteria should also be subject to change in terms of the self-evaluation endeavors of both the learner and the instructor. As resulting changes come about from this self-analysis, changes in performance and evaluative criteria will evolve. A learning value system is developed as the team members develop the evaluative checkpoints.

Factors affecting performance assessment checkpoints are:

1. Areas of student responsibilities
2. Identified performance levels
3. Student strengths and weaknesses
4. Identified areas of student performance concentration
5. Program forces and demands
6. Progress toward objective attainment

    7. Unanticipated operational difficulties facing learner
    8. Learner self-appraisal
    9. Operational options and alternatives
    10. Program-teacher-learner conflicts

The evaluative criteria, then, in a sense, become the indicators the team members use to check each one's performance level and the extent to which their performance levels correlate. This extent of correlations is going to have a direct effect on learning effectiveness and performance capabilities. Student success, then, indicates instructional objective effectiveness.

DETERMINING INSTRUCTIONAL STOPPING POINTS

At some point in time, the teacher must change his role from that of instructing, guiding and motivating to that of a demander of performance usage. That is, he must determine the proper time at which he will expect the student to apply the skills and knowledge he has learned in a practical situation selected in terms of the student's capabilities and action expectancies. The extent to which the student meets or exceeds the cooperatively set performance expectation level will determine this success level. Credit for the achievement of the objectives should be given to him at that time. He should be permitted to move on to the next objective without being restricted by arbitrarily set time unit impositions. Progress should be based on achievement and recorded on a form such as Figure 3-1.

Within the traditional program structure and instructional-emphasis limitations, it is often difficult for the performance results-oriented teacher to be an effective demander of student performance application. The program structures must be expanded so that the student has adequate opportunities to apply his learning in practical situations beyond the traditional confines of the classroom. Again, however, this is a situation in which the teacher must reveal his skills in idea creation and implementation because learner performance application is a part of the total implementation of the overall program.

Examples of Student Performance Usage

    1. Increasing assumption of responsibility for developing purposes, objectives, and directions of own learning program
    2. Becoming progressively the primary appraiser of his own learning performance

3. Participation in building level "intern activities" in identified areas of interest

"Junior" assistant instructors working in selected commercial enterprises cooperating with the school

4. Development and completion of special projects according to teacher-student pre-determined specifications and identified usage in practical situations

5. Basic learning skills effectively applied at a higher functioning demand level

6. Satisfactory functioning in sequential courses designed for application of skills learned in a content course—math-shop, English-journalism

As the instructor and the school implement this approach, individualized programming and individualized evaluation become a reality. The evaluative checkpoints will determine "grading and reporting periods." With this approach, teachers will be continuously reporting to parents, but not necessarily to all on a given date. The reporting times will vary as the students vary in their progress toward, and achievement of, objectives.

CONTINUOUS OBJECTIVE ATTAINMENT RECORD

Objective Attained_____	Specific Performances Revealed
Courses Scheduled to Achieve Objective_____	Credit Earned_____
Sequent Objective_____	
Date_____	
Teacher_____	

Figure 3-1

An important point here is that with this instructional approach, both the teacher and the student become much more conscious of the learning process. It is much easier for both of them to relate the process to the achievement of the identified objective. It will help the teacher, especially, to keep all learning aspects in their proper perspectives and needed degrees of emphasis as opposed to the traditional approach of only being concerned about the desired result and written test performance.

This will also help both the teacher and the student to function in teams of learning for present and future application. As the teacher must keep in mind that he must, at some point selected by him and the student, demand result performance, they both must keep in mind the depth of learning of a given skill or content material so that the student can continue to use it in the future without having to relearn it. Careful selection of skills and knowledge the student will be asked to master and their effective integration in the student's total learning continuum will facilitate the elimination of unnecessary repetition, of gapping between learning level and teaching demands, and of personal conflicts.

HOW TO MODIFY THE CLOSED
PROGRAM STRUCTURE

The school program structure, like individual staff attitudes, can deter change for improvement in favor of the status quo for security. Staff attitudes and actions cannot change unless there is corresponding change in the program structure. This change, in order to reach the individual learners, must extend into the functioning interaction levels of the students. In other words, it must result in changes in their courses, in staff demands, and in the ways the students are able to perform in terms of time, conflicting interests and pressures, and self-identified objectives.

An excellent example of this structural flexibility is the expanded program of Littleton High School, in suburban Denver. This school has a typical suburban high school academic program. In addition, however, the school cooperates with an inter-district vocational agency established to help meet vocational needs of students in several districts not having adequate vocational facilities or programs.

The students select and enroll in the courses at the school; they attend classes wherever suitable sites are available. The vocational agency provides staff, material, and sites. It receives funds from both the State of Colorado and the participating districts.

The students spend part of their school day on the high school campus and part of the day off campus in the vocational program.

Figure 3-2 shows examples of additional courses available to the students as a result of the cooperative arrangement.

Figure 3-2

OFF CAMPUS CLASSES

SEMBCS

Vocational Agriculture I

First Semester 91111
Second Semester 91112
8:15-9:05; 10:15-12:05
Full Year, 20 hours credit)
(Elective 10, 11, 12)

Course includes basic instruction in livestock production, care, and management. Students will have an opportunity to gain practical experience in handling and caring for livestock. Basic instruction is also provided in both ornamental plant and crop production, including basic soils, plant propagation, cropping methods, etc. Approximately $1/4$ of instructional time will be devoted to the development of agricultural mechanical skills including basic carpentry, electrical wiring, arc and oxy-acetylene welding, and operation and care of farm machinery.

Vocational Agriculture Mechanics

First Semester 91211
Second Semester 91212
1:15-3:05
(Full Yyear, 20 hours credit)
(Elective 11, 12)
Prerequisite: Voc. Ag. I or consent of instructor

This option is an advanced course in tractor and machinery repair. Students will study advanced techniques in welding, machinery repair, servicing, and tractor overhaul. Students will gain experience working in a practical day to day setting in a well equipped shop working on all types of repair jobs as they come in. At least $3/4$ of the students' time will be spent in mechanical experiences and no more than $1/4$ in related instruction.

Vocational Agriculture Occupations

First Semester 91411
Second Semester 91412
1:15-3:05
(Full Year, 20 hours credit)
(Elective 11, 12)
Prerequisite: Voc. Ag. I, or consent of instructor

This course is designed to provide actual work experience in the student's area of interest. Students will be placed in agricultural related businesses in order to receive occupational experience. Before being placed, students enrolled in this option will complete a pre-placement training program. This in-class portion of the program is centered on job preparation, assessment of skills necessary for the job, employer-employee relations, and career opportunities. The occupational experience will be planned in cooperation with the employer, the teacher coordinator, and the student in order to meet each student's specific needs.

Vocational Agriculture Production

First Semester 91611
Second Semester 91612
1:15-3:05
(Full Year, 20 hours credit)
(Elective 11, 12)
Prerequiste: Voc. Ag. I or consent of instructor

This course is designed around problem-centered situations arising out of the day by day business of livestock and crop production. Students are placed in the position of determining problems and needs, evaluation, decision making, planning and doing those jobs and activities required to conduct the business of operating the Vocation Farm. The level of responsibility and difficulty of tasks increase as students develop skills and aptitude. Students accept more of the managerial responsibility, thus receive advanced training in the economic, business, planning and technical areas of the farm operation. Students may work individually, in teams, or in large class groups as the situation dictates. Most large group activities are engaged in the search for new, different or improved methods of carrying out production practices and the advancement of agriculture and agricultural leadership. Individual students are allowed opportunity to work in interest or need areas, thus time spent in different production areas i.e., (livestock, crops, mechanics) will vary with individual students.

Horticulture I (Ornamental)

First Semester 91711
Second Semester 91712
8:15-10:05, 10:15-12:05
(Full Year, 20 hours credit)
(Elective 10, 11, 12)
Prerequisite: 1 Unit Science)

The student of Horticulture will receive instruction in botany and plant physiology, plant propagation, identification and classification, planting and transplanting, soils, plant care and maintenance. Students will carry out experiments and investigations on fertilizers and pesticides. A unit of study on licensing requirements will also be covered.

Horticulture II (Ornamental)

First Semester 91811
Second Semester 91812
10:15-12:05
(Full Year, 20 hours credit)
(Elective 11, 12)
Prerequisite: Horticulture I

Ornamental Horticulture II builds on the content offered in Ornamental Horticulture I. Students will again cover a study of the structure of plants, trees, shrubs, and fruits, as well as the identification and classification of ornamental plants. Instruction in Horticulture II will include: physical soil analysis, plant composition and classification, insect identification and control, as well as problems related to greenhouse and nursery management practices. Skills to be learned by students will include: the selection of plants and shrubs, planting and transplanting, shaping, and care of ornamental plants and shrubs. Instruction in landscaping will cover such items as planting, types of landscape designs, and lawn installation care and maintenance.

Cosmetology

First Semester 96111
Second Semester 96112
8:15-12:15, 1:15-5:15
(Full Year, 30 hours credit each full year)
(10 additional hours of credit for summer school)
(Elective 11, 12 — When possible 2nd year students should be scheduled 8:00-12:00 noon)
Prerequisite: 1 unit math, 1 unit science

This is a two year program in which the students of Beauty Culture will receive instructions and practice in hair styling, cutting, and coloring. Manicuring, shampooing, facial makeup, and scalp treatments are other areas in which instruction will be given. Instructions in sanitizing of the salon and sterilizing of the tools and instruments are very important. The techniques of hair shampooing and rinsing will be taught as well as hair setting, hair cutting, and permanent waving. Manicuring, involving the care of hands and nails, will be one of the many skills taught in this course. The cutting of hair will involve thinning, blunting, tapering, nape shaping, and will cover the dry scissors and wet shaping methods. Both semi-permanent and permanent hair coloring will be incorporated in instructions. Techniques of reconditioning hair and scalp are an important phase of this course. Conditions, such as falling hair, oily or dry scalp and dandruff, must be corrected by the beautician. The removal of superflous hair is another aspect of beauty culture. Another area of instruction will be in wiggery. The instructional program will deal with fitting, grooming, styling, and care of the hair piece. The operation of a beauty salon, including financing, operation, decorating, ordering, advertising, and compliance with state law will also be a part of the course.

The cosmetology program will be conducted in cooperation with beauty schools in the Littleton and Englewood areas. Students will receive instruction and related experience in an actual beauty salon. The instructional program will consist of four consecutive clock hours, Tuesday through Friday, with a minimum of 32, eight hour Saturdays. In addition, there will be an individually programmed 250-300 hour summer program designed to provide the State-required minimum of 48 hours in each of the months of June, July and August. The course will require a minimum of 1,650 hours for completion.

Food Management

First Semester 92111
Second Semester 92112
10+15 a.m.-1:45 p.m.
(Full Year, 20 hours)
(Elective 12)
Health examination and chest X-ray required

This program will focus on development of the knowledge, skills and attitudes relating to successful employment in the field of food preparation and restaurant services. Group and individual interaction and instruction in formal as well as informal weekly meetings, and point of performance instruction provided at the cooperative field experience center will be utilized to instruct students in the following areas:

Communicable diseases and food spoilage, equipment, Basic Cooking I (beef, pork, lamb, poultry); Basic Cooking II (seafood, game, dairy products, sauces and seasonings); Advanced Cooking I (meal preparation breakfasts and lunches); and Advanced Cooking II (dinner design and preparation)

Students will receive realistic training in the food management-chef training area by actually working and producing in a successfully operating business.

Child Management Specialist

First Semester 96611
Second Semester 96612
8:15-10:05, 10:15-12:05, 1:15-3:05
(Full Year, 20 hours)
(Elective 12)
Prerequisite: Health examination

The Child Management Specialist program will focus on the development of knowledge and skills relating to the care and guidance of young pre-school age children. Skills which the students will be expected to develop as a result of their experiences include the following:
1. Guide and supervise children in such activities as outdoor play, dramatic play, art, music and health activities.
2. Be aware of experiences and assist children in the development of cognitive skills through the stimulation of intellectual attention.
3. Assist teachers in the conduct of teaching-learning processes by the operation of learning equipment and carrying out instructional duties under the supervision of the teacher.

Students will receive realistic "on-the-job" training by working with pre-school children under the direction of an early childhood specialist.

Nurses' Assistant-Hospital Orderly

First Semester 96511
Second Semester 96512
8:15-11:05
(Semester, 15 hours)
(Elective 12)
(Also 6 week summer session)

Students in this program learn to assist in the care of hospital patients under the direction of nursing and or medical staff members.' This includes answering signal lights to determine patients' needs, serving and collecting meal trays, helping patients walk to treatment units or transporting them in wheelchairs, assisting during examinations and treatments of patients, taking and recording temperatures, pulse and respiration rate, bathing, dressing and undressing patients, and performing other services for patients. After initial training a student may desire to specialize in a specific area such as Geriatrics, Maternity, or Medical Surgical. Students will be required to serve five full days at the Center or in a nursing home during the spring semester on nonschool days.

Expanding the program structure is not limited to just the idea of adding or deleting courses, though a receptive staff does this. Just as important, are the availability and practicality of the course offerings in terms of learning readiness and need demands. If the program is developed in terms of learning human beings, it rules out such preconceived notions as cut-and-dried dividing lines pertaining to limitations of age, or grade, or level, and the need for "special" programs or facilities. What is particularly needed, however, is involvement of staff members who know how to generate, implement, and evaluate ideas. A number of possibilities come to mind here. They are not necessarily new, but perhaps have not been tried in an effective manner or by a capable staff with reference to what the staff was trying to do.

EXAMPLES OF OPEN-ENDED
PROGRAMMING METHODS

Requireds/Electives: Instead of being rigidly defined with consequent limitations in scope and gapping in learning articulation, these could, perhaps, be more effective if the particular areas of study for an individual student were identified in terms of his revealed capabilities, needs, and levels of achievement. Particular short courses could then be selected from a wide variety of offerings. The program of studies could be tailored to the individual. It would be much easier to schedule extended help courses for a given individual because time would be flexible and the wide assortment of offerings would not be developed in terms of grade or other arbitrary categories.

Open choice selections by the student could be made more easily by the learner and more easily adapted to his areas of concentration by his advisor because there could be developed, at all levels, particular areas of skill emphasis that would not have to be tied to subject matter content. Special teacher-learner concentration on just one or more learner weaknesses could easily evolve. Time allotments here could be devoted to such study endeavors as helping a student master the needed performance skills before he went into the actual course content studies that would require him to use these particular tools without additional instruction.

Through an approach such as this, both the teacher and the student are forced to analyze the needs of the student, the particular instructional and learning techniques required, and the overall program of studies in order to select intelligently the singular areas and levels of study that will be of most use to the learner. Emphasis is on the student.

Open-need Classes: Building-level programs need to have incorporated in them such a concept as the open-need classroom. In such a place, students could be given the opportunity to request special assistance in self-identified areas. Of course, these requests could be related to such academic approaches as tutoring, but perhaps the open-need areas could prove to be more effective if the students were given opportunities for requesting help in their areas of concern beyond content limitations. If the school staff subscribes to the idea that personal concerns of students must be given added attention because they greatly affect individual academic performances, then the open-need approach can have a distinct impact on the personalizing of the school program.

This area could very easily be staffed with counselors, empathetic teachers, district resource personnel, and qualified lay help as determined by the school personnel. These people would be available to provide personalized assistance to individual students in a wide variety of areas. In some ways, perhaps, it could be looked upon as a guidance center, but yet there are other areas of student concern where young people just want to discuss issues with someone without desiring any action.

The open-need classroom approach offers all kinds of possibilities for both students and staff. The particular operational approach would vary according to the singular needs of each school so no "best" way of organizing will be mentioned here. The important idea here is that the school staff is providing time and talent to assisting students with concerns they have beyond the academic confines of the classroom. They are attempting to expand the educational environment so that it becomes much more an integral part of the daily lives of the young people. After all, pupils not only desire, but seek, instruction and direction beyond subject matter. If given the opportunity, many of them will take advantage of it.

Challenge Courses: A common practice in schools is to assume that all students in a given group should be exposed to a given area of instruction for the same amount of time. There is little or no consideration of their individual backgrounds in a given subject. This is inconsistent with the results-oriented philosophy.

Each student should be given credit for what he knows and the skills he can perform. Consequently, if a student has shown that he can perform satisfactorily in relation to the stated objectives of a given course, he should be given credit, without regard for time or where he learned the skills or content for that course. He should then be permitted to continue in sequence along his time line.

Figure 3-3 presents an example of a combined procedure and record-keeping form related to the challenge process:

Course Title	Course Objectives	Skill/Content Demands
Method of Challenge	Student Performance	
	Objective Achieved	Level of Achievement
Student_____		
Appraiser_____		
Approval_____		
Date_____		

Figure 3-3

If a pupil is required to attend a class, the requirements of which he has already mastered, he is forced to waste his time. The result is dissatisfaction, frustration, and at least passive conflict. The school goal is continuous, not arrested, education. If content and skills are looked upon as learning tools to be used in the attainment of specified student objectives, then performance is the key, not time spent in a formal class setting or the name of a course on a form in the counselor's office.

Extension Classes: There is no all-encompassing reason why all students must attend classes within the same daily time schedule.

By extending the instructional times available, a school district can reduce overcrowded conditions, better correlate instruction with students' out-of-school activities, and make better use of available facilities. A school district can obtain results such as these by permitting students to pursue the prescribed courses of study through attendance in evening classes or through correspondence courses. They could be set up as an integral aspect of the regular program.

The incorporation of evening and correspondence courses at the secondary level would help the school staff in their efforts to work with potential dropouts, to maintain continuity in learning for students with chronic illnesses, and to develop more realistic programs of study for working students. This incorporation would also enable staff expansion through the scheduling of classes that could be taught by qualified lay persons.

The Las Vegas, Nevada, School District has implemented an extended-day approach that permits students to attend classes in the evenings. This arrangement can be particularly helpful to students who are working or whose peak functioning times are later in the day. It also helps reduce overcrowding facilities by extending the time the buildings and staff members are available to the students.

Instruction and Application: Students are concerned about being able to use what they learn; they want to see a direct relationship between what they learn and what they can do. Consequently, it is imperative that academic courses be tied more closely to the practical arts courses, for example, at the middle level of education. Taking simple measurement as a case in point, students are taught how to use a ruler in a math class, but when they are asked to draw plans and build a project in shop, they have trouble. The complaint is students don't know how to measure a piece of wood.

There needs to be a closer working relationship developed between the academic-oriented classes and the activity-oriented classes because there is commonality of demands, of skills, and of performance levels.

The same holds true at the upper secondary level. School personnel should make an effort to develop a closer working relationship with industry. As the two function separately, there is a gap between what a student is expected to learn in school and how he is expected to function on the job. A much closer correlation by the school and industry would result in the development of a modified on-the-job training approach that could serve as a transitional stage for the graduating student.

It is important, then, that there be cross-planning, sequential instruction related to different class demands, and dovetailing of content area preparation. This is necessary because what is taught in one class often is considered as a pre-requisite learning skill in another class the student is taking at the same time.

Distributive education programs have been implemented in various school districts throughout the country. However, with the new and expanding interest in career education, there is a need for school-business cooperation to be extended into the middle level of education. The following is an outline of this type of program that has been successfully implemented.

Goddard Middle School
Littleton, Colorado

Plan of operation for SCOPE (Student-Community Observer Program and Education).

Purposes of the program:

1. To provide a communication link between the community and the youth of Goddard Middle School.
2. To expose students to the operations of community services and enterprises.
3. To offer a forum for student expression of concern about actions in the community.
4. To provide realistic experiences for students from which they may later make career judgements.
5. To offer a viable alternative to the traditional approach to career counseling.

Mechanics of operation:

1. Students will be placed on a self-interest basis in a community business or local government agency which has been contacted in advance and has expressed an interest.
2. Students are serving as volunteer observers at their assigned agency from 2:00 P.M. to 4:00 P.M. two days a week for a nine-week

period. This time period involves two hours of school time and two hours of the student's own time.

3. Participating students would be scheduled for a seminar to be held at least once during the nine-week period. The purpose of the seminar is to allow the student an opportunity to discuss his participation and the effects of that participation on future courses of action.

4. Agencies are also being invited to submit written evaluation reports regarding the program. This will foster ongoing improvement and continuous communication between the community and the school.

Sample activities in which students are participating:

1. Assisting with activities involving small children at pre-schools.
2. Observing and discussing the operations of the police and fire departments.
3. Doing some simple filing and routine office work, such as answering the telephone.
4. Assisting and observing medical doctors and veterinarians.
5. Working and observing at gas stations, pet shops, and elementary schools.

Ways SCOPE could be introduced into the regular curriculum:

1. SCOPE could be offered through the Social Studies program, through the mini-course approach.
   a. This would be for Social Studies credit and would bring career education into the normal curriculum.
   b. This program would emphasize the skills and attitudes needed in the business and service communities through student participation and observation in the community, combined with seminars and case studies in the classroom.
   c. This program would emphasize student initiative and responsibility as well as introduce him to the attitudes and values of the community.
   d. As for the courses' relation to civics and social studies; issues of the relationship of business, government, social and community responsibility, and questions of government control could be examined.
2. This program could be integrated into all disciplines quite easily.
3. To be expanded, this program would need district money and support for planning, counseling, and teaching of the program.

HOW TO EXTEND THE RESULTS APPROACH
BEYOND THE BUILDING LEVEL

Instructional Calendar: The traditional method of developing yearly calendars is to build it around such concerns as holidays, grading periods, and summer vacation habits. Little, or no, concern is shown toward the anticipated time demands of individual school programs. Regardless of the differences in program structures or levels for which programs are designed, they all must, by tradition or convenience, begin and end at the same time.

If the basic concern is for the development of a learning program best designed to fit learner needs and demands, lock-step time should be eliminated. In its place should be the adoption of learning calendars built on the basis of learning time demands. This results in such variances as primary students and senior high students "beginning the year" and "ending the year" at different times. This is logical, for since their singular needs, characteristics, and time demands differ, their study calendars should differ.

The year-round school program serves as a facilitating force for the development of individualized learning calendars. The year-round program structure can provide the extended time and flexibility in student scheduling to provide for individual student needs and interests. Perhaps, one of the major aspects of the year-round school is that both staff and building resources are available to learners for a longer period of time and, consequently, learner time demands can be met more effectively.

The year-round quarter plan of Atlanta, Georgia, and the 45-15 plan of the La Mesa-Spring Valley District in La Mesa, California, are cases in point of improved time use potential for students.

Atlanta Quarter Plan—Secondary

1. Full programs are offered for four quarters
2. Students have the option of attending any three quarters or all four quarters
3. All four quarters carry equal weight as far as course credits are concerned
4. The dichotomy between regular and summer sessions is reduced
5. Specific courses are required of a student only if his objectives demand the content covered by the courses
6. Students can vary the length of time they are in class each day
7. In terms of course development, the program is ungraded

La Mesa-Spring Valley—Elementary

1. Students are placed in four school attendance groups according to geographic location
2. Three groups attend nine weeks of school while one group is on three weeks of vacation

3. Local building needs are stressed, rather than total district conformity in program innovation
4. Inter-session courses are offered during all of the vacation periods

    A. These are staffed by district teachers on vacation or by available teachers from outside the district

    B. Course lengths vary from one to three weeks

    C. Individual courses vary in their daily meeting times—from one to four hours

    D. Enrollment is optional

    E. Tutoring and student contracting approaches are used

Basically, the type of program structure and the functioning effectiveness of the students working within the structure should determine the instructional calendar for the particular school. It follows, then, that the calendar should be one of the last parts of decision-making to be considered. This should be considered only after careful consideration has been given to such important aspects as projected learning time expectations, program continuum continuity, and staff-student performance levels.

This variation in calendar can result in such positive effects as forcing the staff to consider time allotments in terms of student performance capabilities, individualization of building programs at different levels as well as within buildings, force closer coordination of different level and building programs, and provide flexibility of individual student programs by contributing to the need for keeping instructional centers open longer.

District Testing Programs: There is a growing concern on the parts of many educators and parents about the value of standardized testing. Regardless of the more theoretical questions, one concern is very real—the limited extent to which the typical teacher uses, or even understands, the test results.

Teachers, like students, tend to want to become familiar with those tools and techniques for which they can see a practical use and that apply directly to them as individuals. The typical standardized test approach seemingly does not do this though there is certainly merit to the selective use and application of various tests.

At least in conjunction with carefully selected standardized tests, school staffs could glean much useful information as a result of the school district's developing their own localized K-12 performance achievement tests that are based on and emphasize the what, how, and why of their own programs.

The State of Colorado, and other states, have in a way, given impetus to the development of district testing programs through the passage of accountability legislation. School districts are involved in developing methods and procedures for determining instructional effectiveness. They are involved in developing specific subject area learning objectives and subsequent student performance sub-objectives to determine student use levels of content and skills. This approach also provides ready identification of instructional areas needing improvement.

The use of such a testing program would provide the personal involvement many teachers want. As a result, they would be more likely to use the results. This consequent increased use would also provide the school district with valuable information concerning how well the instructional program reflects the values of the local community and meets the needs of the student population for which the school district is directly responsible.

Implementing this localized evaluation process actively involves staff members in the construction of, administration of, and evaluation of the testing tools. Consequently, more specific indicators can be built into the tests and they are more reflective of the areas of emphasis, effectiveness of techniques and methods used, and of local areas needing improvement. The evaluative instruments are also more adaptable to the changing characteristics of the community resulting from population mobility, economic variations, and program revisions.

Inter-Level Interactions: Sincere educators are always concerned about the lack of articulation and coordination in their K-12 courses of study. They are also concerned about the lackadaisical attitude many staff members have toward meetings involving teachers of the different levels. As a result, a great deal of attention is devoted to eliminating vertical gapping. Results are limited, however.

Again, at least part of the problem here is the fact that many teachers do not feel personal involvement with the concerns of staff members working at other levels. Before progress can be made here, staff members must be made aware of the ways that many concerns and problems are not peculiar to one level alone.

Generally, attempts to create this awareness is done through content development. This works for a short time, perhaps, but as soon as the individual staff members return to their own spheres of operation, separation by space, by level, and by traditional emphasis wipes away the concern.

Administrators, department chairmen, and others responsible for curriculum development must involve their staff members in other ways if the articulative concern is to become an integral aspect of a teacher's functioning. For example, staff members of both the sending elementary school and the receiving middle school could be involved in the decision-making concerning the advancement and retention of students. Cooperative decisions could be made in terms of the functioning effectiveness of a given student at both levels. As these are explored, the staff members, and parents, can better make decisions concerning the probable functioning level of a student than can one teacher or one group of teachers at the same level who are not familiar with the demands of the program of the other level.

Another way of developing this awareness is to assign teachers of one level to work on converse content development for another level. This makes them aware of the concerns of the other staff members and also gives both groups an opportunity to build in preparatory and sequential activities that are based on the areas of emphasis, techniques and methods, and concerns of both teaching levels.

Adult Courses: Parents like demonstrations. Perhaps one of the most effective ways of showing parents just what goes on during a class session is for the school to schedule duplicate classes for parents; they can take the same courses students take. This not only provides lay people with some added insight as to just exactly what is being taught in their school, it also can give them some idea of the problems faced and the efforts made by the teachers to bring about effective learning. Strong parallels can be drawn here because the teachers would face similar dilemmas at both levels of instruction.

Of course, this approach could be of advantage to the school staff in another way. It could serve as an in-service activity for parents. Parents could eventually become effective teacher aides as a result of their becoming better acquainted with the daily functioning of the school and they would become more aware of singular talents they possess and could use in working with a teacher.

Public Education Seminars: In this modern age of change, population mobility, value conflicts, communication problems, and "generation gaps," educators find themselves in the position of paradox—they must keep up with change to meet the present and future needs of students, and yet provide some stabilizing influence in which the public can have confidence; school staffs must reconcile relevancy and accountability; educators must increase educational effectiveness and reduce costs.

Most parents are concerned about their children's education, but they have little in-depth knowledge about learning and the education process. They are given little opportunity by educators to gain this; yet, surveys indicate the better-informed and educated parents are the more supportive.

With this in mind, school districts can develop and schedule public education meetings for the purpose of better informing members of the school community about the total educational program and about the more specific aspects of education as they are seen, developed, implemented, evaluated, and changed by a district's certificated staff.

This approach could contribute to bringing about such results as:

1. Bringing parents "in" more, rather than their merely being on the fringe.

2. Helping taxpayers become more familiar with the concerns of the district staff in terms of developing a sound K-12 educational program.

3. Helping parents develop a better understanding of the value, use of, and results of various "different" instructional methods, techniques, and approaches used in the school district—team teaching, variable scheduling, and many other possibilities—I just use these as examples.

4. More quickly acquaint people new to the district with its educational programs.

5. Taking the program to the people.

6. Possibly give us some indication of the public's interest in gaining more in-depth knowledge about their educational structure.

There is value in identifying such possible topics as the following:

1. New approaches to curriculum development.
2. How courses and content are selected for addition to and deletion from the instructional program.
3. Supreme Court meetings and effects on school operation.
4. Explanation of course content, and reasons why, in the various subject areas.
5. Differentiated staffing, pupil-teacher ratios.
6. How a K-12 course program is developed.
7. Types of school organization, length of school year.
8. Required and elective programs.
9. Changes in education as affected by a changing society.
10. Results-oriented instruction.
11. Library and textbook selection criteria.
12. Other topics suggested by other administrators.

The involvement of supervisors, other central office personnel, and administrators and qualified persons from various other schools at all levels could make valuable contributions through their participation in these meetings.

This approach could be started and kept at the single school level or it could be expanded. The emphasis would not be on just one school, but it would relate to the various levels, to the district, and to modern education as a whole.

Local Budgeting: Just as school calendars should be developed in terms of program instructional demands, so should school budgets. Tradition and bookkeeping convenience are now being played down in favor of such approaches as planned program budgeting systems. This places emphasis on specific program implementation costs, but it can stop there unless district personnel are willing to build district budgets that recognize differences in building programs and that individualized funding is essential to individualized programming and instruction.

A relatively common occurrence is that of individual parents, or isolated groups of parents, asking if a particular aspect of a building program could be included if parents were willing to pay for it. It is also common practice for parent and other public groups to make donations and gifts to schools. These often pertain to one area of instruction, such as music or athletics. Little or nothing has been done to facilitate this on a truly school-wide basis.

It is true there must be consistency in a district program. However, if the community and school personnel subscribe to differentiated programming and individualized program budgeting and they recognize that it is entirely possible for different attendance areas within the same district to have differing value and educational emphases, then the next logical step would be the exploring of possibilities, local and legal, for the parents of a given attendance area to fund, or further fund, a program they desire to see added to, or expanded, in a particular building. If these programs reflect interests and values of a given school attendance and are consistent with existing district-wide concerns, they should be given consideration. Supplementary budgeting procedures could be feasible.

Utilizing Student Appraisal Options: There is relatively common acceptance of the statements relating to the inadequacy of present grading procedures. Part of the cause of inadequacy relates to a breakdown in teacher-parent communications pertaining to student progress descriptions and explanations. There is often a lack of complete satisfaction on the parts of both teachers and parents following progress conferences as as a result of this lack of communication.

Many schools have examined and adopted various ways of reporting student progress. The school staffs have been stymied, however, because these various ways have been adopted as standardized procedures for all teachers to use for all students with all parents.

Again there needs to be individualized flexibility that parallels the program structure and the performance demands imposed on, and by, the teachers. Staff members, then, need to be given the freedom to develop and/or use a variety of reporting techniques and procedures. Teachers need to be given the leeway to select the particular reporting technique that will best facilitate teacher-parent communication. This could result in one teacher using, for example, the traditional letter grade approach with one parent, the anecdotal approach with another parent, and an objective achievement approach with still another parent.

This approach requires that the parent and the teacher sit down and discuss processes that will facilitate their own understanding before they begin to discuss the student. This can help them and the student, and consequently, result in better, continuing public relations.

As a rule, the nature and general characteristics of a course are indicators of the, or types of, assessment procedures that should be used. As a rule of thumb, however, a feasible basis from which a staff can begin to develop an optional grading system would involve consideration of:

1. Use of the performance objective approach for overall performance
2. Content—A-F
   Skills—pass/fail
   Personal—anectodal
3. Descriptive analysis of performance

As they work with, and use, these, staff members will find that (1) the dividing definitive lines between each one begins to fade and teachers begin using various combinations and (2) effective teachers gradually phase out of use all except objectives and performance.

HOW TO STAFF FOR IMPROVED EFFECTIVENESS

Open Staffing: Traditional staffing practices result in teachers being assigned full time to a particular building with possible exceptions of special teachers such as elementary instrumental teachers, all instructors, and support personnel such as speech therapists. By and large, these assignments are by necessity rather than by individualized programming.

With individualized programming and budgeting, and open-attendance boundaries and other practices that work toward breaking down the closed structuring of building programs, there can be definite advantages to using open staffing practices. This approach involves assigning staff members to programs rather than to just buildings. If the emphasis is on program development, then qualified staff members should be assigned to function within specified areas of their particular specialties in more of an instructional complex approach.

The staff assignment practice can be particularly effective, for example, in school districts utilizing the short course structure, in districts with extremes in population turnover and consequent student achievement levels, and in districts implementing innovative pilot programs. This practice enables the district to assign staff members according to changing staffing needs and to match teacher strengths to changing student needs and interests. It also prevents inbreeding which can occur when there is very little teacher turnover in individual schools.

Multi-Level Staffing: School administrators may well find it advantageous to consider developing staffing practices that will enable them to assign qualified staff members up and down the K-12 ladder according to the relationship of teacher strengths and greatest instructional needs. This approach involves not consistently assigning teachers to just the senior high for example, but to assigning them anywhere along the educational continuum where their talents and characteristics can best be used. This could vary anywhere from the upper elementary level to the advanced placement level. Many teachers are capable of teaching at the intermediate, middle, and senior high levels. Why arbitrarily restrict maximum use of their capabilities?

Multi-level staffing offers the same advantages that open-staffing does. It also can facilitate instructional and program development continuity because teachers develop a functioning familiarity with the different levels of program implementation.

This functioning familiarity with the different program levels, both staff and student, contributes to the improvement of learner and teacher performance because staff members are directly involved in the development, implementing, and appraisal of the curricular framework, the teaching demands, and the learning demands. The fact that the faculty set specific performance objectives, identify the methods of achievement, and the consequent procedural framework means that they commit themselves to a results-oriented program for both staff and students.

Some Action Guidelines

Program:

1. The results curriculum is based on identification of individual performance. As the school staff develops the operational structure, they must also develop at each stage corresponding personnel and performance demands. Basic to this are the delineation of

   basic purpose(s) for inclusion of each aspect of the program

   sequential objectives for each program stage

   staff roles and responsibilities

   performance characteristics of each aspect of the program as it is developed

2. The basic aspects of the program development are related to structural framework, personnel functioning, and consequent performance results. One cannot be developed effectively in isolation from the other two. As a result, as staff members consider specific program structure characteristics, they must also consider the specific programmatic effects on personnel and results.

3. Because the emphasis of the structural development is on results, traditional subject area divisions should not be used as basic programming determiners. Instead, purposes, objectives, roles, responsibilities, and performance results must be primary determiners of structure.

4. The program structure, to facilitate practical performance application by the learner, must be developed so that participating community institutions are included. This includes such areas as purpose, methods of utilization, and assessment. Procedures and standards must be developed for participating institution selection.

5. Development of the program structure must include the staff's serious consideration of the programming effects on the learners. As a result, the program demands should facilitate change in staff functioning as their effectiveness indicates the teachers are being progressively less needed by individual students. Included here would be such aspects as

   identification of changing roles of the learner

   flexibility in learner time demands

   development at the building level of criteria and procedures for adding and deleting program aspects in terms of changing student needs.

Personnel:

1. The program structure demands certain functioning skills of the staff. As each phase of the program framework is developed, an inventory of existing staff skills should be made to ascertain such programming implementation aspects as

   time and rate of implementation

   anticipated effectiveness level

   additional in-service needs

   new staff talents needed.

2. Identification of the specific staff skills and talents will provide a reliable basis for selection of program facets. Program development must be based on what the staff has shown it can do well. Program development is sequential, built on existing strengths of the staff. Implementation of an innovative aspect requiring immediate, drastic change in total staff functioning demands should be avoided.

3. Anticipatory planning is essential in programming because of the consequent probable changes in staff functioning demands. As subsequent programming changes are identified, so should the expected staff performance change expectations be identified. This helps reduce the possibility of performance failure caused by a gap between program demands and personnel capabilities.

4. Too often, performance delineation is limited only to staff members assigned to the building full time. The same attention must be given to the development of roles, responsibilities, performance demands, and assessment of support personnel because their performance can greatly affect the effectiveness of the resident staff.

Performance:

1. Appraisal of program effectiveness necessitates the appraisal of individual performance. This individual assessment must be done in terms of the specific program demands, identified roles and responsibilities, and objectives because appraisal of the staff member is also an appraisal of the program. Criteria must be developed that will reveal the capability of the staff member to function within the program structural demands.

2. Appraisal must go beyond the broad program and staff functioning areas. It must also consider such aspects as

the types of options and alternatives available to staff and students

the levels and kinds of anticipatory planning by staff members

changes brought about by staff and learner effectiveness

extent and kind of unidentified conflicts materializing as a result of sequential program phase implementation.

3. Definite consideration must be given to the development of procedures that will reveal the relationship between programming, staff and learner effectiveness, and funding. Cost and performance results should be closely correlated.

4

DEVELOPING A PERFORMANCE-ORIENTED STAFFING FRAMEWORK

The degree to which a program is implemented is determined by the extent to which the staff can function effectively within the program structure and its performance demands. Change in program operational demands necessitates a consequent change in staff functions. A results-oriented curricular structure, then, requires the parallel development of a performance-based staffing framework.

Too often, educators attempt to implement a new type of program without making the necessary consequent changes in the existing framework demands that will provide supportive force for the success of the new approach. Generally, change demands related to staff functioning are neglected because of faculty focus on content organization and on the mechanical structuring of the program.

One of the major problems in education is that faculties are continually attempting one of two things: (1) to implement open-ended methods and programs by persons with closed-space ideas and consequent lack of practical know-how, or (2) force persons with open-ended ideas to function "effectively" in dead-ended programs. Too little effort is made to eliminate closed-space ideas and dead-ended programs and match open-ended people with open-space ideas. Mismatches often end in loss of prestige by both persons and programs.

DEVELOPING OPEN STAFF ROLES
AND RESPONSIBILITIES

Traditionally, school programs are planned and implemented on the basis of a closed philosophy. Such closed development of concepts, as rigid required/elective lists, teacher classification as elementary *or* secondary, and staff assignments according to subject matter specialization, contribute to the evolution of an instructional approach that relegates staff members to operational niches, and learners as outsiders who must prove their adaptive worth before they can be accepted as a functioning member of the educational society.

Many educators are aware of the "locking-in" process that results. In their attempts to do something about it, however, they tend to work with only one aspect, either staffing or programming. One affects the other. In reality, the program structure and emphases determine the roles, responsibilities, and operational patterns of the faculty. Since, traditionally, program structures are isolated and compartmentalized, it is only natural for staffs and staffing patterns to assume the same characteristics.

Much less time and attention has been devoted to staffing patterns necessary for open-ended programming than has been devoted to program structuring. This leads to consequent imbalance of emphasis.

The author served as a consultant to a school staff involved in developing a differentiated staffing framework. This staff was sincere and capable, but during the time they were developing the framework, they had not fully identified different staff responsibilities and objectives. The staff members were devoting more time to identifying ways and means to reduce their clerical and other non-student-teacher activities. They were looking primarily at individual staff concerns as separate from the inter-related desired staff objectives and consequent programming needs.

Each individual staff member's operational effectiveness is directly related to the extent his functioning patterns dovetail with the operational demands and forces of the program structure. Therefore, if there is to be articulation and coordination in learning and instruction, the program structure must be developed in terms of an overall learning continuum, not solely in terms of content compartmentalization. Once this is done, staffing patterns must be developed to coincide with this continuum structure. This involves the use of the open staffing approach.

The role of the faculty member functioning within the open staffing structure is somewhat different from that demanded by the traditional staffing structure. In open staffing, the staff member is not so much responsible for a restricted aspect identified within subject content limitations as he is with student progress within a particular phase of the learning continuum. His responsibilities are identified specifically around the skills-content-behavior composite. He is directly concerned with a student's progress and position along the continuum as these relate to the student's profile of performance. More specifically, the teacher's role and responsibilities can be described as the continuous interaction of the continuum of the program, of the learner, of the subject matter, and of change.

Since open staffing involves the assignment of a given teacher to a program rather than to a building, his specific talents can be utilized wherever they are needed. Following is an example of a reading teacher's schedule in two different program stages.

Talents and Skills
1. Training in remedial reading
2. Can communicate with students at all levels
3. Possesses an outgoing personality
4. Knows how to design individualized programs
5. Views reading as a basic tool rather than simply his subject specialty

School A	School B
1. Teaches a short course in "Fun Through Reading" to seventh-grade students	1. Chairs a committee of teachers to develop a pilot reading program for 14 tenth-grade students functioning below grade level
2. Serves as a resource reading person to math and science departments	2. Meets with involved students to ascertain their individual needs and learning objectives

3. Works with four new students who have both reading and social adjustment difficulties

3. Meets with the parents and students to develop individual learning programs involving "at home" reading activities
4. Works with building Language Arts personnel to integrate pilot program with other building and inter-building departmental demands

Sample Characteristics of Operational Learning Structure

Program Demands Continuum	Student Functioning Continuum
1. Decision-making	Patterns of learning
	learner
2. Emphasis on learning	Interests, needs, motivation
	progress
3. Performance and objective emphasis	Achievement level desires
	objectives
4. Patterns of expected behavior	Value systems
	Adjustment to program demands

Change continuum

Subject matter sequence continuum

Phases of K-12 programs
Learner operational skills
Performance level demands
Objectives

A primary role of the teacher is to develop and maintain an instructional learning structure that facilitates an alternating current effect between the learning continua. In order to do this, a parallel structure must also be developed that describes the instructional functions. A dovetailing of the two sets of continua, then, defines the courses of action for both the learner and the teacher.

STAFFING ACCORDING TO PROGRAM FUNCTIONING DEMANDS

As the program and content continua are developed, such aspects as those in the diagram are built into each sectional phase. Automatically, the desired, and expected, teacher functioning emphases are defined. Staffing, then, is done on the basis of the matching of the described staff functioning with talents and skills of the teacher. Assignment is not done on the basis of subject matter preparation alone. Individual staff assignments are made on the bases of student grouping evolving from the identification of priority areas within interacting continua framework. A given staff member can be assigned at different levels and within different continua anywhere along the total program continuum.

PROGRAM EMPHASES	STAFF OPERATIONAL SKILLS
1. Flexibility	1. Use of options/alternative approach
2. Individualization	2. Functioning in terms of specific performance objectives
3. Variable scheduling	3. Use of continuous individualized curriculum design at the learner level
4. Performance results	4. Utilization of open-ended instructional techniques
5. Innovation	5. Application of combined student-teacher self-appraisal procedures
	6. Operating more in terms of people than in terms of subject matter

STAFF TALENTS NEEDED

1. Skills in human interaction
2. Capability of originating, developing, implementing, and evaluating approaches to meet individual student needs
3. Ability to initiate and maintain change
4. Capability of attaining specific performance objectives
5. Ability to recognize learner changes and to develop sequential learning experiences in terms of these
6. Capability, and confidence, to function satisfactorily in a flexible framework that offers no security through routine, authoritarian structuring

Within this overall framework, a number of variations can be worked out according to the individual needs and desires of a given building. The basic requirement here is the development within the staff of the capabilities of facilitating learning within different structural frameworks and at different, but sequential, levels with emphasis on the learner, not on content.

In one school, within the open-ended short course programming structure, individual staff members identified student needs and interests, then each quarter developed courses related to the teacher's strengths and selected student needs or interests. Courses were continued, added, or deleted according to changing student demand.

The following are examples of ways a teacher's schedule can change as a result of the emphasis on the learner and his needs.

FIRST QUARTER	SECOND QUARTER
1—Math Skills	1—Algebra—Team
2—Math Skills	2—Algebra—Team
3—Social Studies	3—Social Studies
4—Social Studies	4—Social Studies
5—Art History	5—Beginning Oil Painting
6—Beginning Oil Painting	6—Human Relations

USING SUPPORT PERSONNEL TO IMPROVE INSTRUCTION

Out-of-building support personnel must be considered as part of the building staff if they are involved in activities that directly affect the day-to-day functioning of the school. As a result, their roles and responsibilities must also be structured in terms of the specific type of program being implemented in a given school. There cannot be a dichotomy between the way they are expected, or desired, to function and the way the teachers in the building must operate. If there is, by extension, there is a split in the staff.

There is no doubt that subject matter specialists and coordinators can play an important role in school program development. However, their restriction to content emphasis contributes to the gapping of total learning program development and implementation.

UTILIZING THE "HOW-TO" SKILLS OF SUPPORT PERSONS

There is a definite need for support personnel who can help staff members increase their effectiveness in the other aspects of instruction—techniques and methods, personnel management, and performance recognition, to name a few. Content could become involved here only in a satellite sense. Major emphasis should be on the "how-to" approach that affects development, implementation, and evaluation of mechanics, skills, and approaches.

This, in no way, is bypassing the school administrators for they are support personnel in this way. They would also be directly involved in the identification of the need for specific specialists, for coordinating, directing, and appraising their work, and for developing program structures and frameworks within which the support people would function.

Staffing often is equated with cost alone, rather than in tandem with objectives and effectiveness, with accountability, and with effective use of time and talent. Increased effectiveness is not a discount item. It is, instead, a priority that demands attention, more so perhaps, at the outset, from the standpoints of time and talent utilization rather than from the monetary viewpoint. With this in mind, the following suggestions are made concerning specific support personnel roles and responsibilities.

EXAMPLES OF SUPPORT PERSONNEL UTILIZATION

Methods and Techniques: A support person could be of value by helping teachers individually and collectively to become more proficient in the selection and mastery of instructional and learning techniques methods, organization, and management. The primary emphasis here would be on the improvement of teacher skill use levels related to adaptation of materials, to dovetailing learning and teaching patterns, to personalizing instruction, and to individualized diagnostic testing, for example.

The support person here would not necessarily be a subject matter specialist, but rather a person who was skilled in the developing of on-the-job professional skills, of retraining, of motivating change. His primary approach would be through human interaction, demonstration teaching, and practical in-service activities. In order for him to be able to work at all levels of the district K-12 structure, he would have to be well acquainted with the singular instructional demands and needs at each level, be aware of the unique characteristics of teacher groups working at the elementary, middle, and senior high levels, and be competent in working for change within a traditional framework.

Ways and Means: This resource position could be particularly effective at the building level. It would involve a staff member in the building being assigned at least one-half of his time to research and development, with emphasis on building needs. This person could be assigned such responsibilities as developing and coordinating continuous program evaluation procedures in terms of state and federal accountability guidelines, organizing and coordinating adult volunteer aids, research, and digesting information on new techniques in terms that could be further developed by individual teachers or departments; this could be more of a clearing house function. He would also serve as a resource person for building curriculum committees. In addition, he could be assigned other duties that are vital to the effective functioning of the building program, but that are short-term in nature such as district-initiated study reports and parent-staff-student advisory groups.

Again, he would not be assuming the principal's role or responsibilities. He would, however, take some of the routine work from the principal who would have more time to devote to his primary roles of instructional leader of program development and of quality control.

Clerical Pool: Any discussion of results-oriented staffing patterns must of necessity include the use of clerical support people. From the practical standpoint, clerical assistance is effective only if it is available at the time of need. Since adequate clerical aid is vital to the smooth functioning of the teaching-learning processes, the providing of a volunteer clerical pool available to the classroom teachers should be considered an integral part of program staffing.

Pre-planning on the part of the teachers is essential, however, if their specific needs are to be met. Each staff member must be able to anticipate his needs accurately enough in terms of specific clerical skills, times of priority need, and clerical personality characteristics, so that he can write a clerical job description in terms of his singular situation. Once this, and the corresponding performance skill and availability description are completed by each volunteer, it is relatively easy to match talents and skills, and to maintain a ready supply of clerical help.

No attempt has been made to present a complete open staffing structure at the support level. The examples given do, however, present enough of a picture to show the possibilities and variations that are possible in terms of a results emphasis approach.

In one school, stressing the use of parent volunteers, staff pre-planning in terms of lay help needs and the consequent development of lay job roles enabled the Coordinator of Volunteers to make available to the staff 227 hours of volunteer time each week.

	Number Volunteered	Number hours per week
TUTORS	22	63
ART LAB	8	28
PRIDE	5	10 (Could be more)
CLINIC	5	22
	(6 substitutes)	
OTHER:		
Counseling office		12
Ditto		10
Typing	66	12
Music, Math,		
Misc. Depts.		50
(9 persons did 81 hours one week on one project)		
(7 persons did 50 hours on a two-week project)		
Coordinator	1	20
Totals	107 persons	227 hours per week

HOW TO IMPROVE ADMINISTRATIVE SKILLS
THROUGH OPEN STAFFING

Educational literature is filled with suggestions related to what the building administrators can, and should, do to increase their instructional leadership effectiveness. There still exists, though, gaps between what many administrators should do and what they actually do. These gaps occur because of such causal factors as lack of a managerial structure, job skills use levels limitations, and a tendency to perform at the mechanistics level rather than at the initiating leadership level.

Generally speaking, situations such as these are maintained at the problem level because of the administrative penchant for functioning in terms of semi-isolation, of being concerned primarily with intra-building operation and neglecting the imposing and emanating influences that result from the confluent effects of the various district programs.

Because of the nature of their roles and responsibilities, the building administrators cannot function effectively in isolation or in terms of individual interests, strengths, and comforts. They are judged accountable according to the overall effectiveness of their school programs. Consequently, they must possess the skills needed to increase both building and district effectiveness. In order to acquire these skills, administrators need to be given opportunities to function at both building and district levels.

It is not an uncommon practice for school districts to establish various structures that utilize teacher and subject area groups and committees to develop K-12 content guidelines; and assign administrators to the various committees to serve in liaison or advisory roles. This grassroots approach stresses both staff involvement and teacher-administrator teamwork. Too often, however, direct concentrated administrator involvement in the K-12 guideline implementation at the teacher-student level loses impetus beyond this committee stage.

To prevent this loss of impetus, school districts could find it advantageous to activate building administrator groups to continue working with individual K-12 programs from such standpoints as expected teacher performance patterns, possible staffing characteristics and needs, carry-over influences into other content areas, and methods of dovetailing implementation procedures at the different levels of the K-12 continuum.

Possible Administrator Activities

1. Identification of expected teacher performance patterns in a newly-developed K-12 guideline
2. Development of best staffing pattern related to new program implementation
3. Detailing interdisciplinary aspects of a single discipline guideline
4. Developing specific accountability procedures for each level of the K-12 structure
5. Working with subject matter committees to develop accountability criteria for each discipline

This approach enables the building administrators to expend concentrated efforts on specific instructional objective-oriented activities involving their own and other levels of responsibility. It facilitates the evolvement of the specific outcome of providing ways for the administrators to become better acquainted with more of the specific content continuum, to work more closely with persons assigned to the stages, or levels, and to provide more active leadership in program implementation, thereby helping them become more aware of the overlapping influence and effects the various school programs have on each other.

Rotation of administrative personnel to committees concerned with content areas outside of their own major subject area specialization provides still more opportunity for the administrators to develop better understanding of the singular demands, approaches, and needs of each major content area. As a result, they can work in a more constructive manner in coordinating the various sub-units of the building programs so that improved staff and program cohesiveness, identification of total staff objectives, and interdepartmental articulation can become practical realities rather than just remain theoretical desires.

HOW TO BEGIN DEVELOPING TOTAL STAFF PERFORMANCE OBJECTIVES

Staffing according to specific learning needs and program emphasis along a continuum facilitates, through identification and priority leveling of objectives and processes, implementing of the performance results concepts. The singular emphasis on the development of specifics from the standpoints of identification of program, learner, and content continua, of variable staffing patterns, and instructional area functioning descriptions related to the phases of the continua help set the framework and guidelines for the development of performance results objectives. This emphasis also provides some structure for the development of expected staff/student functioning patterns.

From here, the next logical step is the faculty's developing of staff sub-group objectives, and from this the development of total staff performance results for a given year. The continued emphasis on specifics as the staff moves from individual to group results objectives can present developmental problems because of the progressive involvement of more people who, as a group, must continue to reject the consequent tendency to become more general in thinking as a result of added individual input.

Following is a basic guide for developing faculty objectives:

I. Purpose
   A. Give direction for program development
   B. Provide framework for staff development of individual instructional objectives
   C. Provide bases for
      1. determining staff effectiveness
      2. developing guidelines for
         a. relevancy
         b. accountability
   D. Identify individual and staff performance emphases
II. Procedure for Staff Members
   A. Familiarization with school philosophy and clarification of individual staff member's philosophy
   B. Identification of needs of students in terms of
      1. Present and future
      2. Staff talents
      3. District program
      4. Community outlooks
      5. Student characteristics
   C. Self-appraisal of individual and staff functions in terms of
      1. Learning emphases
      2. Student needs
      3. Individual teacher performance patterns
   D. Identification of
      1. Present performance levels and characteristics of staff
      2. What staff wants to accomplish as a group
      3. Consequent possible functioning demands
   E. Development of specific staff objectives
   F. Identification of procedures to attain objectives
   G. Development of assessment criteria and monitoring system

One faculty with which the author was involved, using the above approach, developed total staff objectives for a school year related to

1. Development of staff self-appraisal procedures related to performance objectives
2. Involvement of students in learning activities selection
3. Implementation of a short course approach in the Social Studies and Math Departments
4. Continued in-service endeavors related to improvement of staff skills in planning and implementing individualized learning programs

5. Development and implementation of procedures to reduce intra-departmental and inter-departmental instructional gapping

At the end of the year, the staff felt that, though there were varying degrees of objective attainment, the fact that their identification of, and focus on, specific areas of concern was a primary contributor to both staff and parent feeling of increased learning effectiveness.

DEVISING IN-SERVICE ACTIVITIES
FOR DEVELOPMENT OF STAFF OBJECTIVES

The degree to which a staff can work together to develop results objectives depends, of course, on a number of factors. Important among these are the extent to which individuals are willing and capable of accepting total staff objectives, the degree to which each individual can dovetail with the staff objectives his own instructional and personal objectives in an expanding, sequential manner, and the level of sophistication the individuals have in working with results objectives.

A new program cannot be implemented and be effective unless the staff members involved in the implementation are able to practice and to apply adequately the particular functioning skills that are demanded by that program. An innovative program placed within an unchanging tradition structure by staff members using methods and techniques of another structure and emphasis has little, if any, chance of succeeding. Unfortunately, too many faculties find this out through sad experience; then often the program per se rather than human error in application, is identified as the cause of failure. The same holds true for the development of total staff objectives.

Moline High School in Moline, Illinois, has implemented a unified science program designed to provide opportunity for success for every student enrolled in the program. The structure emphasizes individual student differences in needs, interests, and capabilities. Success of the program was dependent on the science staff's revealed capabilities to function effectively within a framework of team teaching, performance objectives, and individualized learning. In this case, effective articulation of program design and staff skills resulted in improving learner functioning.

The experience this author has had in working with staffs attempting to develop staff objectives has helped him to identify a number of causes of development difficulties. Among these are

1. Lack of staff experience in effective sequential developmental planning at the total staff level—beyond content and grading period time limits.
2. Conditioned over-concern with the mechanical program operations level and with daily problem areas.
3. Lack of skills needed for the development of priorities through the rejection and options processes.
4. Lack of experience in working with results objectives and planning ahead for group results.

Though working to develop total staff results objectives may be a new experience for a given faculty, it is, perhaps, one of the most effective ways for the school staff to structure and implement quality control procedures. Even though most teachers have worked, in one way or another, with "general" and "specific" objectives, they have dealt only in a superficial manner with quality control. The more in-depth working with staff performance objectives requires teacher participation in in-service activities led by effective leaders who can function within the framework limitations of staff experience, desires, and potential. This is essential, for the staff must learn the singular skills and techniques of developing and implementing processes that are demanded by the identified performance objectives.

The school staff becomes directly involved in effective quality control as they work to

1. Develop performance results objectives
2. Master skills necessary to implement desired program changes
3. Identify satisfactory performance standards for staff and students
4. Develop effective appraisal systems
5. Develop structural organization in terms of priorities, time, and talent
6. Parallel staff operational patterns and program functioning demands
7. Identify job descriptions, roles, and responsibilities of both staff and students

Once a staff has become oriented to these approaches, has gained an understanding of the concepts, and has gained some skill in developing and implementing total staff objectives, they will find they have also made definitive progress toward solving such problems as intra-staff isolation, personal and departmental philosophical splits, priorities, identification, and program budgeting. There is also more undivided understanding of what the total staff will be trying to do, and how and why. This is certainly farther down the road of accountability than most staffs have traveled in the past.

DEVELOPING TEACHER PERFORMANCE PATTERNS ACCORDING TO PROGRAM DEMANDS

As a school program is developed, the roles, responsibilities, and functioning patterns of the teachers are defined and described in relative detail. Just as the organizational pattern must be developed in terms of the results desired, staff job delineation must be done in terms of program demands and forces. Individualization is involved here just as it is at the student performance level.

The various sequential stages of the program continuum have their own singular sub-demands and sub-forces that affect the performance patterns of the teachers working within these stages. Because of certain similarities of characteristics between stages, there will be functioning demands common to all stages. Though these are all important, it is the delineation of the differentiated functioning patterns, and consequent techniques and method implementation, that play such an important role in increasing learning effectiveness.

Program Characteristics	Staff Functioning Characteristics
1. Individualization emphasis	1. Personalized student/teacher interaction
2. Continuous progress structure	2. Planning for and managing changes
3. Performance results base	3. Instructional design in terms of continuous self-appraisal
4. Open-minded programming	4. Functioning at idea level as well as implementation level

| 5. Direct staffing structure | 5. Functioning skill-content-personal levels according to changing student needs |

These differing functioning patterns are determined by, and in a way, selected by, such identified characteristics as learner patterns, difficulty of content in relation to learner skills, teacher skill use levels, results objectives selected, and relationships between learning skills needed, content studied, and class activities selected. These differentiated patterns are also identified in terms of the teacher's expected level of student learning effectiveness. This expected level of effectiveness is, unfortunately, translated by most teachers to mean "expected level of achievement"; it is not necessarily synonomous. Effectiveness refers primarily to how well a student learns in terms of application and benefit, in terms of relationship to his own recognized needs and interest, and in terms of his own desired level of societal functioning. This, often times, is not in harmony with the level of achievement expected by the teacher, which he uses as a gauge of his own success.

One of the major factors contributing to this gapping is the developmental characteristics of the classroom power structure. Too often, this evolves into a subtle conflict between students and teacher. It is important that each teacher, as he develops a classroom learning structure, takes into account the need for considering ways to reconcile the opposing forces so that the power structure is conducive to learning as well as to teaching. Part of the staff member's responsibility is to develop and manage the power structure.

Learning Structure Characteristics	Classroom Power Structure Characteristics
1. Performance level demands	1. Group learning patterns
2. Patterns of expected behavior	2. Past levels of success and failure
3. Continuous progress structure	3. Attitudes toward learning and authority
4. Teacher/student team planning	4. Social interaction skills
5. Peer group discipline approach	5. Clique leadership influence

| 6. Emphasis related to learner and content | 6. General group personality and individual personal values |

Job delineation is also determined by course descriptions, value, and place in curriculum. A problem here is that course descriptions are usually written only in terms of content to be covered, special requirements, pre-requisites, and the like. Little is said about specific value to the learner, how the course will be taught, what will be expected of the learner, and the course level placement in the content continuum. From this standpoint, perhaps, it is only natural to expect that the instructional job description would be content-oriented. Perhaps, also, this is why educators have developed the habit of developing delimiting role descriptions rather than developing area frameworks within which the expected functioning patterns, roles, and responsibilities are identified.

The following role and responsibilities objectives that do provide guidelines for expected staff functioning were developed by a staff developing the program structure for a newly-organized middle school in the Boulder, Colorado, School District.

GOALS FOR THE LOUISVILLE MIDDLE SCHOOL

The faculty and administration of Louisville Middle School will:

A. Help all students develop/maintain a self-image as responsible persons of value.
B. Develop programs that will recognize the wide variations in social and academic levels of development of the students.
C. Provide the students with the materials and facilities necessary for learning.
D. Nurture respect and understanding for people, environment, and ecology.
E. Focus planning and instruction on the needs of individual students.

PROCESS OBJECTIVES FOR TEACHER-ADVISORS

A. Apply basic skills in human relations when interacting with students, parents, staff, and administrators.
B. Provide assistance to students as an active *listener*.
   1. Recognize a student who needs assistance.
   2. Recognize the problems and needs of students in terms of the student's experiences in relation to today's world.

    3. Aid students in self-understanding.
    4. Aid students to recognize and respect individual differences in others.
    5. Recognize when a student should be referred to a counselor.
  C. Work closely with the counselor to meet individual student needs.
    1. Aid students in selecting courses and planning their schedules to fit their individual interests and needs.
    2. Assist counselors with interpreting standardized test information for students and parents.
  D. Guide the student in learning how to learn.
    1. Provide an atmosphere that is open and comfortable for the student's communication.
    2. Help the student develop confidence in his own ability to learn.
    3. Help the student learn problem-solving techniques.
    4. Bring to the classroom a personal and creative approach toward implementing these objectives.

Course descriptions, of course, need to be written. Teachers should not try to write them in isolation, however, just as they should not attempt to teach courses in isolation from the human factors that influence learning effectiveness. Again, course descriptions and job delineations should be developed in terms of instructional, learning, and content continua. When this is done, role and responsibility application is emphasized and job descriptions, per se, tend to be phased out of the instructional picture.

Basic Determiners of Functioning Patterns

    1. Emphasis of subject matter
    2. Functioning pattern of administrator
    3. Level of teacher-learner interaction
    4. Teacher feeling of competency
    5. Teacher-need time demands of students
    6. Objectives to be attained
    7. Student learning patterns
    8. Program structure demands

Following is an example of a course description approach that describes the roles and responsibilities of the teacher and the learner.

COURSE: Advanced Sewing—
    Each student will decide what garment she will make in terms of her sewing skill and fashion interest. She will follow the pattern directions.

She will select the style and colors that are becoming to her. She will be given the opportunity to participate in a fashion show wearing her own creation.

ANTICIPATED VALUE TO LEARNER—
1. Further development of her sewing skills
2. Opportunity to make some of her own clothes
3. Opportunity to consult personally with a local department store Teen Consultant concerning the style, colors, and material that would be most becoming to her.
4. Experience in modeling
5. Increased knowledge about her personel clothing needs

LEARNER RESPONSIBILITIES—
1. Selection and purchase of material and pattern
2. Setting of standards of sewing excellence
3. Identification of areas of competence and areas of needed instructor help
4. Development of specific criteria for appraisal of her work
5. Development of anticipated garment completion schedule
6. Identification of reference material
7. Identification of planned ways of applying knowledge and skills gained

TEACHER RESPONSIBILITIES—
1. Help students select garments in terms of learner strengths and weaknesses
2. Provide sewing advisory help as needed
3. Identify individual student need time
4. Provide students opportunities to make their own decisions
5. Schedule with students progress appraisal checkpoints
6. Provide opportunities for students to wear and display garments
7. Develop self-appraisal criteria related directly to learner performance
8. Stay out of students' way when observed student progress is satisfactory

In practice, traditional job descriptions have a limiting effect on performance effectiveness because they are usually written from the teaching standpoint and because they generally emphasize functioning limitations rather than performance capabilities. Also, many times, job descriptions are restrictive because they cannot be written, or changed, to encompass the varied, and changing roles and responsibilities thrust upon the teacher by the learner.

Typically, so-called teacher job descriptions include such responsibilities as the following:

1. Obligation for continued self-improvement
2. Preparation of lesson plans
3. Serving on professional committees
4. Completion of inventory, attendance, and other forms
5. Making selves available to meet needs of students
6. Communication with parents
7. Assumption of certain non-teaching assignments such as grounds supervision

The above are general, vague, and pertaining to mechanics. Though they do provide some kind of job accountability, they have little to do specifically with performance effectiveness. Consequently, they should be replaced in priority listing by such action guideposts as the following:

1. Identification of specific objectives to be attained
2. Development of individual in-service programs
3. Development and implementation of teacher-learner performance standards
4. Development of functioning roles and responsibilities related to learners, other staff members, and program
5. Identification of what the individual staff member can do to make himself a more effective and positive force in the organizational structure
6. Clarification of what level of performance can be expected of him in terms of his existing skills and potential

DEFINING BASIC ASPECTS OF
EFFECTIVE PERFORMANCE PATTERNS

In setting performance guidelines, delineating of roles and responsibilities is essential. Along with this is the identification of the singular staff qualifications necessary to these roles and responsibilities. The problem of inflexibility arises here, however. That is, definition and description can result in a "locking-in" of job requirements and qualifications that can inhibit initiative and creative effectiveness. Though there must be some consistency in terms of both staff member and student, it is not realistic to assume that job requirements cannot change. Job requirements must be subject to a flow effect that allows the performance activities of the teacher to vary and to change in terms of learner progress. Since it is impossible to stop the learner's change, it is only sound reasoning to plan a performance framework that allows a paralleling changing of teacher performance specifications with changing learner characteristics. It follows, then, that if a teacher expects to work in an effective manner with students, he cannot be satisfied with the status quo. The status quo exists only for the present, and should not be prolonged, as it often is, in relation to the educational process.

Perhaps, all this points out the need for another important characteristic school administrators should have and should look for while interviewing teacher applicants. That is the drive for success—the capability of defining and recognizing progressive success, the ability to function so that success is attained. Success in this respect should be considered in terms of the extent a staff member progresses in effectiveness beyond the identified performance satisfaction point for the program framework within which an individual is functioning.

In delineating jobs and function patterns, a great deal of consideration should be given to descriptions of the individual's roles, responsibilities, authority, and accountability. Every staff member must work within these inter-related, yet sometimes separate, frameworks. So often, these areas are considered in practice as terms only, becoming job realities only when an individual feels his academic freedom, for example, is being encroached upon; yet, it is these very definitive aspects of his performance expectations, properly applied, that can help prevent many intra-staff conflicts.

In too many cases, the so-called "typical" educator sees his job primarily in terms of authority, in terms of what he thinks his superior expects of him, and in terms of possible conflicts between himself and his appraiser. Little attention is given to how the appraiser views these aspects or how they are affected by the program demands. Role, responsibility, authority, and accountability must be delineated from all three standpoints. After delineation, both the individual staff member and his superior must work in terms of the resultant framework.

As a consultant, this author has been asked often to clarify role, responsibility, authority, and accountability in terms of the specific situation in which the groups with which he was meeting were working. As a result of this, and consequent discussions with each group, it has been his experience that the following basic definitions of each one can serve as a starting place for any individual staff working to clarify them within its own program framework. Though the staff may work with each one separately, as the faculty progresses, it finds these four concepts are very much inter-related, as the following definitions will show.

Role: The primary functions of the teacher are to help each student function in a more positive manner at present, to help prepare him to function effectively in the future, and to make himself progressively less needed by the student. The role of the teacher, then, is to work with each student in such a way as to help the learner become more independent and more proficient in decision-making, and in dealing in a satisfactory manner with the various types and levels of conflict that he meets in daily living. His role is working with the learner to help him become proficient in recognizing, solving, and managing problems peculiar to his own way of life within a common social structure.

Responsibility: The basic responsibility of the teacher is to provide each student with an educational framework that gives him opportunities to work with various option and alternative processes and procedures which will help the learner develop his own functioning patterns to facilitate achieving his desired results. The teacher's responsibility is to provide opportunities and learning situations that will help each student develop an open-ended learning approach which will help him develop and maintain positive learning behavior.

Authority: Effective teaching authority is reflected in the learning framework rather than developed as a separate, threaten-entity. Consequently, authority is apparent and applied in terms of the methods and procedures used in the classroom. These practices are developed in terms of human interaction, in terms of self-set objectives by both learner and teacher and in terms of mutual understanding of the need for common learning values.

Accountability: The teacher works toward the achieving of accountability as he works to gain results by the student. A basic starting definition of accountability, then, is the teacher's gaining results from the students that are of benefit to the learner and are in accord with the value structure of society. This involves effective decision-making, learning performance, and directly or indirectly, all aspects mentioned under role, responsibility, and authority. Perhaps, however, there is more lay involvement in the definition of accountability than in the other definitions because, in the last analysis, it is the public that determines the extent of accountability.

FACTORS AFFECTING TEACHER DELINEATION OF ACTION AREAS

Each teacher is responsible for developing his actual functioning framework within the broader program structure. He does this through his day-to-day performance levels and patterns. Unfortunately, in most cases, these evolve only as a result of habit, rather than through conscious effort. The result is a pattern of operation that shows consistent progress only in routine.

In order to avoid this exercise in open-ended inefficiency and ennui, every staff member must be constantly aware of basic personal factors that influence the development of his functioning patterns. These will, of course, vary with each individual and with each program, but, by and large, they generally will relate to the broad categories of attitude and skill.

One of these basic factors is the extent of acceptance of the overall program delineation. The degree of agreement will be determined by how well each individual can function within the program forces and demands, how well he can adjust personal and program differences, and how much personal performance satisfaction he gains from working within the program structure. Honest acceptance precludes performance satisfaction.

Another factor that affects individual staff delineation is the teacher's cognizance of the various aspects of his own instructional management system—as different from his routine and habitual functioning patterns. Unless the teacher can define, and justify, his own philosophy and consequent methodology, he cannot expect to function effectively within a broader program continuum. Some of the basic concerns here are identification of realistic objectives, self-oriented and program-oriented, planning and group directions, emphasis on performance results, and patterns of personal behavior.

Aspects of a Personal Management System

1. Ways in which support personnel are used
2. Decision-making techniques and emphases
3. Performance monitoring methods

4. Instructional design procedures
5. Identification of roles and responsibilities
6. Types and levels of objectives set
7. Personal performance patterns
8. Utilization of time
9. Human interaction capabilities
10. Adaptability to changing situations and conditions
11. Planning, organizational, and implementation capabilities
12. Idea generation

A final example of a basic aspect affecting individual delineation is that pertaining to performance functioning. This relates to the ways an individual prefers to function as opposed to the ways he must function, either because of personal limitations or because of imposed program structure limitations. It can also relate to ways a person thinks he is functioning as opposed to the manner in which he is actually performing. Both of these attitudinal aspects can cause conflict between the individual and the program structure unless the teacher develops a self-appraisal process that helps him ascertain such important characteristics as his personal and programmatic strengths and weaknesses, his action area skills and skill use levels, and his singular types of objectives, and degrees of emphasis related to results and process. Not to be excluded from this area is the ego level a person possesses related to his present and desired positions on the staff totem pole.

Program Demands	Functioning Preference
1. Applied student use of learning	1. Cognitive teaching level
2. Team teaching	2. Self-contained classroom
3. Departmental-wide use of a single final test	3. Individualization of instruction
4. Instructional methods selected in terms of learner functioning patterns	4. Variations of methods according to past teacher success

It has been the writer's experience that the identification of the personal factors related to performance are the ones least considered as a staff works to improve effectiveness. The development of staff self-appraisal criteria which correlates each staff member's functioning patterns and emphases to job demands at each stage of program development, helps emphasize the importance of personal performance factors as major determiners of program development direction.

There must be a clear understanding on the part of each staff member of the dovetailing relationship between the actual performance demands of program structure and the ways he sees himself functioning within the curricular framework. As both program and personal delineations are developed, and reduced to writing, the dovetailing relationships become more obvious and the necessary overall job delineation becomes a practical, functional reality.

This applicable format also can serve another vital function. It can provide the initial guidelines and impetus for teacher self-appraisal, with a direct relationship to the way a staff member functions, from such standpoints as professional concerns, flexibility, creativity, professional relationships, desire to improve, areas and aspects of functioning emphases, and planning methods. Job delineation provides built-in appraisal criteria for both the program and the person functioning within it.

DEVELOPING A PROGRAM ORGANIZATIONAL CHART

It is a common practice for a school district to develop an organizational chart showing line and staff members. Though there is purpose for this type of chart, it has limited implementation value at the building level. There is more value in the development of an organizational flow chart that would delineate the building instructional program. The primary value here would be to the teachers because in developing the chart, they would have to analyze, identify, and sequentially organize the varying emphases, sub-programs, and roles and responsbilities of the school staff.

A building instructional flow chart also offers some advantages in such areas as public relations, inter-departmental endeavors, in-service programming, and teaching performance expectations. These result because staff members have an outline from which they can organize their own instructional activities, coordinate and articulate inter-class and inter-departmental activities and emphases, identify desired functioning patterns of both staff and students, and consequently be more specific and consistent in their interpretation of the program to parents and patrons. There is no question about the need for individual faculty skill improvement in all of these areas.

Types of questions each individual staff member needs to answer for himself here are

1. In what specific ways do my efforts and responsibilities contribute to the total school effectiveness and to the attainment of community goals?
2. To what extent do my activities go beyond my own specific subject matter assignment? In what ways do I reinforce other departmental emphases?
3. Are my expectations of my students and of myself reasonable? Are they within both my students' and my capabilities?
4. In what specific areas do I need in-service help? Are they primarily skill, content, or behavioral areas?
5. In what areas can I help myself and in what areas do I need resource help?
6. In what ways do my philosophy and functioning patterns coincide with program philosophical and operational demands? In what ways do they differ? What am I going to do about these differences?
7. To what extent does my teaching performance agree with the performance levels demanded by my stated objectives? Am I capable of functioning effectively at higher objective levels?
8. To what extent can I effectively design, implement, and manage the type of learning structures needed by my students?

Though the building organizational chart will vary from school, the example in Figure 4-1 will illustrate various aspects of the school program that can be delineated through this means.

This type of organizational flow chart can be expanded as much as a given staff feels is needed to clarify the school program. For example, if the faculty so desired, specific courses within a department could be listed with a structure paralleling the above example developed for each course. This detailed approach could be an extensive undertaking, perhaps, but it would be worth the effort in the long run because of the resulting need for more specificity in program development, in objectives development, and in personnel performance expectations.

This phase of program delineation can also be used as an aspect of program quality control. The identified areas can be used to help clarify the various levels of objectives, to help develop minimum expected satisfaction points, and to help identify progress checkpoints along the instructional continuum. In like manner, it can have satellite effects on identification of differ-

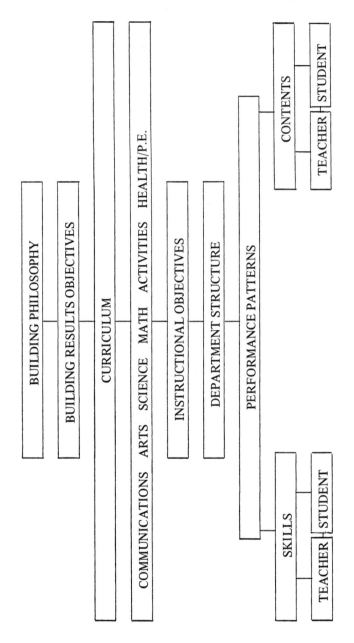

Figure 4-1

entiated staff characteristics, accountability, program evaluation and revision.

This approach can also have a positive influence beyond the building level in terms of staff selection and support-staff utilization. Staff members should be selected in terms of their potential capabilities to function effectively in the program. Since the various aspects of the program are identified and defined in the organizational chart, it is much easier for the prospective teacher and the interviewing administrator to analyze the skills, traits, and potential of the teacher in terms of the program demands. Matching of skills and demands becomes more reliable.

In terms of support staff utilization, the flow chart helps the school staff identify resource persons who can most effectively work within the program because their skill needs are identified. Also identified are the specific program areas and levels at which resource persons can be asked to serve. The efforts of the support personnel can be more productive because their specific talent and skill needs are identified and because they can more readily gear their activities to specific curricular aspects and levels on a continuing basis.

The performance results emphasis necessitates an individualized structural framework that not only stresses the matching of staff talents and skills to identified program functioning roles and responsibilities, but also emphasizes the changing of identified individual staff member roles and responsibilities as new learner needs dictate. Since both learner and teacher performance effectiveness is directly related to how well individual staff members are assigned to meet specific learner needs, the individualized open staffing approach provides a method for implementing a results-oriented staffing framework that facilitates the fuller implementation of the learner performance-oriented curricular structure.

Some Action Guidelines

Program:

1. Program development is a process involving change for a purpose. It is a process of selection, addition, and deletion. When a sub-structure or approach is added to the existing program framework, usually it is added to improve the operational status quo, to replace a procedure, sub-structure, or process that has proved inadequate. As the new

approach is added, the corresponding ineffective approach should be eliminated. This is the continuing developmental acceptance and rejection process in which the effective staff engages.

2. The staffing structure is developed in terms of desired results, just as is the program structure. Program structure and objectives characteristics determine the staffing structure framework.

3. Staff selection procedures must be developed primarily in terms of individual revealed performance results, demonstrated capabilities, and effectiveness potential.

4. A staffing structure must be spelled out in writing. In addition to immediate staffing needs, a staffing schedule should be developed indicating probable future staff needs, qualifications, and performance expectations.

5. Staff selection should be made in terms of specific performance needs as revealed by the extent of objectives attainment.

Personnel:

1. Too often, out-of-building support staff schedules are developed primarily on the basis of the number of buildings the staff serves. To be effective, the support staff schedules must be developed on the basis of identified building needs and consequent identified roles, responsibilities, and desired results.

2. Individual, and total faculty, in-service activities must focus on providing staff members needed "how-to" implementation skills. Theory should be included only as it facilitates the learning of the functioning skills.

3. The performance-oriented structure necessitates the staff's continuous appraisal of objectives attainment and the resultant learner-need changes. These efforts will be effective, however, only if the staff also recognizes the consequent need for changes in staff utilization, and if consequent changes in staff roles and responsibilities are made to correspond with these new learner demands.

Performance:

1. The performance results curriculum stresses staff-learner functioning effectiveness. Staff appraisal, then, must be done in terms of how well the staff, and each individual faculty member, function within the demands of the program structure. Identification of these operational requirements is a prerequisite to appraisal criteria development.

2. Effectiveness assessment must also identify the correlation of staff utilization to results attainment and the consequent dollar cost. Cost

should not be the basis criterion, of course, but it does give an indication of operational efficiency. Also, in the minds of parents and patrons, it is an important accountability factor.

3. Identification of differing areas and levels of functioning responsibilities is a form of differentiated staffing. Cost accounting should also involve the identification of differing salary schedules related to the levels of operational responsibility *and* the related extent of results attained.

5

TEACHING EMPHASIS FOR
PERFORMANCE RESULTS

The module curriculum is an action-oriented, performance results-oriented program. It demands major changes in teacher functioning patterns and action strategies in such areas as personal interaction techniques and procedures, the designing and implementing of various program aspects, and the attitudinal and philosophical emphases of each staff member. These operational changes relate specifically to the development of an organizational approach that facilitates learner action by keying to learner varying performance needs as determiners of staff performance patterns. Changing learner-performance demands necessitate the school staff's developing skills related to the improving of overall staff operational efficiency, the matching of specific teacher talent with individual student needs, the implementing of continuous student/staff scheduling, and the developing of integrated student-teacher program appraisal procedures.

ESTABLISHING AN ACTION
STRATEGY FRAMEWORK

A teacher working within a program that emphasizes performance and results must, of necessity, be as much concerned about subsequent learner activities and schedules as he is with the present learner endeavors. These cannot be allowed simply to evolve—because of the relatively obvious shortcomings of this "approach." Effective student functioning requires the teacher to take time to plan and design programs of learning so that they are geared to the specific individuals who are expected to perform within the programs.

All this means the teacher must dovetail the present and the immediate future. He must develop broader action programs for students rather than limited study endeavors. To do this, the staff member needs to keep in mind that he must work within both short and long range objectives, he must utilize positive approaches that are based on what a student can do, yet lead to the elimination of individual student learning problems. Emphasis must be placed on the designing of programs based on present success rather than just on past limitations.

To do this, the instructor must look at both the total program and the "whole student." An action strategy framework is built in terms of what a student can, and is expected, to do. Both student and teacher focus on actions related to student implementation of the learning design. Unless the individual student is able to implement the program in terms of his own strengths, limitations, and objectives, the program structure reverts back to a teaching, rather than a learning, emphasis. The student becomes a passive, rather than an initiating, force within the school framework.

The following illustrate some basic differences between a teaching and a learning action structure.

TEACHING EMPHASIS	STUDENT CHARACTERISTICS	LEARNING EMPHASIS
1. Arbitrary identification of requireds and electives	1. Present student needs and functioning levels	1. Course selection according to identified student needs
2. Teacher selection of instructional methods	2. Differing learning patterns and demands	2. Matching teaching methods to learner operational patterns.
3. Teacher selection of learning purposes	3. Learner-identified "needs for knowing"	3. Teacher-student development of objectives

4. Staffing according to course offerings	4. Individual learner instructional demands	4. Matching staff talents to student needs
5. Scheduling according to program mechanics	5. Individual learning systems	5. Course sequencing according to "readiness levels"
6. Teacher imposition of instructional design	6. Increasing assumption of responsibility for own actions	6. Student implementation of learning design

The designing and implementing of a learning program takes time, and skill. Since more control of time is available to the teacher than he, perhaps, realizes, he needs to devote an increased amount of his time to priority areas, such as design, rather than to such mechanical aspects as grading of endless sets of papers. This is not to imply that within a traditional structure sincere teachers do not devote time to planning. It does mean, though, that staff members need to plan more effectively and probably in different ways.

A primary area in which the instructor should do much of his planning is the learning-functioning area. As he attempts to work out a program structure in which his students can function and progress along the various continua, he will tend to view content more as a means and less as an end in itself. As a result, planning and design tend to center around what a student can do, and what he needs to do, rather than around what the teacher is expected to do only within the confines of a textbook or a course guideline.

FORMULATING ACTION TECHNIQUES

As the staff member devotes more attention to the learning-functioning area, he will also find that he is spending more time planning in terms of people. He will be spending more time planning with people—with the student, with the parent, and other teachers with whom the student has classes. As the student and parent participate in this planning, under the teacher's leadership, the teacher will quite often find it is the learner and the parent who become more involved with subject matter and content selection in terms of objectives. The teacher's time here is devoted more to guidance and counseling.

In this way, the teacher is continually involved with the student in terms of developmental learning techniques and program selection as well as in the formal learning endeavors. An important aspect here is that the teacher has many more opportunities to work with the pupil in a more indirect way to help him develop such priority skills as decision-making, self- and personal-program selection, evaluation, and progress.

The staff member is also working more closely and consistently with the parent in the same ways. Through this approach, the parent is more directly involved in the educational process. Consequently, he can become more cognizant of the strengths and weaknesses of the student and more aware of the problems and challenges facing the teacher. As the parent attempts to deal with the various aspects and levels of his offspring's educational functioning, he is better able to see and understand the role and responsibilities of the teacher. He also becomes more aware of the need for both relevancy and accountability in education. The subsequent increased appreciation for what the teacher is attempting to accomplish with the student leads to better public and personal relations.

Through this approach, the parent is more directly involved in decision-making pertaining to his child's educational program in such specific areas as

1. Course selection
2. Performance demands and application
3. Progress appraisal methods
4. Identification of learner needs
5. Identification of student-teacher-parent responsibilities
6. Selection of priorities
7. Identification of instructional demands

A new student, transferring to one school in which the author worked, came in with his father to get his class schedule. Instead of their simply sitting and waiting while the counselor filled out a schedule of classes, the student, the father, and the counselor spent some time discussing the school program structure and demands, objectives and purposes of the different courses, and other subjects pertaining to the school staff and program.

The discussion soon turned to an emphasis on the boy's and the father's roles and responsibilities in the program framework. Both the student and his parent were somewhat surprised to find themselves attempting to answer such questions, among others, as the following:

1. What did both the boy and his father expect from the school?
2. What functioning levels did the father feel he and the teachers could reasonably expect the boy to attain?
3. What responsibilities did the father feel he had to assume in order for the boy to attain these levels?
4. What did the student feel his areas of strengths and weaknesses were? What did the father feel these were?
5. In terms of the student's past performance, what should be the order of learning priority emphasis for the boy?
6. From the listing of available course areas, which ones could, perhaps, be of most use to the student in terms of his and his parent's stated objectives?

As would be expected, perhaps, answers to these questions were not readily obtained. By the time the initial conference was over, however, the student and his father were aware of the needs and interests of the boy, the ways in which both could, and would, contribute to leaning effectiveness, and what they could expect from the school.

This information was also given to the student's teachers. They used it as the basis for their instructional planning related to this student. It was also used as the basis of the student's progress reports in the later-scheduled parent-student-teacher conferences.

Following are the learning priorities, class schedule, and parent responsibilities developed for the boy's first session, the second quarter of the school year.

Learning Priority Needs

1. Reading help
2. Physical coordination
3. Adjustment to new peer groups

Class Schedule

1. Developmental Reading Through Literature
2. Introduction to Gymnastics
3. Woodwork
4. Human Relations
5. Personal Business Math
6. Factors Influencing Local Weather

Parent Responsibilities

1. Helping the student with oral reading at home
2. Meeting with counselor and teachers every other week for progress evaluation
3. Taking time each day to discuss with the boy his daily experiences and reactions at school
4. Working with the boy to help him develop specific achievement levels in each course

Results

This boy withdrew from his classes at the end of the first semester, at the completion of the above schedule, because his father was transferred to another state. During the time he was in this school, however, he accomplished the following:

1. He has begun to show more interest in reading, with less urging from his parents and teachers
2. He had learned to use hand tools satisfactorily
3. He had made some friends and was referring to the school as "his school"

As the teacher works to design and implement an action program for the student, he must of necessity rely on the skills and talents of the counselor. By no means is the teacher expected to develop and coordinate the various program aspects by himself. It is his responsibility, however, to develop his own methods of operation in such a manner as to make it possible for the counselor to be actively and consistently involved. Too often, staff members reveal a tendency to consider it a weakness to ask for help. In reality, it is only common sense to take advantage of the help available from support personnel.

Modern education is not a simple matter or process. Just as it is no longer possible for students to be exposed to equally effective learning techniques and skills in all subjects in a self-contained classroom, it is not realistic for the teacher to expect, or be expected, to possess all the skills, or the time, to meet the varied needs and demands of the student.

CHANGING THE TEACHER ROLE
IN PARENT-STUDENT CONFERENCING

Planning determines action. Within the performance-oriented module curriculum structure, the teacher must master the techniques of planning and of holding conferences. Planning and conducting learning conferences with students, instructional conferences with associates, and informational conferences with parents furnish a key to the success level of the teacher and of the student. There is no magic ratio of conference time allotments to numbers of students. Time involved here will be dependent upon such things as student-need time, teacher and student skills, continua level emphasis, and subject matter difficulty. Conferences should not be held simply to satisfy some kind of time requirement. Like faculty meetings, they should be held only when there is a clearly evident purpose and objective. All students do not need equal conference time.

These conferences are an integral part of the overall individualized curriculum design. As a result, the teacher needs to concern himself with the various ways of organizing and holding conferences that will be of most value to the participants. Conferences, by and large, should not be content-oriented, though this surely would be an important aspect. The meetings should also include such aspects as student time use, the development of present and future student/teacher schedules, student learning techniques, and organization of available student resources. In other words, the conferences must be developed in terms of the learner. As a result, they emphasize more "how to" developmental characteristics, with the teacher serving in the counseling, coordinating role and the student, (and parent) gradually, as he develops the skills and maturity, assuming more of an initiating participant role.

To involve each parent in the educational process through conferences, the teacher must make an effort to get the parents to identify

1. The parental role in his child's learning program
2. His child's needs in priority order
3. The rate and level of progress he anticipates his child will achieve
4. What should be reasonable performance expectations
5. How he evaluates his child's performance
6. How he views his child's learning patterns
7. What he can do to help the student and the teacher

This approach not only actively involves both the student and parent in the educational process, it also helps commit the parent to a continuing cooperative support role. It can result in increasing teacher and learner effectiveness as well as maintaining school-community relations through individual teacher-parent contact.

The following individual parent-teacher conference breakdown for one quarter, at Goddard Middle School, indicates the parental interest that can be developed through personalized involvement. The count represents an average of six conferences for each parent. The school is on a seven-period day.

Department	Total	5th Grade	6th Grade	7th Grade	8th Grade	9th Grade
ENGLISH	883	293	130	156	200	104
SOCIAL STUDIES	680	110	202	113	110	145
SCIENCE	447	115	118	115	51	48
MATH	510	120	112	99	94	85
MUSIC	182	61	31	45	24	21
PHYSICAL EDUC.	279	116	40	47	33	43
INDUSTRIAL ARTS	41	-	-	1	35	5
HOME ECONOMICS	46	-	-	-	44	2
ART	22	-	-	-	9	13
IMC AND AV	2	-	-	-	2	-
COUNSELING	95	21	22	20	18	14
GODDARD TOTALS	3187	836	655	596	620	480

IMPROVING TEACHER ORGANIZATIONAL PROFICIENCY

Throughout the previous chapters, at least indirectly, reference has been made to specific talents and characteristics a teacher must have to be effective beyond the so-called minimum satisfaction point. In the type of program structure discussed in this book, there are a number of teacher characteristics and traits that are common to all teaching-learning situations. There are other characteristics, such as those following, that are important in other curricular structures, but are often neglected. Within the module curriculum and results-emphasis concepts, such characteristics are vital aspects that are keys to the success of both program and people. Consequently, they must be given priority emphasis in the selection of staff and in day-to-day staff functioning. These abilities determine the ways in which a staff member actually works with the learner.

1. Basic, of course, to this is the teacher's organizing his teaching-learning endeavors around each student's characteristics, his strengths, his talents, his patterns, and his continua graphing. Once these are identified, the teacher can then put together a relatively complete picture of a student's present position, the direction in which he is going, and the consequently needed performance details, tools, and techniques. This organization goes beyond just arranging teaching sequences and test schedules. It involves the analysis and synthesis of the total program, of the individual student's program, and of the role of the teacher.

2. The teacher must be adept at developing results objectives in terms of the present learner situation and in terms of what he expects the situation will be at a pre-identified learning progress checkpoint. This means that the instructor must develop the skill of recognizing present and evolving pupil functioning patterns and of preparing the consequent learning options and alternatives that not only allow the student to work in a clearly defined framework, developed on the basis of his existing level, but also provide the flexibility for variation according to student change.

3. The teacher must be able to view his area of responsibility from the standpoint of a coordinator. In order to attain his stated results, he must become efficiency-oriented. He must devise ways and means to coordinate effectively the time, talents, and priorities of the student, of the other teachers working with him, and his own. Also, he must be able to schedule and coordinate the various instructional resources available to himself and to the learner. Unfortunately, most staff members tend to function only in terms of isolated coordination; that is, they tend to relate a film, or guest speaker, for example, to a single lesson or unit or they devise a test that pertains only to one phase of instruction. The result is a lack of continuity in the learning process, though these may be sequenced. A primary responsibility of a coordinator is to provide instructional and learning continuity.

ESTABLISHING A PERFORMANCE DATA FILE

All of this, of course, means the teacher needs to develop and maintain data files—(1) of content, of materials, and other information he may deem of potential use and (2) of information pertaining to the learner himself. Grade books and lesson plan books, traditionally the primary "record" books, are only small parts of the files. These data files, in general, need not be overly complicated. In effect, overall, there would be little difference between the amount of time and paperwork devoted to maintaining data files and the time and paperwork involved in traditional record keeping. The primary difference is in the areas of emphasis.

Major emphasis should be placed on the aspects and phases that pertain directly to student performance characteristics and progress facilitators and limiters. The learner performance file should be set up on the bases of such aspects as the specific performance results objectives set, the consequent selected learning activities, anticipated and real gains, skill and content needs, and continua placement. As this file is continually updated, student performance appraisal is also done.

Continuous updating of the data would include the following:

1. New objectives set
2. Areas of learning difficulties
3. Priority areas of instructional emphasis
4. Changes in student performance patterns and functioning levels
5. Extent of parental involvement
6. Progressive skills mastery and consequent application capabilities
7. Needed changes in teacher functioning
8. Anticipated changes in learning program design and changes in demands for teacher-need time

Traditional record keeping is time-consuming because there is duplication of activity by the teacher in grading papers, in preparing materials, and in appraising student progress on the basis of isolated units rather than in terms of continuous progress. Also, when primary emphasis is placed on content changes rather than on student growth, there is greater difficulty in keeping records accurate enough to provide valid bases for curriculum development, for prognosis of student programming, and for appraisal of teaching effectiveness.

INCREASING EFFECTIVENESS THROUGH FLEXIBLE STAFFING PRACTICES

Because of the module emphasis on learning, there is an equal stress on the learner. The consequent instructional concern facilitates the matching of staff talents to student needs by the building administrator. He is able to follow a direct staffing approach rather than use the indirect method where he only makes staff assignments according to pre-enrollment figures and on the basis of staff size according to some pre-determined ratio. There are times when the ratio approach forces the principal to create a teaching load in order to keep a surplus staff member.

Direct staffing involves selecting and assigning each individual staff member according to a specifically identified need, or a combination of needs, related to the singular characteristics of the student body. As in the open staffing concept at the district level, direct staffing within the building means that there can be changes in staff assignments as the needs and characteristics of the student body change because the staffing is done, also, in terms of the human elements rather than just a prescribed course of study.

Examples of Direct Staffing

STUDENT NEED	STAFF SKILLS NEEDED	SCHEDULE NEED
I. Supervised work experience	1. Understanding of student desire for functioning beyond school confines	Student assignment outside of building part time
	2. Ability to interest and involve businesses in school program	Courses designed to dovetail with student "job" needs and social development needs
	3. Primary interest in student development, not content, as an objective	
	4. Recognition of student conflict areas	
II. Expansion of academic program	1. Anticipating student performance and projecting programming needs	Independent study
		Flexible time scheduling
	2. Development of short-term need courses	Changing of courses
	3. Identification of maximum student points of functioning efficiency	Scheduling into community resource areas
	4. Individualized program development	

Direct staffing will also have an effect on teacher functioning within the classroom because faculty members tend, in a number of ways, to develop classroom operational procedures and patterns that parallel those of the school structure. If the faculty assignments are made in terms of identified learner needs and attributes, it is relatively easy for each teacher to reduce them to the learner action level. By extension, then, this staffing approach has a direct effect on the identification and attainment of performance objectives at both the teacher and learner levels.

It must be recognized that every school has a differentiated staff and a differentiated student body, whether or not the program structure and salary schedule reflect this. Failure to develop teaching and learning frameworks in terms of this unavoidable aspect is deliberately to build delimiting effectiveness factors into the learning program. A consequence, here, can be the placing of a teacher in an instructional situation he really is not equipped to handle, by training or by temperament. In all honesty, it cannot be fully justified in terms of relevancy or accountability if, for example, a school professes to be concerned about individualization of instruction or program emphasis on the learner as a person. There is a serious inconsistency between what the school staff professes as a philosophy and as a mode of operation and the way the staff is assigned. There is recognized student body differentiation, but no admitted staff differentiation.

Various aspects of the school program demand differing types and levels of skill from certified staff members. These levels must be identified and considered when staff assignments are made. Following is an example of program and staff level and skill identification.

PROGRAM LEVELS	SPECIFIC FUNCTIONING SKILL NEEDS
1. Theory	1. Needs assessment
	2. Program force and demand recognition
	3. Objectives identification
	4. Research and development
2. Planning	1. Organizational skills
	2. Creative talents
	3. Programming coordination
	4. Idea development

3. Implementation	1. Reducing ideas to learning action
	2. Developing functioning skills in learner
	3. Change and conflict management
	4. Objectives achievement
4. Appraisal	1. Status quo, progress, and change recognition
	2. Priority identification
	3. Knowledge of program subsystems
	4. Knowledge of planning and design

ORGANIZING FOR LEARNING PERFORMANCE

A curricular structure that is developed in terms of learner characteristics must, of necessity, be an open-ended structure because the students are maturing, are expanding their outlooks, and are becoming responsible for their own actions which involve personal and social decision-making. If learning is to occur, teacher action must be consistent with, and responsive to, learner function patterns. Instruction, then, must also be open-ended.

Success in using the open-ended approach is dependent, as much on teacher attitude, as it is on effective use of such instructional techniques and skills as options and alternatives, delegation of responsibility to students, independent programming, and so on. This is especially true in the four continua areas—change, total program, student growth, and content. The teacher must be constantly aware of modifications occurring in each of these and be able to correlate consequent changes demanded in, and by, himself. Conflicts between closed teaching attitudes and procedures and open-ended learner patterns will result, through attrition, in the learner's being forced to adapt to the limitations imposed by the dominant applied authority of the instructor.

The use of the options and alternatives approach is essential in a program where emphasis is placed on dovetailing structure with learning, rather than with teaching. In actuality, the teacher who desires to improve his teaching effectiveness has little, or no, choice but to implement the options and alternatives approach simply because differing students function and learn in differing ways. So do teachers.

Many teachers are rather adamant in their desires to be given more freedom and authority to function as they see the need. This is a valid position, however, only if they are willing to extend this same functioning consideration to the learners. Again, though, the teachers have little, or no, choice if they really want to improve their performance levels because their improvement is determined by learner improvement. Also, only through allowing students to make decisions can the teacher make himself progressively less needed. This decision-making cannot be relegated to a simple multiple choice approach, wherein the student is merely given the freedom to select techniques, procedures, and methods from a list compiled only on the basis of teacher interest and emphasis. This is not only hypocrisy; it is built-in obsolescence.

DEVELOPING THE BASIC
LEARNING STRUCTURE

An unfortunate situation in education is that too many certified staff members do not know how to organize and maintain a learning structure and to function within it. Part of this, of course, is a result of the ways that teachers have been trained, partly because of the way they are expected to function by those to whom they are responsible, and partly because it is less complicated to develop a teaching structure than a learning structure. A consequent result of this situation is that many teachers unconsciously assume the role of an obstructor to learning rather than a facilitator, a coordinator, and a manager of learning endeavors. They know how to participate in teaching activities, but not in learning processes.

The following memorandum was given to the author by a Social Studies Chairman after his attendance at an in-district meeting concerned with curricular innovation. It reflects his concern about the need for an organizational approach that stresses the importance of each building staff's assuming responsibilities for program development in terms of learner need as well as in terms of district-wide program review schedules.

It appears to me that all participants at this meeting are receptive to innovation and change; our differences arise over:

1. The definition of change; . . . . at what point does enrich-

ment become change and worthy of district scrutiny?
2. How best to inaugurate and implement change efficiently
and effectively.

It was conceded that most teachers embellish and enrich the
prescribed curriculum, playing to their own areas of expertise,
student interests, and the topicality of the subject. Yet, when we
try to identify the above for the student and let him choose areas
of in-depth study in which he is interested, we are told that our
program does not follow district curriculum and that our procedures for implementing the program are not in keeping with
district guidelines.

It is my considered opinion that a district, which is indeed
concerned with innovation and change, cannot superimpose a
structure upon its change agents which require from six to
eighteen months to deal with mechanics which can be more
effectively and efficiently handled at the building level. I propose
that, in keeping with the spirit of accountability, the district
formulate committees of teachers and administrators who will be
charged with rewriting the objectives for each grade level in
measurable behavioral terms. The committee will also draw up a
testing instrument. Each school and department will be held
strictly accountable for failure to reach those objectives. At the
same time, each building and department will decide how best to
utilize its manpower and time in order to reach and hopefully
surpass the objectives of the district.

Within the results-oriented module curriculum framework, the
teacher needs to develop the skills for developing and implementing the learning framework. Perhaps, at the outset, the most
convenient manner for a teacher to implement this structure is to
place primary emphasis on the development and writing of
learning performance objectives. This identifies need, direction,
and priority aspects for both the student and the teacher. From
these learning objectives, the teacher can, then, develop his
instructional objectives. These, of necessity, will have to be
developed within the functioning construction of the learning
objectives.

There are various ways the teacher can reveal an emphasis on
development of learning performance objectives. Among these are

1. Identification of student needs and consequent individualized
course selection

2. Delineation of teaching roles and responsibilities in terms of recognized learner demands
3. Selection of performance appraisal criteria stressing applied performance
4. Setting personal instructional objectives
5. Selection and use of student-oriented functioning classroom procedures that place the teacher in a support role
6. Methods of using specialized support people such as the reading teacher, the speech therapist, and tutors
7. Development of lesson plans that put primary stress on the identification of what the learner will accomplish rather than on what the teacher will attempt
8. Identification of specific ways the teacher plans to make himself progressively less needed by the student
9. Development of a personal in-service program designed to improve teaching performance results rather than just improving content mastery
10. Correlation of individual desires to program demands
11. Placement of performance emphasis on implementation action
12. Involvement in the planning, design, and appraisal levels of program development as well as involvement in the implementation level
13. Projection of future functioning demand in terms of present operational effectiveness

In this manner, the learner and the learning objectives receive top priority. The role and responsibilities of the teacher are delineated in terms of the learner. It is relatively easy, then, for the teacher to select his own direction, procedures, and methods of operation because specific guidelines have already been established. As long as the teacher maintains this priority sequence and functioning framework, it will be a rather uncomplicated matter for him to maintain a learning-oriented approach on a day-to-day basis.

Another area that must receive increased attention from the teacher is program structuring for the individual student. This means that each staff member becomes less concerned about the make up of a "class" and more concerned about the unique, and common, characteristics of the particular students to whom he has been assigned. Class size and enrollment ratios become much less important when decisions are made in terms of what a teacher should be able to do with the specific needs and characteristics with which he is expected to deal. These, together with the identified program, instructional, and learning objectives, become primary bases for individual and overall program development when individualized performance is emphasized and and when the curriculum is geared to the inevitable changes that occur within people and within society.

UTILIZING PERFORMANCE CONTRACTING

The performance results structure stresses accountability, by both the teacher and the student. This involves the development of student-teacher results objectives and consequent specific methods for achieving them. It also involves the delineation of the roles and responsibilities of the teacher and the learner so that each has a clear understanding of what is expected of the other. Once the instructor and the learner agree on their objectives, their roles, and their responsibilities, a performance contract, in effect, has been created.

The next step is for the parties to the contract to develop the specific means and methods by which the performance contractual obligations will be met. Several operational options are available to the contractual participants here. Three primary approaches are involved here.

1. Student-teacher performance contracting (Figure 5-1)
2. Teacher-administration performance contracting
3. Industry-school performance contracting

Student-teacher performance contracting involves the cooperative development by the instructor and the learner of specific learning objectives, limited in scope, but sequential in nature, that emphasize student action. They are geared to the learner implementation level. The instructor objectives are developed more from the support standpoint. In many cases, performance contracting at this level is done in terms of specific individual student needs and for content demands.

Examples of Possible Personal Teacher Performance Contract Areas

1. The teacher will plan, develop, and implement an individualized learning structure in a seventh-grade reading class. The agreed success result level will be—two-thirds of the class will have increased their reading competencies by two grade levels in six months.

EXAMPLE OF A BUILDING CONTRACTING FORM

Present Situation _____ _____ _____	Agreed Upon Desired Situation (Objective) _____ _____
What Student Will Do _____ _____ _____ _____	What Teacher Will Do _____ _____ _____ _____
Progress Checkpoints _____ _____ _____ _____ Date _____	Date for Objective Attainment _____ Student _____ Teacher _____ Parent _____

Figure 5-1

2. The counselor, during the coming school year, will develop and coordinate a sub-system structure within which the 15 formally classified "emotionally disturbed" students in the school can function more effectively. This program will include utilization of personnel from the municipal mental health center, district psychological service personnel, and private medical doctors selected by the involved parents.

   The agreed upon success result levels will be

   reduction of average student out-of-class time by 30 percent

   reduction of total number of discipline referrals from this group by 25 percent

   increase in family therapy participation by five family groups

   extension to full day school attendance by four students

3. The four identified teachers will plan, develop, and implement an interdisciplinary social studies-English-science sub-program, involving 75 students identified as "average" performers, that will meet major

district content requirements as stated in the three subject area guidelines, but will expand and increase student functioning capabilities in the use of writing skills.

The agreed upon success levels will be

60 percent of the students will score at least 75 percent on the district-approved tests in the three subject areas

80 percent of the students will be able to successfully meet the composition requirements of all three departments as evidenced by their passing grades on their written work in each of the three subjects

60 percent of the students will be able to apply their skills successfully to practical situations as evidenced by their performance ratings earned from working in selected commercial concerns—a scientific equipment supply house, a newspaper office, a library, a museum, the Police Department, and the county Social Service Department

The identification of success levels demands that the contracting staff member be aware enough of the specific needs, past and present performance levels, and general functioning patterns of the students to commit himself to an expected instructional results level. Since he is also committing the learners to this same success level, it is essential that the teacher recognize that the contract is a team approach, stressing the assumption of responsibilities by both teacher and learner.

Teacher-administration performance contracting is directly related to student-teacher contracting but, generally, is developed with more emphasis on the instructional level. Here, the teacher and his supervisor come to agreement on the objectives to be attained by the teacher through the cooperative efforts of himself and the students assigned to him. Objectives here are geared to the teacher, and to teacher/student attainment. Performance results are delineated over a broader spectrum of student needs and program demands but are still specific in nature in terms of teacher functioning.

Industry-school performance contracting involves the utilization of a business firm that guarantees to raise student functioning skills to a particular level in certain agreed-upon academic areas. Emphasis here tends to be on the use of programmed material with a focus on output—the extent of progress a student makes toward the pre-determined performance objective and the revealed performance level of the student within the scope of the contractual framework.

These three approaches have several common characteristics such as an emphasis on specified performance objectives, concern for applied performance as an aspect of accountability, and the utilization of basic approaches that extend beyond the traditional instructional framework and, consequently, demand the implementation of differing instructional tools. Variations occur in such areas as utilization of instructional talent, degree of skill/content balance, and learner performance pattern demands.

All three of these approaches have basic functioning emphases that make them valuable teaching/learning vehicles within the performance results framework. The extent of their operational effectiveness, however, will be determined by the ways they are used, the skill with which the teachers and students can use these approaches, and the confidence they have in the contractual framework.

DEVELOPING OF STUDENT AND TEACHER SCHEDULES

Within the module curriculum structure, both teacher and student schedules are flexible and open-ended, but this does not mean that the school must use modular scheduling. Its use is optional. Both staff and learner schedules are developed on the bases of need and progress, rather than just on academic course offerings.

Because learner needs and progress do not lend themselves to rigidly defined guidelines, the developing of teaching and learning schedules must be a continuing activity. Of necessity, then, these schedules must be tied directly with the development of departmental schedules and offerings which evolve as a result of the staff's recognizing, and anticipating, needs and progress. It is only sound and consistent to maintain paralleling schedule modifications if the staff feels, and functions, on the basis that learning itself is a progressive process and that it results in changes in the individual.

The following shows how flexible module scheduling can be developed in terms of changing student needs and existing course guidelines. The cited overview is from the Littleton, Colorado, public schools social studies guide.

EIGHTH GRADE

THE MODERN NON-WESTERN WORLD
Overview

In recent years, educators have become aware that the non-western world is influencing world activities more and more. An important part of a student's education is to be aware of the ideals and values of these societies as they relate to events in the world today. Insight into political, cultural and economic developments in these nations provides a basis for understanding the complex world in which we live.

These countries will be studied selectively in separate units to illustrate culture areas and patterns that exist in the non-western world. As the course progresses, similarities and differences within this area will become evident. By the end of the course, the student should realize that, as in all the world, man is as he is because of the ideas and events that preceded him; and he is now shaping and contributing to the world of tomorrow.

LEVEL	ECONOMICS	HISTORY	GEOGRAPHY
Eighth	Man's effective use of human and natural resources is a determining factor in a nation's stability, worth, and effectiveness.	The history of the non-western world is composed of the cultural and philosophical developments of this area. The contact of the West and non-West has produced a mutual exchange of ideas and illustrates the interactive quality of history.	Physical and geographical conditions are important to a country's historical progress. Land structure, natural resources, water, climate, and other geographical factors influence cultural behavior.
	POLITICAL SCIENCE	SOCIOLOGY	ANTHROPOLOGY
	The change of political power reflects changing cultural and historical patterns. Conflict has been a basic and fundamental factor in the growth and development of civilization.	Every society develops a culture of its own even though some of the ideas are borrowed from other cultures.	Adjustments on a local basis to differences arising from contacts with other cultures have accelerated changes in life.

Proposed Mini-course titles

8th Grade

The Economics of the Developing World
Politics of the Emerging Nations
Religions of the World
The Rise and Fall of the Japanese Empire
African Anthropology
Population Pressures
Oriental Art
   Colonization and Imperialism
The Chinese Revolutions
The Vietnam Conflict
Religion in Conflict: Hindu vs. Moslem, Arab vs. Jew
Japan's Economic Miracle
Social Orders of Asia-Africa

PROCEDURE FOR DEVELOPING
TEACHER-LEARNER SCHEDULES

All this de-emphasizes the importance of the traditional master schedule structure. In its place, there evolves a master framework including the courses offered, staff role and responsibilities, and individual staff and student schedules (see Figure 5-2). In effect, what results instead of a rigid master schedule, is a well delineated mode of operation for both staff and students, which can be as viable as the people who are expected to function within the school.

This does not imply that there is no structural consistency within the school framework or that everyone involved can make decisions according to his own interests or desired levels of functions. Continuity, consistency, program identity, and results effectiveness could be lost if this were so. It does mean, though, that student and staff scheduling must be flexible enough to be consistent with the maturation and educational growth changes that are occurring in the learners. The desired consistency and direction are derived from student and staff functioning patterns, from the stated performance objectives, and from the cooperative planning of teachers, students, and parents within the established operational framework.

Scheduling involves more than just the identification of the subject each student will take each period and assigning of an "adequate" course load to every teacher. Scheduling entails the

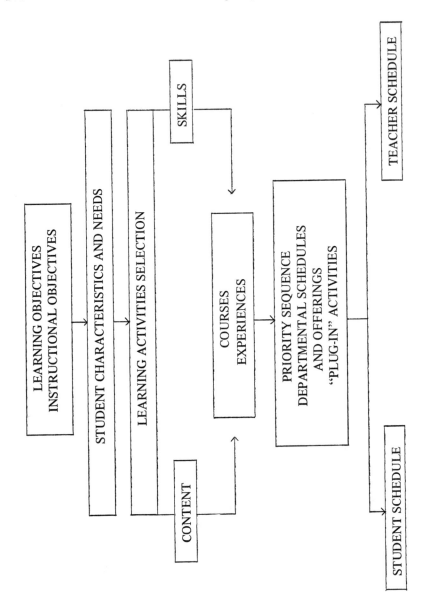

Figure 5-2

day-to-day functioning of each person in terms of his role and responsibilities. Consequently, because of the necessary interaction between students and staff members, no one person develops his own schedule. Its development is the result of the meshing of several persons' talents, time, efforts, and thinking. This coordination can best be done, perhaps, through the use of the systems approach, which, after all, is an important aspect of the module curriculum structure.

By using a systems approach, each functioning phase of the school's operational program is spelled out in detail. It is much easier, then, to coordinate the various phases for consistent, continuous progress toward the overall objectives. This approach also helps the staff to avoid needless repetition and conflict resulting from a lack of communications and a lack of direction. Such clearly delineated systems as *budgeting, staffing, scheduling, grading,* and *communications,* for example, are important aspects in direct relation to the effects they have on individual student and teacher functioning. Since these are felt to be vital phases of the program, they need to be carefully developed and described in terms of the operational procedures and purpose of each system and in terms of its contribution to the effectiveness of the total program.

Major Phases of the School's Operational Program

    Instructional/learning performance
    Staff development
    Curriculum development
    Planning and design
    Results assessment
    Organizational management
    Change implementation

By the nature of his job, the teacher is responsible for helping the learner progress through the educational program. Consequently, it is he who should be most familiar with the student's operational characteristics. Unfortunately, in many schools, the teacher has limited input or participation in decision-making relative to student scheduling. A most useful source of information is thereby left out of the process.

As the teacher functions within the module curricular framework, of necessity, he must become more involved in the development of individual student schedules. In order to do this effectively, he must become more concerned, more knowledgeable, and more active in instructional areas outside the specialized limits of his own particular field of preparation. This is essential because the teacher has to know the total needs and progress demands of the student if he is to make intelligent decisions concerning student programming effectiveness in his own area. This is particularly important because the total staff must become more aware of the similarity in demands, functioning patterns, and areas of study emphasis among various departments. It is also important because the student becomes more prone to function in terms of total program continuity rather than in terms of isolated subject matter or system units.

STUDENT SCHEDULING AND CLASS SIZE

There are certain mechanical factors in any type of program structure that also have decided effects on teacher and learner scheduling. One of the most important of these is the procedure used to determine the number of students a teacher can work with most effectively. There are a number of factors that influence this number. The number of different courses a teacher is assigned, the level(s) of difficulty of these courses, singular student characteristics, and district staffing standards are a few aspects that must be considered.

Perhaps, though, in determining the number of students with which a teacher can most effectively work, even more consideration should be given to the specific objectives of the course(s) and anticipated teacher-need time by the pupils. From these, course job descriptions for both students and teachers can be developed. The projected number of students for the class can be partially ascertained, then, on the basis of the expected functioning patterns of students and teacher. Within the module curricular structure, courses can be offered as often as necessary so there is little, or no, reason for an overly large number of students having to take a given course at the same time.

IMPROVING THE CURRICULUM
THROUGH STUDENT SCHEDULING

Class and student scheduling activities in the module curriculum become an integral part of curriculum development. This results

COURSE DEMANDS	CLASS SIZE RANGES
I. Basic skill need emphasis, 70%-80% teacher-need time, low student functioning level, oral technique demands	10-15 Students
II. Skill-based learning, extended-time needs, 60%-70% teacher-need time, teacher-led activities, cognitive-rote structure, low skill levels	10-20 Students
III. Analysis, synthesis, creativity, project development, content-affective oriented, 20%-40% teacher-need time, high skill use levels	15-25 Students
IV. Content-affective oriented, academic objectives, 40%-60% teacher-need time, performance demands within existing skill ranges of the students	25-35 Students

because of the continuing curricular alterations and changes that must necessarily be made as the learners reveal varying degrees of change and progress.

To keep the program of learning up-dated in terms of student needs and demands, various courses must be added and deleted, at least temporarily. In making these additions and deletions, the school staff constantly needs to make decisions on the basis of learner need and achievement. There is constant evaluation of individual courses and series of courses in terms of their relevancy. As courses are added to meet new or changing needs, staff members are also involved in specific course and general curriculum development. In addition, staff members must constantly evaluate the overall program to keep it balanced in terms of student need, in terms of staff talents, in terms of the different continua, and in terms of the types and number of courses offered.

DEVELOPING A PROGRESS APPRAISAL SYSTEM

There are three viable areas that must be considered in progress appraisal. They are separate, yet so inter-related that the appraisal of one involves the appraisal of the other two. These three are the student, the teacher, and the program. Unfortunately, in most cases, evaluation, or appraisal, is attempted in only one function area with little, or no, attempt to include the other two. Traditional grading focuses upon the student, in-service training concentrates on either the staff or the program, and local evaluation of the school centers primarily on program interpretation. A useful and valid appraisal system must be so designed that the effects, influences, and forces of all three must be considered. Also, the system must be designed to be as viable and flexible as are the student, the teacher, and the program.

Appraisal systems must be designed and developed. In too many instances, teachers utilize methods of evaluation that have simply evolved, that have no consistent pattern or basis, that they cannot delineate in detail, and that they have difficulty in interpreting. To help overcome these weaknesses, school staff members will find it helpful to take time to deliberately design an appraisal system that best fits their particular situation. However, it must be remembered that interpretation of the system will be done also by people outside the school—by parents, by personnel in other schools to which students transfer, and by potential employers, among others.

With all this in mind, a school faculty, and district personnel, will find it most helpful, as they develop an appraisal system, to consider continually the following as valid concepts on which they can develop an effective appraisal system.

1. Balance of emphasis on the change, learning, content, and program continua
2. Procedures for both student and teacher self-evaluation
3. Applied performance by the student
4. Extent of relevance and accountability
5. Attainment of objectives

These are relatively broad areas. More specific details within each area should be developed by individual faculties because they will vary from school to school. No single standardized outline can be developed that can apply satisfactorily to every school. If this were possible, the school staff would be faced with the same weaknesses mentioned earlier in this section.

The primary purposes of an appraisal system are to provide an effective means by which both teacher and learner can ascertain the present functioning level and to provide the necessary information to give planning direction for consequent desired action. A simple reporting procedure is not sufficient.

For an appraisal system to be effective, the school staff must build into it a continuous feedback system that permits each teacher and student to be aware of his daily progress and functioning levels. Again, performance graphing is a useful technique here because it is necessary for the teacher to identify the specific areas, force factors, specific objectives, and achievement expectancy levels and other factors before he is able to plot functioning levels. Graphing is useful here, also, because it can provide immediate feedback information to both the student and the teacher for identifying necessary program changes according to present learner needs.

The particular design and areas of emphasis of the appraisal system will determine the role of the instructor in the appraisal process. Since there is no way the teacher can avoid at least reflected evaluation at any level—learning, instructional, or overall program—he should be very much concerned about his role in the appraisal process and the extent to which he has input. Within the module curriculum structure, it is essential that his role be that of an analyst as well as a consequent action initiator beyond the teacher-learner interaction level. If he does not accept this proffered responsibility, someone will do it for him.

As an analyst, it is necessary for him to be able to look at the separate, yet inter-related student, teacher, and program levels in terms of present and anticipated effectiveness and direction at each level. Following this, then, he must be able to plan courses of action in terms of his analysis of the existing situations. As he does this, he becomes more involved in making decisions that affect his own functioning demands and consequent total program direction. This involvement is essential to the improving of learning effectiveness and is a key to performance level determination in the module curriculum approach.

An example of this can be mentioned, in part, in terms of a second quarter progress assessment a math team made, and gave to the author, concerning their implementation of a skills-based, ungraded, continuous progress math program involving grades six through eight.

1. Low ability students are having success. Fewer than 1 percent received an F quarter grade.
2. Brighter students are being challenged.
3. Parent response is positive.
4. Student response is positive.
5. Discipline problems are minimal.
6. Small groups are available for students with special problems.
7. Each student is aware of his individual needs and progress.
8. Fewer personality conflicts exist between teacher and student, and between students.
9. Student motivation has increased.
10. Multi-teacher input to evaluate student.

We feel however, that the following problems exist and that solutions must be found:

1. Team planning time together during the day is limited causing:
   a. Communication breakdown
   b. Coordination deficiencies
   c. Too much before-and-after-school meeting time
2. Teachers have difficulty identifying student names and personalities.
3. An occasional student is misplaced or not placed.
4. There is poor communication with, and ineffective use of, parent volunteers at times.
5. Make-up work is difficult to arrange.

The primary functioning emphasis for the teacher, and the student, must be on the attainment of specified results through satisfactory job performance. Performance efficiency is directly related to the correlation of the program organizational structure, teacher operational skills, and staff practices in terms of identified learner results objectives. Results attainment indicates progress and change which dictate new performance demands. These new demands require the staff to be concerned with maintaining functioning effectiveness through continuous adjustment, and development, of instructional processes that facilitate continuous learner progress. Herein, is organizational efficiency.

Some Action Guidelines

Program:

1. In developing a new program, it is very easy for the staff to become so concerned about teacher functioning *or* student needs that the structuring of the operational demands for one can evolve into an impractical situation for the other. Care must be taken to be sure that the new operational demands are within the functioning capabilities of both teacher and student.
2. The basic emphasis in program development is the provision of a learning structure. In order to accomplish this, the staff must use such primary guidelines as
    > learner needs
    > programming purposes
    > projected desired learner development
    > student performance roles and responsibilities
    > teacher-student set objectives
    > identified teacher management functions
    > progressive appraisal system
3. Program development must be done in terms of the capabilities and needs of the people who must function within the structure. Primary emphasis must not be on content, mechanical techniques, or unquestioning conformity to "past successful practices."
4. There must be a paralleling of objectives development, programming flexibility, and teacher implementation practices. Providing an individualized program structure and demanding that all students follow a single time schedule, or meet common deadlines, is difficult to justify.
5. Staff concern must be devoted to the development of both staff and student operational efficiency. Lack of a close coordination of mechanical programming demands related to record keeping, non-productive meetings, and conflicts between staff sub-groups with desired personnel functioning patterns and stated results objectives can seriously inhibit performance results attainment.

Personnel:

1. Performance demands of students and of teachers must be developed in concert. Developed separately, they can reveal decidedly different functioning demands. The result is operational conflict which seriously limits performance effectiveness of both staff and learners.
2. Often, staff members and students must change their role and responsibility emphases to maintain progress toward objectives

attainment. The staff must take care in writing their objectives and operational procedures so that semantics and highly structured learning demands do not lock teacher and/or learner into an unchangable mode of operation.

3. Each staff member must be continually alert to the need for the use of options and alternatives in terms of the constantly evolving satellite results, and consequent student demands, that result from revealed learner progress. This need can necessitate the teacher's modifying his sequential short-term objectives and performance requirements.

4. Every staff member must learn to develop, implement, and manage an effective performance plan. Conflicts between what a teacher wants, what he can do, and what he states as desired results can result in little more than teacher and learner frustration.

Performance:

1. Support personnel can greatly affect performance results attainment. In many instances, however, their functioning is not subject to building appraisal. Consideration should be given to development of criteria that assess their contributions to identified building objectives and the objectives of individual staff members with whom the support people work.

2. Emphasis must be given to the implementing of appraisal practices that facilitate staffing according to specified purposes, functioning in terms of identified roles and responsibilities, and progress attainment in terms of specific results attainment.

3. Appraisal of all sub-systems must be done in terms of their needs and influences toward the attainment of the identified primary overall building objective(s).

6

INSTRUCTIONAL PLANNING
FOR PERFORMANCE

Instructional planning for results requires that teachers design their classroom structures and related teaching-learning endeavors, not just adapt them from whatever content resources are available. This designing of the teaching-learning action endeavors demands that teachers assume directing and managerial roles in classroom curriculum development. This approach necessitates the staff members' designing classroom structures that parallel the overall program framework using the learners as the basis for planning, then delineating the results objectives, the consequent teacher-learner performance functions, and the methods of determining personnel progress extents. Effectiveness of design affects extent of results attainment.

In the past, schools and individual teachers have not, if present indications and trends mean anything, adequately proved their effectiveness and financial worth to the public—and learners are part of the public. Now, proof of effectiveness must be done at both the total program and individual teacher levels. This demand for proof requires different, more detailed approaches from the design standpoint.

These approaches will, of necessity, be varied in style, structure, and direction according to the singular dictates of school program, staff talents, student characteristics, and community emphases. By and large, however, there are general factors that must be considered as bases for program structure and curriculum development common to all schools. Included in these are

1. Personnel—students and teachers
2. Performance results
3. Planning and design techniques
4. Implementation effectiveness
5. Appraisal criteria and techniques

USING THE LEARNER AS A BASIS FOR PLANNING

Effective lesson planning cannot be done in isolation from the learner, the person *for* whom the planning is traditionally done. The basis for lesson design must, of necessity, be the persons who are expected to act according to the design. These individuals can act in terms of the design only to the extent that their roles, responsibilities, spheres of action and the aspects of teacher-student interaction are delineated.

The teacher, of course, is the person who is primarily responsible for learning design effectiveness. In order to carry out this responsibility, he must know the learner characteristics well enough so that he can develop teaching-learning operational demands which parallel teacher-learner patterns and forces. He must, of consequence, then, develop his plans in terms of what both he and the learner are capable of doing. To do this, the teacher, in these developmental endeavors, needs to assume the role of analyst and manager.

As an analyst, the teacher must be able to identify functional reasons for the learner to participate in the specific endeavors being planned. This involves the instructor's relating learning demands to present student living and values, and then projecting learning demands in terms of how he, the learner, and the parent view the student's ambitions and future activities. In this same role, the teacher must be able to determine relevant ways in which a student can reveal achievement through performance by application.

The demand for student applied performance, coupled with a built-in "need for knowing," requires that the learner recognize the specific skills, areas of knowledge, and operational techniques needed. This involves the teacher's use of singular dovetailing approaches that relate to motivation, to relevance, and to accountability. This is basic to effective teaching-learning design because it requires the instructor to recognize and define specific aspects of each, to compare present achievement with anticipated future needs, and to identify particular techniques to bridge the gap between planning and performance for both teacher and student.

DEVELOPING THE TEACHER'S MANAGEMENT ROLE

The teacher must assume the role of a manager or coordinator because he is responsible for the development of plans, processes, objectives, and activities in direct relation to both teacher and student time and talent, to efficient use of facilities, material, and equipment, and to human potential. In addition, he must be able to relate the use of all these to idea generation and implementation, which is the fundamental basis of the teaching structure. In many cases, this approach must receive direct in-service training emphasis because of the tendency of teachers to work more at the content level than at the idea level.

Following is an example of a staff in-service activity designed to help teachers develop the skills of using the learner as a basis for program planning.

PROPOSED PROGRAM FOR GODDARD
MIDDLE SCHOOL IN-SERVICE
(By Dr. Maxwell Jones, Participating Psychiatrist)

PURPOSE: To increase students' assumption of responsibility for discipline

FORMAT: Three initial training sessions are proposed to orient and prepare the staff for implementing the program. Thereafter, the following format will be utilized: Once weekly, for a period of one-half to one hour, teachers will lead a discussion of problems of discipline with their students—covering topics such as causes of misbehavior and ways students can take more responsibility for their own behavior. After school on the same day, the entire faculty will meet for at least 20 minutes for a "Group Review" of the discussions with the students, to share their experiences, secure help and support from one another, and learn from the ideas and experiences of others. One resource person will be assigned to each grade level, to observe the class discussions, participate as teachers request, and to feed back to the Group Review the process they observed in the class discussions.

ORIENTATION SESSION 1: The session will begin with a general introduction to the proposed program, its format and purposes. After this brief introduction, the session will focus on the specific purpose of this session: to improve teachers' skill in observing behavior in the classroom. The format will be a demonstration of a teacher introducing the idea of a class discussion on discipline to his/her students. The demonstration will include examples of the teacher not listening in depth and not perceiving non-verbal behavior and the student behavior that results. The demonstration would be repeated with variations suggested by the Goddard staff. This demonstration would have the additional function of helping the staff think through how they would wish to introduce the program to the students. The session will end with a simulation of a "Group Review" using the preceding demonstration as the focus and the entire staff as participants; this would serve to acquaint the staff with the function and format of the "Group Review."

ORIENTATION SESSION 2: The specific focus of this session will be the differences in teachers' and students' perceptions of disciplinary problems. The staff will be divided into two groups—one to assume the role of Goddard students, the other to be themselves. Each group will be given copies of a description of a discipline problem facing a school such as Goddard and will be asked to come up with a solution. The groups could then report their solutions to one another, discussing how the solutions differed; or the groups could exchange roles and repeat the task. Two other concepts would be stressed in follow-up discussion: examples of the "students" utilizing their untapped potential and the effect of teacher expectations on pupil behavior.

ORIENTATION SESSION 3: This session would focus on the three systems of norms that control students' behavior: teachers' expectations, peer-group expectations, and parents' expectations. Through discussion, the staff would be encouraged to consider the need for compromise and complementarity if a satisfactory approach to discipline problems is to evolve, and would be asked to consider ways in which the three systems might be integrated. This session is not expected to produce quick and final answers to these issues; instead, it is intended as a starting point for the regular class discussions and Group Reviews to follow. The session will include discussion among the staff to develop consensus on the long-term plans for the program.

Idea Functioning Levels

1. Development of new approaches to meet new change demands
2. Programs of future functioning needs and patterns
3. Management effectiveness
4. Program design and development
5. Objectives development
6. Appraisal results utilization
7. Decision-making

Since a primary responsibility of the teacher is to make himself progressively less needed, it is essential that he master the skills necessary to instructional functioning at the idea level. Also, since a basic function of the teacher is to gain learning effectiveness through the efforts of the student, it is necessary for the instructor to develop instructor-learner objectives and activities that enable the student to function also at the idea level, according to his capabilities, mental and emotional. This is a more difficult task for the teacher, but it is important because it has a great deal of effect on learner effectiveness, attitudes, and action. It is also important because it is consistent with the structural emphasis of the module curriculum concept.

Instructional-learning design, planning, implementation, and appraisal, then, should be done, indeed, must be done, in terms of the particular skill and idea levels at which the teacher and the student can function and in terms of the relationship of what the teacher and program demands and what the student is capable of doing.

DESIGN ACCORDING TO OBJECTIVES AND PERFORMANCE

In too many instances, lesson plans are written in terms of a textbook, a district course of study, possible team teaching situations, test schedules, parent-teacher conference schedules, and other forces that come primarily from a teaching emphasis or the mechanical aspects of the school program. A common sight is a teacher sitting in the faculty lounge, with an open lesson plan book and an open textbook in front of him. From such settings, lesson plans evolve. Many of the results of the efforts put forth here are little more than outlines to guide the teacher in spending class time. Little or no consideration is given to the reasons, bases, or implications pertaining to the outlined activity. There is little evidence of action learning consideration.

There are some cornerstones on which a teacher writes his outlines or on which he designs a program for action learning. The primary difference as to whether he simply outlines some activities or whether he designs and implements a learning program depends on how well he can identify these specific cornerstones and on how effectively he can translate the ideas to action. The aspects on which the instructor must build are philosophy, objectives, and status quo. To ascertain the extent to which he has been building from these, a teacher can analyze his previous year's plan book. It would not be out of the realm of reason to expect that he would find differences in his professed and applied philosophies, gaps and inconsistencies in his instructional continuity and articulation, and an emphasis on teaching activities rather than on the attainment of learning objectives.

Philosophy: In designing for action learning, the staff member must be able to have a working knowledge of the philosophies that govern the student's and the parent's educational reactions, as well as having his own philosophy clearly defined in his own mind. Only in this way, can the teacher recognize the forces that these beliefs can bring to bear on the teaching-learning situation. Only in this way, can he develop a learning environment that takes advantage of the aspects of agreement of the three philosophies and that is developed with specific philosophical differences in mind. On the surface, this seems to be an impossible task. However, most teachers, within a short period of time, depending upon the extent of purposeful contact, can give a fairly accurate description of the ways a student and his parents feel about a particular teaching-learning situation.

A person's philosophy, or pattern of beliefs, is going to govern his action patterns. As a consequence, it is imperative that the teacher be aware of the differences in what he expects and what a student can do. The same, incidentally, holds true for the parent. The teacher must develop a realistic philosophy which facilitates the designing of a structure that provides for a realistic, practical performance framework for each individual student. It does no good to force a student to learn given facts and provide no way, or opportunity, for him to use what he learned. Unless he recognizes, and accepts, a reason for learning a given fact, memorization, rather than learning, becomes a dominant aspect of his functioning.

The more general philosophy of the school itself must be considered here, also, because this can be a limiting or facilitating force acting upon the teacher's philosophical implementation. Causes here relate to the impracticality of the school philosophy as it relates to the student body and/or to the extent of dovetailing of the school philosophy and the teacher's, student's, and parents' philosophies.

Objectives: A learning structure must be designed in terms of identified attainable performance results if there is going to be any consistency in direction, if there is to be any continuity in progress, if there is to be any application of learning, and if there is to be valid basis for performance appraisal. Again, there must be identification of specifically desired results that relate directly to the performance of the teacher, of the student, of the total staff, and of the district. A primary responsibility of the teacher is to develop a plan of action that meshes these various objectives, that provides reasonable sequencing and that promotes the attainment of these multi-level objectives. Success, here, is dependent on the planning done at the individual teacher level.

As a teacher begins to identify specific objectives, he reveals a tendency to make them terminal; that is, they are not sequenced or developed with change in mind. If an educator accepts the premise that learning reflects a change in behavior, he must, of necessity, make his results objectives sensitive to learner change.

Specific change aspects with which the teacher must deal as a result of his instructional endeavors are growth changes in the student, changes in learning needs and conditions, progressive changes in student and parent objectives, and changes in the student resulting from his mastery of particular skills and content and his achieving identified objectives. Change, then, is an integral aspect of learning design.

Status Quo: Instructional planning is not done in limbo. Planning and design at the classroom level must be done with several things in mind; student, teacher, program structure, required content, and community values. Objectives set the direction for the design implementation. The learner status quo determines the starting point or the departure point for progress toward the specified objectives.

The status quo is more than just "where the student is." It implies that he is "x" number of skills and achievement levels from where attainment of objectives specify that, hopefully, he should be. Determination of a learner's status quo involves the identification of his places on the continua in comparison to where the projection, in terms of his singular skills, potential, past and present progress indicate he should be along the composite program continuum. He could be ahead of, behind, or on schedule. Regardless of his position, the individual learner status quo reveals particular situations, problems, and possible directions for subsequent individual program design.

The author worked with a staff that had utilized the performance objectives approach for two years. In his progress conferences with each teacher, the teacher's progress toward the attainment of his identified objectives was discussed in conjunction with the staff member's completed self-appraisal form. In this way, both the administrator and the teacher knew the original teaching-learning status quo position, extent of progress, new status quo position, and anticipated teacher plan of action in terms of the existing situation. Consequent classroom learning and management emphases were identified in terms of the conference decisions.

At the end of the second year after their introduction to the performance results approach, lesson plans written three years before were returned to each staff member. Almost every person observed how incomplete and how instructor-oriented his old lesson plans were. Reactive comments, such as the following, were reflective of their present concern with learners.

"This certainly doesn't tell me what I wanted to accomplish."

"I wonder what the students were being asked to do."

"I was only thinking about what I was wanting to do."

As in similar cases in many schools, these old lesson plans dealt primarily with only the time span for which they were written. There was little, or no, revealed concern for sequential planning in terms of present student learning and consequent learner functioning changes.

Typical of entries in these old plans were

1. Pop quiz over ratio, pages 98-103
2. Review—discussion over short stories, emphasizing theme, plot structure, and character development
3. Devote period to class development of purposes for study of next unit on poetry
4. Faster group work on electrical unit—using laboratory equipment
   Average group—outline Chapter 5
   Slower group—small group discussion of Chapter 5

USING TEACHER SELF-APPRAISAL AS A DESIGN DETERMINANT

An important task for the teacher, and of the student and of his parent, is to identify the specific reasons for the existence of the student's status quo position. Analysis, here, always needs to be done in terms of potential progress, not just in terms of why a student is not at the expected status quo position along the program time and progress line.

In general, analysis of student progress factors is done by the teacher within the framework of the student's functioning. This, of course, has validity, but it is only one aspect. The teacher also needs to analyze student progress within the framework of his own functioning. It is not unusual for a staff member to find that some primary limiting factors to student progress fall within the instructional functioning framework, often specifically within the planning stage. This, however, is directly related to teacher self-analysis pertaining to what he has contributed to the existence of the status quo and what he can do to help the student advance his position along the program continuum.

This self-analysis related to instructional planning and design implementation on the part of the teacher pertains directly to what he, as the instructional leader, is going to do about the situation. In order to develop an effective action guide for himself, the teacher is going to have to answer, in terms of his own function, such questions as the following:

1. What are the specific limiting and facilitating factors pertaining to planned student progress?
2. Why do these factors exist?

3. What actions can the teacher take to dovetail the forces of these factors into a common progress force?
4. How will the teacher identify student problem areas and causes as the learner moves from the status quo toward the desired objectives?
5. What does the teacher hope to accomplish for himself as well as for the student?
6. How can the teacher determine differences between
   a. a problem and a lack of motivation by teacher and learning
   b. dislike and a lack of motivation by teacher, by student, or by both?
   c. failure and poor program planning?
   d. performance and teacher effectiveness?

Learning program design entails the developing of teacher functioning guidelines as well as student functioning expectations. A lack of adequate planning for teacher functioning can inhibit the learning process much more than many educators realize. Lack of learning performance is not always the fault of the student alone.

Following are some examples of teacher functioning guidelines related to the facilitating of performance. These guidelines relate to the teacher function in a support role to the learner.

1. The teacher should serve in a facilitating, motivating role. He should not function in a domineering manner, though he must impose demands pertaining to student conduct.
2. The teacher should identify learner needs, objectives, roles and responsibilities, then identify his mode of operation from these.
3. The teacher needs to plan as much in terms of what the student is capable of doing as in terms of what the learner is not capable of doing.
4. The teacher must be able to identify the specific reasons he is needed by the student.
5. The teacher must select learning activities in terms of student need and capability rather than just in terms of teacher preference.
6. There should be a gradually increasing transfer of learning responsibility from teacher to student during every classroom unit of study.
7. The success of the student determines the success of the teacher.
8. Lesson planning must be done in terms of pupil need, not just in terms of content requirements.
9. The teacher must be aware of what the student needs, and expects, from him as well as what he expects from the student.

10. Learning begins "from where the student is." Instruction should also begin from this point.

11. A high correlation between student needs and teacher weaknesses related to a given unit of study necessitates at least a temporary change in teaching assignment.

A department chairman in a suburban district used the following question guideline as he worked with his department to clarify staff support areas.

1) Definitions of the following:
   a. course
   b. unit
   c. program improvement
   d. curriculum change
   e. curriculum revision
2) Where does enrichment fit into the present K-12 program?
3) Must teachers teach what and only what is in the curriculum guide?
4) If a teacher achieves the objectives as outlined in the curriculum guide, is he free to pursue other areas of student interest?
5) Can we not set the objectives for the District and leave it to the Building Departments to decide how they will reach those objectives?

DESIGNING A CLASSROOM PERFORMANCE FRAMEWORK

A classroom performance framework is built around the four basic areas of objectives, skills, content, and activities. Learning effectiveness is determined by the ways the teacher organizes the performance demands of the particular aspects of these four areas and the extent to which they interlink in a sequential manner. This framework is the result of the teacher's deliberate analysis, evaluation, selection, and implementation of the options available to him in each area. Add to this the teacher's careful development of a viable mode of operation for both teacher and learner, and a performance framework begins to take shape.

When these various details are worked out, both the student and his instructor can more readily ascertain the desired learning environment and the functioning conditions peculiar to the learning environment. This is essential because the instructor and the student need a clearly defined picture of the performance setting and functioning patterns expected of them before significant learner progress can be made.

Instructional design necessitates continual and consistent decision-making by the teacher from the human standpoint more than from the academic standpoint. The instructor, for example, needs to make decisions relative to specific selection of contributory learning tools in the skill, content, activities, and subobjective areas. In terms of the performance objectives identified, the teacher must make decisions relative to such as the following:

1. What particular skills and areas of knowledge must the student have?
2. What other skill and content aspects can be included to help the student to gain the needed skills and knowledge?
3. Are these two levels of skills and content clearly identified and sequenced?
4. Do all of these facilitate specific learner progress or are some of them nothing more than time "fill dirt"?

Answers to such questions as these are directly related to the teacher's own philosophy, priority objectives, and educational value system. Hopefully, there is no dichotomy between what he says and what he does.

HOW TO USE THE FLEXIBLE STRUCTURE APPROACH

Much has been written about the different domain levels, cognitive, affective, and psychomotor and the need to consider them in the development of learning endeavors. The same need holds true in the instructor's development of activities in which a student is expected to engage to help bring about learning progress. Far too few educators spend enough time organizing instructional activities to correspond to the differing learner levels present in the classroom.

Recognizing that students do vary in their learning patterns, processes, and rates, even from chapter to chapter within the same textbook, it is essential that classroom program design allow for individual student time demand variations. Time demand is often indicative of level functioning. Therefore, it is important for the classroom teacher to develop his learning units and activities on several different levels which correspond to individual, and group needs. The instructor must consider, here, the possible need for level development, also, in terms of learning processes and teaching techniques that can be of best use to the student.

This level development cannot be done in isolation from the

pupil's placement on the program continuum. If it is done in isolation, there is very likely to be instructional gapping, or unnecessary instructional repetition is often imposed by the instructor in repeating material, processes, or skill techniques that were not effective learning tools. Though, perhaps, extended concentrated time needs to be devoted to the learning of a particular skill or content, surely the approaches should be changed to meet the student's revealed functioning level.

The selection of instructional techniques receive much less attention from the teacher than they should because there is a definite inter-relationship pertaining to the type of lesson, the specific objectives, the teacher expectations of the student, and the tasks the learner is given to do. A gapping or breakdown in consistency, here, contributes to a limiting effect on the student's progress, an effect imposed on him by poor selection of teaching methods and learning job demands. In order to do an efficient job in this respect, the teacher, again, needs to continue in his role as analyst to determine needs and the subsequent teaching tools that can be used most effectively. The author has found that to ascertain the specific instructional techniques and methods that can be most effective in a given learning situation the teacher should endeavor to answer such questions as

1. What methods, procedures, and activities are best suited to this student and this particular learning task?
2. How do they compare with the progress made by the student using these methods and techniques in the past? To what extent were they facilitating learning?
3. What time allotments will the student need?
4. What is the anticipated amount of teacher-need time?
5. Are these methods and techniques consistent with the applied performance demands and with my appraisal techniques?
6. What will be my teaching role?
7. What will be the learner's role?

As the teacher designs the teaching-learning framework, he must not forget to involve the learner in the process. The extent to which the student should be involved will vary according to the type of learning tasks involved and the degree to which the student is capable in terms of knowledge of task, understanding of needs and demands, and capability of planning his own learning program. In general, however, the student should have some say in the selection of priorities and alternatives, and in making choices pertaining to learning activities and techniques that parallel his own known skills and learning patterns. When the teacher insists on making all these decisions himself, he insists on assuming the dominant initiating role. He is assuming, and keeping for himself, the role that should be gradually delegated to the student within each learning unit as well as within the overall program.

The departments of the school where the author is Principal have used such approaches as the following, as bases for program design and teacher functioning delineation.

> Continuous progress, skill leveling, ungraded
> Topic approach as opposed to survey
> Electives, various courses teaching similar skills
> Department requirements based on the achievement of skills (achievement will be the constant; time will be the variable)
> Mini-courses
> • Interdisciplinary
> • Non-graded, advancement will be based on achievement
> • Teaming

IMPLEMENTING THE PERFORMANCE PLAN

As every staff member designs his instructional-learning program, there are a number of characteristics he needs to build into the program if he really expects to achieve results objectives relative to relevancy, accountability, and learning progress. Some of these characteristics will vary according to the singular situations within which each school must function. There are others, however, that can be considered as important basics in any learner and results-oriented program.

Flexibility: At the same time the teacher needs to be concerned with consistency in direction and emphases, he also has to build in flexibility that will permit both him and the student to continue to function along the continua as learning change and forces occur. If the instructor, through design or oversight, fails to incorporate change possibility aspects in such areas as sub-objectives, activities, continua placement, and learner functioning levels, he will find himself, and the student, locked in by time. Unfortunately, time as allotted through traditionally constant mechanisms such as master schedules, carnegie units, and required units in a course guideline becomes very difficult to change. Desired changes at the learning level, then, are difficult to bring about. Flexibility use, at the outset, helps to eliminate this boxing in.

Sequential coordination: To insure continuity and consistency in the learning process and in the various program continua, the program designer must pay particular attention to sequential coordination of the individual learner program with satellite learning and interaction areas. For example, the teacher needs to be aware of any overlapping of emphasis, skills, and content into other instructional areas. A skill taught in one class level can, possibly, be a performance demand pre-requisite in another class of the same level—measurement taught in math, but used daily in shop. This same situation can occur within the various activities and demands of the same unit of study. Consistency between student capabilities and teacher expectations within the same module course is basic to learning effectiveness.

Demands and forces: A viable learning environment comes into being only to the extent that the student, teacher, program, and time forces are developed into a congruous intermesh in which both teacher and student can function and with which both can deal. In order to bring this about, the instructor must be able to identify these singular forces, agreeing and opposing, and organize them into parallel force action. Examples here are interest-emphasis, achievement-expectations, skill need-skill demand, pop test-discipline. The teacher, also, must be able to anticipate new demands and forces occurring as a result of learner progress. Those which, perhaps, have not been present in the past, must be integrated into the new present situation in order to maintain learning continuity.

Examples of Emergent New Demands and Forces

1. Conflicts relating to differences between content difficulty and student achievement level and progress
2. Need for utilization of differing teaching/learning methods
3. Changes in learner job delineation as a result of subject matter guideline revision
4. Need for student rescheduling as a result of student achievement
5. Need for reassignment of a teacher to another stage, or stages, of a continuum level because of changing learner needs
6. Sequential change in teacher role and responsibilities as determined by student performance

Along with this, there must be teacher anticipation of probable decisions that either, or both, teacher and student will have to make as a result of the changes that occur. Crisis or spur-of-the moment decision-making, of course, cannot be entirely avoided, yet, through projection, many of these decision-making areas can be identified fairly accurately by both teacher and student. Examples here are possible areas of enrichment or remedial action, time alternatives, difficulty of content, and teacher-need time.

Progress expectations: A traditional approach in determining student progress is the teach-test method. A problem here is that the teacher exposes the learner to pre-selected material, asks him to participate in certain activities, and then tests the student as to what, if anything, has happened—if any, and how much, learning has occurred. In a number of instances, the teacher could probably make a relatively accurate guess on extent of learning without the use of the test. None of this really tells the teacher very much, however, because he has not taken the time to identify a starting point for the student's progress, nor has he made the effort to specify an expected achievement level for him. Without these specification points, it is much more difficult for the instructor to determine learner progress and teaching effectiveness.

Two methods the author has found effective in helping to identify specification points are (1) set anticipated performance levels that can reasonably be considered as "satisfactory" for the student and for the class, in terms of teacher objectives, and (2) determine where the particular unit of study fits on the program continuum as compared to the student's location. Any differences here will be of great help to the teacher in making decisions and selections pertaining to specific teaching-learning techniques, methods, and procedures. They also provide a consistent method of progress feedback for the teacher and the student.

EVALUATION ASPECTS OF THE INSTRUCTIONAL DESIGN

Every student and every teacher reveal certain functioning characteristics, positive and negative, as affected by the program structure within which they are expected to function. The program framework has reflected functioning characteristics determined by the manners, and capabilities of the person operating within the framework. As conflicts arise, changes must be made in all, or each, of the three functioning forces in order to maintain, or improve, performance effectiveness. This need for change involves the development of an evaluation system by the teacher and by the school administrator. The first level of evaluation, however, is for the teacher because his actions have a primary effect on the extent of effectiveness revealed by himself, by the student, and by the program structure. In many cases, the program structure, per se, is not the basic cause of failure or lack of effectiveness. A major cause here is the teacher's and student's lack of the necessary skills to function within the program demands.

The program structure is only as good as the capabilities of the people functioning within it. Since change comes about in the people before it comes in structure, perhaps, appraisal of instructional design should start with an analysis of the performance capabilities and patterns of the people involved. The appraisal techniques should be developed so that the program structure and the functioning levels of the persons involved are analyzed as an integral whole, not as isolated units of force and effect.

Though specifics of appraisal procedures and emphases will vary from school to school, depending upon the singular staff, program and community characteristics, several examples of appraisal approach toward the inter-related emphasis of personnel functioning and program structure can be given that transcend many of the singular characteristics of individual school program structures.

USING STUDENT PROGRESS AS THE BASIC APPRAISAL CRITERION

Grading and learning demands: Emphasis has been placed on the importance of correlating program demands with personnel functioning, both student and teacher. Using student functioning as an example, there can be very limited validity in assessing pupil performance if the appraisal criteria are not consistent with the program functioning and learning demands. Traditional letter grade emphasis on the basis of arbitrary quarter-grading periods is not consistent with program and instructional emphasis on performance results and continuous learning progress. Effective program design stresses future student performance levels based on present continua placement; traditional grading procedures stress rating of a student only on what he has done as a result of previous efforts under prior situational demands that can no longer be delineated.

There needs to be clearly defined performance appraisal demands that parallel program functioning demands, student action patterns, and sequential learning activity selection. Academic emphasis on testing as a major evaluative technique is inconsistent with program emphasis on applied performance results.

**Examples of Paralleling Pupil Performance and
Programming Patterns**

PUPIL PERFORMANCE	PROGRAMMING PATTERNS
1. Pre-test evaluation	1. Placement of student within program according to individual skills needed
2. Participation in enrichment short courses and projects	2. Challenge opportunities, "plug-in" independent study activities
3. Number of successfully completed units and levels of performance	3. Adjustment in continuum level, objectives, and available learning options
4. Post-tests in specific content and skill areas	4. Increased performance demands in practical situations

Student progress analysis: Learning progress is not an educational entity that can be categorized or compartmented into arbitrarily determined content and time units. Learning progress varies in level and rate according to the variation in program and instructional forces working on, for, and against the learner. Appraisal consistency, then, must take into consideration such factors as the following:

1. Multi-level student performance levels that allow for areas in which each student can experience
   a. sure success
   b. challenging endeavors
   c. self-innovating initiation
2. Ways for student-keeping of own progress graphs
3. The building of a composite continua time line

4. Specific ways both student and teacher can determine progress
   a. starting levels identified
   b. progress levels—high's and low's
   c. projected finish level

Basic to the area of student progress analysis is the teacher-student team's developing feedback methods that will provide continuous, reliable information pertaining to the functioning patterns and levels of both student and teacher. In order to be useful, these feedback procedures must be developed and organized to provide immediate information return. This process should also be developed so that appropriate feedback information can be available to parents on a consistent basis. Immediate feedback, as opposed to traditional periodic progress checks, is essential if necessary programming changes such as time allotment variation, special help provisions, and content adjustments are to be made in parallel relationships with the changing needs and demands of the learner.

Examples of Practical Feedback Criteria

FROM STUDENT	FROM TEACHER
1. Teacher-need time	1. Extent of success in meeting instructional demands
2. Levels of objectives set	2. Need priorities
3. Satisfactory performance range	3. Continuous performance graphing
4. Most effective individual learning techniques and procedures	4. Feasible options and alternatives
5. Personal learning expectations	5. Observable changes occurring in student functioning patterns
6. Extent of acceptance of program functioning demands	6. Instructional expectations
	7. Changes in appraisal criteria necessitated

Instructional planning for performance results uses the learner as the basic functioning unit. Every phase of the learning performance-oriented program is developed in terms of how it will facilitate learner functioning. The long-run effectiveness of the learning structure will be greatly affected by the effectiveness of the learning support phases, those developed at the instructional level. The worth of these instructional phases will be determined by how well the teacher functions as a coordinator and manager of such instructional aspects as the teacher's operational role, the selection of operation objectives and performance demands, the change forces resulting from learner progress, and the teacher-learner functioning patterns within the broader building curricular structure.

Some Action Guidelines

Program:

1. Planning and design determine the program characteristics. Staff roles and responsibilities determine implementation characteristics. Often, teachers inexperienced in in-depth curricular design will tend to want to develop the program in terms of their past experiences and present skills. To prevent a superficial reworking of the existing structure, the staff members involved in program design need to be sure that a new programmatic approach doesn't become "fail sure" by their attempting to implement a new program demand using only techniques, methods, and skills developed for another program. A new structure demands additional, or new, staff functioning skills.

2. The implementation of a new program results in the staff's having to work with new functioning demands. Effort should be devoted to specifically identifying and detailing the changes being implemented, the specific results expected from these changes, and how both staff and students will be expected to function differently; otherwise staff functions will be in conflict with program operational demands. This negative conflict can cause loss of staff support for the new program concept.

3. Program flexibility must be developed in terms of present programming needs *and* in terms of anticipated change in staff-student performance characteristics resulting from revealed personnel functioning effectiveness.

Personnel:

1. Typically, the traditional staff member views teaching and management as two different functioning levels. Within the performance results concept, the staff member serves in both areas because, by the nature of his responsibilities, he must identify, select, and use

various materials and pieces of equipment, he must be involved in budget item identification, and he must be responsible for the functioning effectiveness of his students. The idea that in the classroom, teaching and management are "different" is contrived reasoning with little effect other than limiting student learning.

2. Arbitrarily-developed teacher functioning patterns are inconsistent with learning program emphases. Teacher operational planning should be done on the basis of anticipated student functioning.

3. Instructional planning must be done in terms of specific objectives and learner needs. Planning involves both selection and appraisal methods. Decision-making related to the determination of techniques to be used in the classroom, for example, involve

an identification of the methods, procedures, and activities that are BEST suited to the given situation

an identification of individual student learning success using these methods, procedures, and activities in the past

a recognition of the consistency between these instructional selections with the applied performance demands and the teacher appraisal emphases

Performance:

1. Learning effectiveness will be greatly influenced by the extent to which the student understands the need for knowing how to use, in his own living, the skills he is being asked to master within the formal classroom structure.

2. Teacher self-appraisal must be done in terms of student functioning *and* teacher functioning if the teacher expects to obtain any useful, reliable feedback related to his instructional effectiveness.

3. Appraisal of performance must result in proof of effectiveness through learner action. Many traditional appraisal methods, forms, and emphases stress desired teacher characteristics and philosophically justified items such as positive learning environment, use of a variety of teaching methods, and the provision for individual differences and, as a consequence, are inadequate for effective appraisal. Appraisal criteria must focus upon the student's actual use of the skills and content learned in an applied situation such as

functioning adequately in the next higher learning level

use of these skills and knowledge within his own sphere of social living

setting and attaining progressively higher personal functioning objectives

7

PLANNING BASES FOR PERFORMANCE MONITORING

To be an effective force in improving staff and student performance, appraisal emphasis must be placed "where the action is," in the functioning results related to students, to teachers, and to program. Performance monitoring must focus on the revealed and desired personnel functioning levels within the program operational demands. Consequently, assessment criteria must be developed in such terms as continuous change, program operational demands, staff self-appraisal, and identified performance success levels.

IDENTIFYING UNDERLYING FORCES
AFFECTING APPRAISAL ACCURACY

Performance appraisal of one area cannot be done in isolation from the direct and indirect forces and demands imposed by the various other facets of the total educational framework. Yet, continuing attempts are made by educators to assess in isolation, in terms of sub-system dichotomies. A typical example here relates to the efforts of many teachers to develop lesson plans at the affective–cognitive level, then teach primarily at the cognitive level. Planning is at the "learning" level and implementation is at the "teaching" level.

AFFECTIVE–COGNITIVE PLANNING	COGNITIVE APPLICATION
Study of "The Death of the Hired Man" by Robert Frost	Oral reading of poem
	Poetic style
a. Theme	Language use—poetry and
b. Poetic style	prose
c. Man's concern for man	Definitions of "house"
d. Value of human life	Setting of poem
e. Success in life	Use of descriptive words
f. Comparison with students' own lives	Character contrasts

If there is any consistency of evaluation in terms of these sub-program characteristics, it is only natural to expect consequent sub-program appraisal isolation. A change in one area, then, does not facilitate consequent needed change in planning and implementation relationships in the other sub-areas of the total structure.

Another area of neglect in the traditional method of effectiveness appraisal is the consideration of change. Generally speaking, a school program is developed on the assumption that if learning takes place, there are going to be changes taking place in, and by, the learners. Too often, regardless of the extent of change that does occur, no allowance is made for consequent change in program structure, in teacher-student relationships, or in staff selection of different techniques and methods in terms of the new learning demands and forces evolving as a result of the learner changes. The result is an attempt by educators to appraise performance of students and teachers as they function in terms of changing teacher-learner characteristics within a relatively static program structure. Extent of change made in structure is not correlated with extent of change occuring in students resulting from their learning new skills, new ideas, and additional knowledge. Evaluation, as a result, has very little pertinence to the identification of developing needs and anticipated future teacher and learner programming for performance.

EXISTENT PROGRAM CHARACTERISTICS	LEARNER PERFORMANCE	NEEDED PROGRAM CHANGE
1. Status quo objectives	1. Attainment of objectives	1. Sequentially higher level objectives
2. Departmentalized content emphasis	2. Increased applied performance level	2. Interdisciplinary functioning
3. Pre-determined required courses	3. Achievement beyond set course requirements	3. Implementation of options approach
4. Pre-determined grading standards	4. Skills and knowledge gained outside of classroom activity	4. Individualized performance progress criteria
5. Teacher-identified student functioning patterns	5. Increasing student program performance pattern conflicts	5. Paralleling of program and learner patterns

RECOGNIZING CHANGE AS AN APPRAISAL FACTOR

Though the traditional approach to staff-student appraisal can, and does, tend to identify problem areas, the emphasis does not extend into the area of future planning or of anticipated changing conditions. Attention, instead, is given to present needs for remediation, with little, or no, attention given to preventive action in terms of new learning forces and demands. Perhaps, this condition exists because the present is easier to deal with in terms of existing, static judgmental criteria rather than with continuous change criteria, which, incidentally, many teachers and administrators do not know how to develop and implement. Figure 7-1 illustrates one method of reducing the gapping between "present" planning emphasis only and continuous change design.

The Colorado Department of Institutions, through the Educational Department within the Division of Youth Services for adjudicated youth, is implementing a curricular structure that emphasizes student progress in terms of integrated student, program, and division objectives. The program is developed in terms of the individualized continuous progress approach. It is a fully prescriptive-based program that stresses individual program development, on the basis of diagnosed learner need, with a consequent specific plan written to provide a specific help for the individual, using learning activities packets.

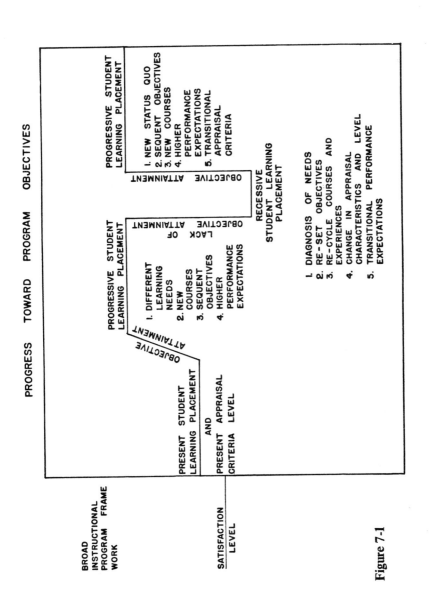

Figure 7-1

The basic appraisal factor is change in student behavior as indicated in the flow chart, Figure 7-2.

DEVELOPING CONTINUOUS CRITERIA

Much of the difficulty lies in the fact that evaluative criteria are developed in isolation from the specific forces and demands of the building program and the consequent expected functioning patterns of the personnel, both staff and students, working within the program structure. These assembly line criteria—broad and vague enough to fit almost any program situation—can serve as little more than mechanical and egoistic pacifiers. Useful and effective learning, teaching, and program criteria must be developed in terms of a specific student body, a specific staff, a specific program, and the performance results objectives developed in terms of them. This is not to imply that differing educational structures cannot have common aspects and similar criteria. It does mean, however, that any criteria selected must have a direct, specific relationship to singular aspects of the particular program framework within which the criteria are to be used.

Continuous criteria, then, must be developed with respect to anticipated change in the learners and the consequent necessary change in program structure. This development of continuous change appraisal criteria must be done with specific procedures, processes, and results in mind. A basic consideration here is the recognition of the importance of identifying the ways and patterns of individual functioning, since results attainment is directly related to the ways a person selects to help him attain his objectives.

Some Basic Areas Necessitating Continuous Change Criteria

1. Anticipation of sequential performance progress toward identified continuum stages
2. Expectation of levels of achievement at each stage
3. Identification of new performance behaviors expected as a result of new student learning experiences
4. Identification of performance and behavior levels expected of a student as he progresses through total program
5. Projection of changes in program structure to meet new needs resulting from student learning
6. Expectation of changes in teacher performance patterns as a result of changes in program structure

STUDENT FLOW IN AN INSTRUCTIONAL-OBJECTIVE BASED CURRICULUM
WITH LEARNING-ACTIVITIES PACKETS

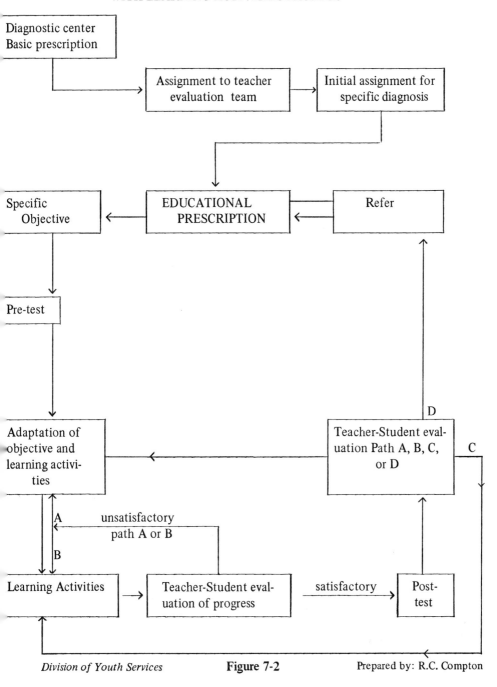

Division of Youth Services **Figure 7-2** Prepared by: R.C. Compton

IDENTIFYING PROGRAM FUNCTIONING
PATTERNS AND DEMANDS

Sub-systems, like the total school program, are developed on the basis of assumptions. A fundamental purpose of an evaluation system is to determine program and sub-program effectiveness. This pertains, also, to the validity of the basic assumptions from which the programs are developed. In reality, the appraisal process of the staff, student and program structures and functioning patterns provides a procedure to help determine the extent of validity of the basic assumptions.

Two basic assumptions pertinent to school program development are (1) the program helps meet the needs of the students, the community, and the staff and (2) the educational framework reflects a learning emphasis. With these in mind, then, any definition or description of the school program will be developed in terms of learner needs and teacher-learner talents. Again, however, the same problem of dichotomy between what is said—philosophy and objectives—and what is actually done—day-to-day classroom implementation—must be dealt with.

It is within this gap between philosophy and implementation that performance objectives play an important role, for they provide the transitional step for reducing philosophical theory to practical application of learning. As these performance results objectives are developed, assumptions are being reduced to more readily identifiable relationships between objectives and results, between process and results, and between learning and application.

Appraisal techniques must be applied to the school's underlying assumptions because static or false assumptions affect the extent of change, of progress, and of effectiveness of the school program and personnel. These basic assumptions cannot be unchanging, though they must be consistent, because the valve systems and modes of operation for society and students change. Too, assumptions must be progressive in direct relationship to the need for program development in terms of pupil progress.

The staff must be able to answer such questions as the following if they are to be able to ascertain continuously the validity of their basic assumptions.

I. Meeting the Needs of Students
    1. Does the curriculum reflect the identified priority interests and needs of the community?

2. To what extent does the school program offer areas for successful functioning by every student?
3. Is the program updated periodically to reflect changes in community characteristics?
4. Does the program structure facilitate staff growth or does it impose limitations of conformity on the teachers?
5. How do the curricular operational demands encourage the teachers' planning for anticipated changes in student learning needs?

II. Reflecting a learning emphasis

1. Do the instructional level objectives describe what the learner will be able to do in practical situations?
2. Is the learner encouraged to participate in decision-making related to his program emphases?
3. Is the program structure flexible enough to allow for operational changes needed as a result of learner progress?
4. Do student performance roles and responsibilities receive primary emphasis in curriculum development?
5. How are teaching support roles identified?
6. To what extent are program functioning requirements reasonable for *all* students attending the school?

APPRAISING AND CHANGING THE SCHOOL'S BASIC EDUCATIONAL ASSUMPTIONS

The appraisal of, and possible need for, change in basic assumptions poses a problem for the school staff. This problem is related to the staff's ability to identify the key points at which the basic educational assumptions should, and can, be changed. The changing of basic assumptions can often involve a challenge to the individual staff member's personal philosophy and value system. Perhaps, one reason there is reluctance on the part of most school faculties to attempt seriously to analyze their fundamental operational assumptions from the standpoint of possible change is that change can produce a philosophical and operational vacuum, and no progressive assumption development process has been devised to fill the void.

This reluctance related to basic assumptions change, by extension, can have a decidedly negative influence on appraisal validity and total program effectiveness, for changing operational forces and demands come into conflict with static foundation ideas. However, a serious assessment approach cannot only bring these conflicts to light, it can also help pinpoint the degrees of change that can provide the staff with possible assumption change direction. For example, conflicts between teaching-learning program demands, community-student-program areas of emphases differences, and direction and extent of change variations as viewed by staff, students, and parents can be indicators of needed assumption change or indicators of the dichotomy between philosophical assumptions and actual practice.

Operational demands imposed by the program structure on the staff and students affect their functioning patterns and consequent assessment procedures and techniques. Again, emphasis here is placed on what is really happening within the building educational framework rather than what is stated philosophically as to what is desired in such terms, for example, as staff creativity, program flexibility, operation by objectives, program learner emphasis, and general curriculum balance. Accountability, relevancy, and effectiveness are determined by actions, not just words.

EFFECTIVE ASSESSMENT AND
PROGRAM FUNCTIONING DEMANDS

The actual observable, measurable extents to which students are progressively less dependent upon their instructors are directly related to the various ways and manners the learners are encouraged, directly and indirectly, to engage in such functioning pattern development aspects as option selection, role and responsibility assumption, time management, and personal decision-making. Identification of these extents, and paralleling them with program functioning forces, contribute to the consistent development of overall, operational functioning demands that can more easily be evaluated in terms of effectiveness and consequent program worth.

Effective assessment is also affected by the ways the basic school program structure encourages the staff to function. What, for example, are the differences between advocated concern for performance results and subject matter emphasis, between departmental curriculum development and K-12 course content importance, and between the actual role of the teacher and the professed role of the learner? Answers to such questions as these will help to identify and clarify the program functioning patterns and demands and the extent of paralleling between what is said and what is actually happening. This, consequently, will affect the extent to which assessment is geared to words or to action.

Another school staff, with whom the author worked, was concerned about the "locked-in" affect the program structure within which they were functioning had on both students and staff. The faculty, in a series of meetings, was asked to explore answers to such questions as the following:

1. How much time per week per grade will your subject area require?
2. Which grade levels will you want to include in your subject area?
3. What type of program would you like in your subject area?
4. Are you considering team, block, or a traditional approach?
5. What are required courses and elective courses that you would want in your areas and in which grade levels?

As a result of their discussions, the staff felt they could begin to open up their program more by implementing a rotating schedule with extended time blocks. They felt this structure would provide the following advantages.

1. Small group instruction, allowing for more individualization of student problems
2. Team teaching brings more expertise to the students
3. The ability to build more interest in the subject areas because all teachers on that team come in contact with all students in the school.
4. Rotation of the time blocks will allow students to be exposed to different subjects during the school year at different times.
5. A better approach to Drug and Health Education because Science and P.E. are grouped in the same block.
6. A continuing of education because all teachers are teaching all grade levels.
7. More emphasis on reading and comprehension skills because reading and language arts are grouped together.
8. Counseling by teachers coordinated by the counselor (note advisory period).
9. The block arrangement allows for team teaching between the discipline and non-discipline areas and also, to some extent, inter-disciplinary team teaching between grade levels.
10. An exploratory activity period for students to pursue interest areas.
11. Ability grouping within certain blocks with the flexibility that students would be able to move between levels.

BASES FOR DEVELOPING SUCCESS
APPRAISAL CRITERIA

Appraisal criteria need to be developed in terms of the specific program to which the criteria are to be applied. As a result, before criteria can be identified, program characteristics must be delineated. This delineation must be developed primarily in terms of the operational facets of the program, the day-to-day patterns that generate the demands and forces with which students and staff must deal as they carry out their teaching and learning duties and responsibilities. These day-to-day operational aspects are primary determinants of the teaching and learning roles, of the ways the teacher should be appraised, and, in reality, of the ways the teacher assesses his students' performances.

Once these specific program characteristics are identified and described, it can be relatively easy for the individual teacher to ascertain the specific ways he is expected to function. Also, the teacher, in cooperation with the building administrator, can much more easily pinpoint the level of teacher performance that can be considered as "satisfactory." This clarification can have direct carryover to the pupil level of functioning because once the teacher's role and performance expectations are described, the teacher finds he has more specific guidelines to follow in developing paralleling expectations for learning performance. In this way, performance assessment can be oriented more to projecting success rather than simply analyzing an unchangeable past.

After the program characteristics and consequent expected student and teacher functioning patterns have been identified, appraisal criteria can be more accurately compiled. This procedure is essential if appraisal procedures, techniques, and emphases are to be consistent with the program structure demands and forces. Increased appraisal validity can result because of the consequent reducing, or eliminating, of the gapping between assessment expectations and actual program functioning demands.

Since, in reality, there can often be overlapping in the ways a teacher is evaluated and the ways he evaluates his students, there is validity in the thought that there should be some similarity in the ways teacher and student performance results are recorded. Again, a logical way here would be to use staff performance graphing in terms of the continua of change, of program, of content, and of individual progress.

Examples of Staff Performance Graphing Criteria

1. Objectives attainment
2. Specific evidence of performance level improvement
3. Continuing attainment of objectives of overall program
4. Instructional program design and organization
5. Implementation and management of need and change structures
6. Contribution to total program effectiveness
7. Development of appraisal criteria relative to self, student, and program functioning
8. Identification of projected needed changes in teacher functioning as a result of previous planning implementation.
9. Development of effective feedback methods pertaining to both teacher and student functioning
10. Capability to function effectively in differing continua stages
11. Correlation of personal characteristics with demands of assignment
12. Effectiveness in program structuring for individual learners

The State of California has eliminated, with the exception of physical education, specific course requirements for graduation from public schools. With this change, California school districts have been given the authority to develop programs in terms of student and community needs. This local authority provides school staffs with opportunities to design and implement learning programs in terms of people rather than in terms of arbitrary rules and regulations.

This dramatic change stresses the fact that courses offered in a school must be justified in terms of the stated desired performance results of the school. By extension, this also can mean that each teacher's role in the school program must also be justified by these stated performance objectives and his ability to attain them.

This California law, Senate Bill One, has identified change as a major school and teacher assessment factor. As a result, school staffs have the opportunity to develop effective programs in terms of student need and staff talents. With this, comes the possibility of wider use of such approaches as individualized instruction, continuous progress, performance results criteria, and open staffing. With this opportunity, comes the responsibility for bringing about, and maintaining, increased teacher and student performance success.

BASES FOR TEACHER PERFORMANCE MONITORING

It is difficult to monitor performance unless specific criteria, specific functioning emphases, and specific assessment checkpoints are identified. These should be developed in terms of the program, of staff talents needed for program operation, and of individual teacher functioning patterns. It is essential, too, that there is a dovetailing of the monitoring procedures and emphases with the program and curricular processes and emphases. Lack of adequate operational dovetailing leads to gapping and consequent lack of appraisal validity and consistency.

Basic to the development and implementing of an effective monitoring system is the detailing of the specific program structure with its consequent singular demands related to staff and student functioning patterns, its particular operational characteristics, and staff objectives and priorities. Once this basic task has been accomplished, it is relatively easy for the administrators and teachers to identify the particular staff talents, skills, and attitudes needed to facilitate teaching-learning progress within the educational framework.

Staffing patterns, of necessity, then, must be consistent with the program functioning demands and with the singular staff talents, skills, and attitudes needed. Teachers who possess all the necessary skills and attributes for a given program are not often found. As a result, if learning effectiveness is to be maintained and validity in staff appraisal is to be gained, participation in a preparation program of in-service activities is necessary for new staff members so that they can gain the necessary skills and modes of operation demanded by the program. Until the new staff members have gained these, there can be only limited consistency in appraisal because of the lack of harmony between program demands and individual teacher functioning capabilities.

Just as there is a need for the diagnostic approach to determining "where a student is" along the learning continuum, there is a parallel need for a diagnostic approach to determine a staff member's position in relation to program forces and demands. This staff diagnostic approach involves determining such characteristics as an individual staff member's unique strengths, weaknesses, and possible conflicts between teacher functioning patterns and program functioning demands. The resolution of conflicts here does not mean the individual is subjugated to the program. It does mean that before individualization of in-service help can be developed, areas of differences must be brought to light.

Through experience in working within the performance results-oriented program structure, the author has found that effective monitoring of teacher performance in terms of program functioning demands and individual teacher objectives is dependent upon the matching of teacher performance level capabilities with singular program operational demands. Reliable functioning assessment cannot be done if there is a gap between what a staff member can do best and what his assignment demands that he be able to do well.

Full reduction of gapping here can only be done through observation of on-the-job functioning. Consequently, a school employing applicants who have completed successful practice teaching within the program can have an advantage here if the staff follows a procedure such as the following, taken from a suburban high school's guide for student teachers.

Benefits From Student Teacher Observations

Orientation to the teaching environment where the student teacher will be working

Management techniques and classroom routine
Awareness of the supervising teacher's style
Understanding of how pupils react to stimuli
Knowledge of content and method
Exposure to the problems of teaching

Learn additional teaching techniques

Techniques of arousing student interest
Identify skills which the student teacher can use
Learn what makes "good" teaching effective
Analyze teaching behavior which seems to be ineffective

Provide a more comprehensive background for the consideration and evaluation of ideas and practices

Learn to evaluate teaching

Recognizing theoretical implications
Determining basic principles associated with teaching
Formulating a valid concept of what constitutes effective teaching

Gain a more comprehensive understanding of students

Comparison of the same student in various school situations
Understanding of the forces that determine student behavior
Case study of special students

Gain a more comprehensive picture of the function of the school

Other grade levels and other subjects taught
Learning experiences which have preceded the student teacher's grade
   level
Experiences which will follow the student teacher's grade level
Relationship of various content areas to one another
Curricula in the school

A program must be developed with consideration of the skills, talents, and potential of the people, both teachers and students, who are expected to function within it. The staff diagnostic approach is more an aspect of the process for selecting new staff members who can contribute more, faster, to the program and who, as a result, reveal a higher potential success rating. The diagnostic approach also provides a method for the administrators and staff to assess in-service training needs more accurately because the diagnostic procedures can, and should, be a continuing aspect of the appraisal system.

Performance monitoring should also be concerned with the ways a person selects to facilitate progress toward stated objectives, and the extent of progress. It involves using a system that provides feedback consistently enough to the performer and to his appraiser so that continuous graphing of performance levels and progress can be done. Occasional or spasmodic observation is not monitoring, nor is it effective. Since, supposedly, performance is an ongoing process, the monitoring process should be ongoing.

Performance monitoring can be a function that is categorized as a staff process only. Performance is concerned with interaction between teacher and student and with the attainment of, or the progress toward, objectives, the extent of which is directly influenced by both teacher and student. The monitoring process has value only to the degree that it positively influences learning effectiveness. Therefore, selection of monitoring procedures and criteria should be done with the idea that they are performance facilitators. This is not meant to imply that emphasis should be placed on student performance as a major criterion for teacher appraisal. It does mean, though, that monitoring processes and criteria need to be consistent with program priorities and functioning demands, need to be specific enough to be of value to teacher and learner, and need to contribute to the two basic requisites of teaching effectiveness: (1) post-objective attainment action and (2) the teacher's making himself progressively less needed by the student.

An effective performance monitoring system involves the individual's participation through co-devleopment of criteria, of self-analysis, and through self- and cooperative-appraisal analysis. This is essential if humanizing and personalizing staff relationships and individualization of performance appraisal are to result. Another primary reason for individual participation in the monitoring process is the need for each staff member to recognize "where he is" in terms of the program demands of satisfaction performance levels and the consequent skill use levels needed.

Self-recognition of present level of performance, compared to program demand level, can be a better motivational factor than many incentive forces imposed on the individual, since imposition does not necessarily result in agreement or honest acceptance on the part of the teacher.

**DEVELOPING A PERFORMANCE
SELF-APPRAISAL FORM**

Before effective individualized appraisal criteria can be developed for a teaching staff, it is essential that each staff member be aware of his status quo position. Basic to the development of this awareness is each staff member's engaging in self-appraisal related to the total functioning demands of the program. Following is a basic self-appraisal guideline that a school staff can use in developing its own criteria.

GODDARD MIDDLE SCHOOL

ORGANIZATION AND MANAGEMENT

1. Teacher implements his plans for individualized instruction by:
    1. Outlining and implementing behavioral goals and objectives.
    2. Develops and administers, in conjunction with department chairman and other teachers, pre- and post-tests for evaluating individual progress.

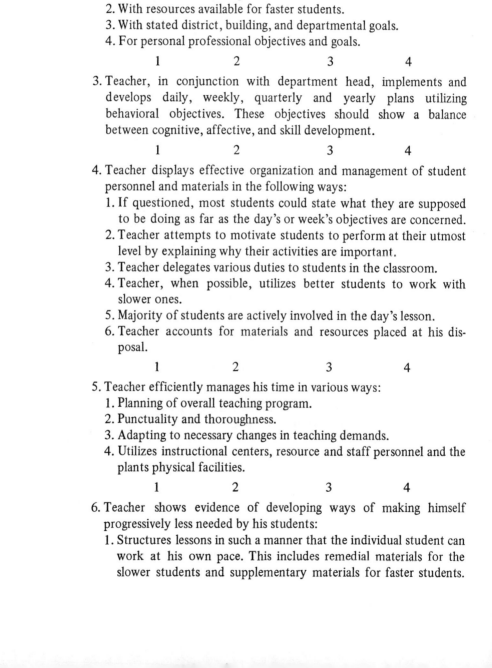

3. Constructing a program which will help students attain individualized goals. Uses and is familiar with special materials such as
program learning, multi-media, and individual progress sheets.

    1   2   3   4

2. Teacher develops and implements a learning program:
1. For minimum student goals.
2. With resources available for faster students.
3. With stated district, building, and departmental goals.
4. For personal professional objectives and goals.

    1   2   3   4

3. Teacher, in conjunction with department head, implements and
develops daily, weekly, quarterly and yearly plans utilizing
behavioral objectives. These objectives should show a balance
between cognitive, affective, and skill development.

    1   2   3   4

4. Teacher displays effective organization and management of student
personnel and materials in the following ways:
1. If questioned, most students could state what they are supposed
to be doing as far as the day's or week's objectives are concerned.
2. Teacher attempts to motivate students to perform at their utmost
level by explaining why their activities are important.
3. Teacher delegates various duties to students in the classroom.
4. Teacher, when possible, utilizes better students to work with
slower ones.
5. Majority of students are actively involved in the day's lesson.
6. Teacher accounts for materials and resources placed at his dis-
posal.

    1   2   3   4

5. Teacher efficiently manages his time in various ways:
1. Planning of overall teaching program.
2. Punctuality and thoroughness.
3. Adapting to necessary changes in teaching demands.
4. Utilizes instructional centers, resource and staff personnel and the
plants physical facilities.

    1   2   3   4

6. Teacher shows evidence of developing ways of making himself
progressively less needed by his students:
1. Structures lessons in such a manner that the individual student can
work at his own pace. This includes remedial materials for the
slower students and supplementary materials for faster students.

2. Structures lessons to provide a balance of individualized, small, and large-group activities.

3. Sets directions for class activities, utilizing individualized and student-led groupings—limiting his own presentation to the minimum amount of time.

    1   2   3   4

INSTRUCTIONAL EFFECTIVENESS PRACTICES

1. Accepts and assumes the multi-purpose role of motivator of students, and director and guide of learning activities.

    1   2   3   4

2. Maintains a positive classroom environment, encouraging dignity in relation to learning activities.

    1   2   3   4

3. Emphasizes experimentation, discovery, originality and creativity rather than conformity.

    1   2   3   4

4. Uses a flexible approach based on the immediate situation and needs of students.

    1   2   3   4

5. Uses a variety of teaching methods.

    1   2   3   4

6. Uses community and consultative resources when applicable.

    1   2   3   4

7. Develops clearly defined objectives which can be applied by the individual teacher in the classroom; and which can be clearly articulated to others.

    1   2   3   4

8. Sets realistic minimum class achievement levels as related to level of students.

    1   2   3   4

9. Develops, implements, and appraises innovation in their subject area(s).

    1   2   3   4

10. Develops activities in behavioral terms.

    1   2   3   4

11. Develops own teaching materials when applicable.

    1   2   3   4

12. Accepts responsibility for program development on a department, school, and district level.

    1   2   3   4

13. Has developed a system of identifying his personal and instructional areas needing improvement.

    1   2   3   4

14. Assists students in setting realistic learning objectives and has developed methods of performance appraisal for both students and educators.

    1   2   3   4

15. Makes teaching activities relevant and interesting in terms of learner levels.

    1   2   3   4

16. Shows evidence that he has helped students develop skills in accepting responsibility, in terms of their maturation, for their own education.

    1   2   3   4

PUBLIC RELATIONS

1. Establishes with student participation and understanding realistic standards of classroom and school behavior, student attitude and student-teacher relationship; and enforces these established standards in a consistent, fair manner that is understood by the students and parents.

    1   2   3   4

2. Enforces compliance with classroom and school policies in a consistent manner that is understood by students and parents.

    1   2   3   4

3. Maintains a consistent and impartial relationship with students which provides each child a feeling of security and personal worth.

    1   2   3   4

4. Strives to maintain exemplary conduct and appearance before the students, parents and public at all times so that he/she will be an asset to the teaching profession.

    1   2   3   4

5. Recognizes and accepts responsibilities to carry out assigned duties for the total school program efforts and effectiveness in duty assignments and committee work.

| 1 | 2 | 3 | 4 |

6. Is able to interpret from observation of student in classroom and other school areas, achievement in class work, student's work habits, peer relationships, teacher and/or adult relationships, the needs and interests of each student to parents.

| 1 | 2 | 3 | 4 |

7. Can clearly express and implement his philosophy of education.

| 1 | 2 | 3 | 4 |

8. Is able to interpret the minimal requirements established for each achievement level in his/her area of teaching, the activities used to meet these requirements, and the techniques used to evaluate the progress or achievement of each student related to his ability.

| 1 | 2 | 3 | 4 |

9. Maintain an open-minded approach when dealing with students and adults.

| 1 | 2 | 3 | 4 |

COMMENTS:

PROFESSIONAL GROWTH

1. The teacher should develop yearly objectives; continuously evaluate his progress toward accomplishing these.

| 1 | 2 | 3 | 4 |

2. The teacher strives to increase his individual potential by all methods available to him. (This might include travel, reading, taking courses both within his teaching and pride areas and in-service sessions.)

| 1 | 2 | 3 | 4 |

3. Maintaining good staff relationships, sharing materials and ideas and assisting others in increasing their effectiveness when requested.

| 1 | 2 | 3 | 4 |

4. The teacher will develop and use new techniques and then will evaluate their effectiveness.

| 1 | 2 | 3 | 4 |

5. The teacher will use all methods of in-service and out-service to achieve a learning environment which is student-oriented rather than teacher-oriented.

>   1   2   3   4

6. Supports positive growth of building, district, professional, educational organizations and committees.

>   1   2   3   4

COMMENTS:

INDIVIDUALIZING PERFORMANCE ASSESSMENT

Too often, educators overlook one of the most helpful bases of performance monitoring. That is the consequent action directions and change in performance levels which can, or should, occur as a result of an individual's participating in staff in-service programs. The assumption here is that these programs are developed with specific skills use and implementation techniques in mind and that in-service programs are developed on a progressive basis; that is, as individual's skills, techniques, and needs become more sophisticated, the in-service programming keeps pace in a sequential manner.

Monitoring bases should include, also, the needed changes in functioning patterns and modes of operational structuring coming about as a result of an individual's revealed effectiveness level on the job. New situations reveal differing needs and new demands. These can occur any place on an individual's continuum, from his philosophy and objectives, to the daily entries in his lesson plan book. Since change and effectiveness are closely related, diagnostic planning and performance monitoring should include specific criteria and procedures for identifying the extent of change brought about and/or needed by the individual.

Another functional basis for performance monitoring is a given individual's own instructional management system. The extents to which he does what he says he is going to do, to which he follows or varies his planning, to which he organizes integrates, and uses his own teaching-learning sub-systems, for example, have a direct effect not only on his own effectiveness, but on the effectiveness of the monitoring system itself. Like the "garbage in, garbage out" term used by computer technicians, poor teacher planning and implementation of the program and human aspects to be monitered can result in ineffective monitoring and ineffective performance. This ineffective performance rating is not automatically the result of poor monitoring.

Again, if performance monitoring is to have an individualized emphasis, more specific monitoring criteria need to be developed in terms of each indivual's own program emphases, instructional structure, and functioning patterns. Arbitrarily developed criteria and processes have limited value because they have not been developed with a specific person, specific operational procedures, specific talents and skills, and specific emphases in mind. The appraiser is a middle man attempting to implement an "absentee appraiser's" criteria and the individual being monitored is one who has no role other than being the object of the monitoring.

DEVELOPING A STAFF APPRAISAL SYSTEM

The author has talked with members of various local education associations about changes within the profession. Topics of conversation have run the gamut from the individual student level through federal legislation. Educators can bring about some of these changes at the local building and district level, and some, not. Unfortunately, some of the practices educators can change locally, they do not, in spite of the fact that logical bases for keeping them have changed, or no longer exist.

Teachers talk about the changing roles of schools, of staffs, and of students. They discuss various methods of improving academic instruction. In various ways and settings, they propose ways of identifying collective professional strengths and weaknesses. They are concerned about the demands on them for relevancy and accountability. Not always are these topics identified on a priority basis, however. Even though one of the important problems that concern educators now is that of finding ways and means of proving educational effectiveness to the public, they, by and large, attempt to maintain the traditional approaches and methods that really do not reveal their functioning effectiveness to themselves. Reference, more specifically, is made here to the methods commonly used to record individual educators' performance histories. When educators are having problems such as this, they can expect to have difficulty explaining satisfactorily how effective they are to the public. Consequently, it is essential that better ways of approaching teacher evaluation are used.

Most teachers, whether they are aware of it or not, desire to be "evaluated" according to their individual values, preferences, and styles of action. Differences of opinion arise when the values, areas of emphasis, and functioning demands of the program differ from either or both. The traditional "teacher evaluation" method is looked upon in a negative way because of such given reasons as (1) ineffective application, (2) non-personalized, and (3) isolated process. Perhaps the first step is to eliminate the teacher "evaluation" idea. It has a negative ring to it and besides it really is not accurate. The performance appraisal approach is more accurate because here the concern is more with action than with theory.

The purpose of performance appraisal is to help a person do his job, to emphasize his involvement on the basis of analysis and improvement; not only just a concern for what has happened. Performance appraisal can be effective when it is:

1. Used correctly and consistently.
2. Used positively—building on strengths.
3. Related to the overall program structure and demands.
4. A cooperative appraisee-appraiser process.
5. Individualized.

A student will learn according to the way he is treated. A staff member will teach as he is treated. These two statements refer specifically to human interaction—to personalization and to indivi-dualization. Performance appraisal should be an individualized function in terms of the specific program demands and structure within which a person is expected to function. As programs differ, so should appraisal expections, functioning demands, and appraisal forms. There are, however, some criteria common to various programs within the same district. These are determined by community values and district policy.

Basically, the primary determiners of appraisal criteria should be:

1. The program structure, demands, and forces.
2. The individual being appraised (be he teacher, principal, director, et al) in terms of what he says he is going to do.

Some preliminary actions that must be taken here are:

1. A description of the program—its demands, its forces.
2. An identification by the appraisee of:
   a. where he is in terms of the program demands and forces
   b. his own level of performance
   c. the extent he wants to improve his effectiveness.
3. Explanation of how the individual is expected to function in this type of program.
4. Definition of performance that is considered as "satisfactory."

The individual staff member, in effect, then, determines his own appraisal criteria by:

1. Determining where he is at present in comparison to where he says he wants to be in terms of job effectiveness.
2. Determining his own areas needing improvement through self-appraisal.
3. Determining what he is going to do about his present position on the effectiveness totem pole.
4. Developing his own personal in-service program.

A major concern here is to change from the traditional "staff evaluation" approach to an approach that involves performance appraisal through the self-setting of objectives and related criteria. This involves each staff member's setting instructional objectives and personal objectives. The consequent primary emphasis is on an individual's identifying what is expected of him within the program, his personal strengths and weaknesses, and what, (and how, and to what extent,) he is going to do about the existing situation and conditions pertaining directly to him as he functions within the program. The appraisal begins with the individual and ends with him in terms of WHERE HE SAYS HE IS, HOW HE WANTS TO IMPROVE, AND HIS PLANS FOR IMPROVING. He makes the commitment and then DOES SOMETHING ABOUT IT.

This does not rule out the role of the appraiser, but it certainly does change it. It changes from the traditional role of judgment making, of directives, and of isolated emphasis to that of counseling, of cooperation, and of teamwork through which the appraiser and the appraisee accept appraisal criteria—primarily identified by the person being appraised. The appraiser and the appraisee are working within the same program structure. A common objective is their working together to increase functioning effectiveness. The effectiveness of one affects the effectiveness of the other. Each helps the other attain his objectives.

The self-setting of performance results objectives with an individualized, personalized emphasis rules out many traditional, standardized procedures such as

1. Common standardized evaluation forms requiring that all staff members be judged against exactly the same list of items—varied only by interpretation.
2. Evaluation in terms that do not pre-identify what can be considered satisfactory performance.
3. Lack of provision for the appraisee being given opportunity for input and determining the output.
4. Lack of an allowance for the varying conditions and demands on the person as he functions within a given framework that will differ from those in which another person is assigned to function.
5. A form made up entirely by persons who are not involved in the performance review.
6. An approach which is not humanized.

This approach does not advocate chaos or a lack of a recognition that there are common aspects to different programs. It does emphasize, however, that in a case, for example, of a school with 50 teachers, there would be 50 appraisal structures developed— each one developed to fit the *individual* situation of *each individual teacher,* the PRIMARY RESPONSIBILITY FOR ACTIVE implementation lying with the teacher.

Times and conditions have changed. Procedures must change with them. Consequently, it is necessary that educators plan in terms of objectives and methods of attaining them. Appraisal of their own performance, collectively and individually, must be done in terms of pre-defined goals and standards of performance *if* educators are to become, and remain, RESULTS-ORIENTED. Obviously, this is related to public accountability.

The performance approach is as much a philosophy as it is a practice. From the philosophical standpoint, it is based on human interaction, on respect for each individual, and on the idea that most of the members of the education profession are capable and desirous of improving their effectiveness, of assuming responsibility for developing and achieving their effectiveness, of assuming responsibility for developing and achieving their own objectives by developing, in general, their school district, and their own building. This concept changes the role of the teacher in "evaluation." It places more responsibility on the individual staff member for analyzing his level of functioning and for developing ways for improving areas needing added attention.

Results appraisal places added change emphasis to the administrator's role in which he must

1. Arrange building organization and methods of operation that facilitate functioning in terms of self-set objectives.
2. Increase his own effectiveness in leadership.
3. Maintain satisfactory levels of functioning effectiveness within the program scope.

This approach changes general faculty-administration interaction because it places heavy emphasis on a cooperative approach which stresses self-control and self-direction and a confidence in human capacities. It also stresses the importance of communication without the obvious pre-judging tendency with which either, or both, appraisor and appraisee enter the traditional evaluation conference.

Performance appraisal cannot be done effectively unless:

1. The acceptance of common criteria based on both the appraisor and appraisee's understanding the responsibilities, expected results, and required functioning patterns demanded by the job situation of both individuals.
2. The elimination of arbitrarily developed lists of personal standards against which one intends to evaluate another and which may not be the same standards by which the person being appraised is using for his action guidelines.
3. Appraisal is closely related to performance levels and results.
4. The appraisal of performance in terms of the present, but with emphasis on consequent action. Appraisal must be a two-way street with emphasis on what is actually being done—on effectiveness and on results.

The performance appraisal approach also affects what is placed in an individual's professional file. Instead of the traditional information, what would be placed in the file would be such information as the person's objectives, self-set, how well, and to what extent he accomplishes these. This does not mean, however, that everything in past and present files should be discarded. It does mean, though, that if there is a need for a negative entry, there should also be a corresponding entry related to the individual's self-set criteria relative to the elimination of this need.

Performance monitoring, in reality, is not a process that is carried out as an endeavor separate and beyond the instructional and learning aspects of the school program. Instead, it is an integral part of the implementation of the program sub-systems through staff and student performance. As such, performance appraisal processes must be concerned with, and reflect, the characteristics, emphases, objectives, and performance demands of the program structure within which the personnel are expected to function successfully.

In order for performance appraisal to contribute to improvement of results attainment, it must be directly concerned with the action areas of the school program, the ways people function. Consequently, performance monitoring must focus primarily on the ways personnel function, why they function in singular ways, the results they are working to attain, the changes staff efforts are intended to bring about, and individual student and teacher growth. Only in this way, will the people concerned begin to see a valid reason for appraisal and be active initiators of performance appraisal rather than simply individuals who must be "evaluated."

Some Action Guidelines

Program:

1. Total program effectiveness is greatly determined by the various inter-relationships of the sub-systems. As a result, appraisal development for any given sub-system of the overall program should include criteria for determining its performance effect on other sub-systems.

2. The structure of each sub-unit of the program determines the operational patterns of the people functioning within the structure. If there are no similarities in these operational demands, limited personnel effectiveness will result because of the inabilities of the teachers and students to work equally well within the conflicting structures.

3. Though program characteristics may be identified, in effect, it is the teacher's functioning characteristics which dominate in the classroom if there is conflict between program and teacher operational

demands. Therefore, it is essential that teacher roles and responsibilities within the program structure are specifically spelled out so that there is no doubt about the individual's areas of accountability and functioning requirements.

4. Effective staff appraisal is based on an individualized, personalized approach. The program structure should reflect the same emphasis. Both program and appraisal emphases are related to the way people function in a given framework. The purpose of the program also gives purpose to appraisal.

Personnel:

1. The program structure can become static through unchanging personnel practices. As student needs and functioning patterns change, so must staff patterns and methods change. Otherwise, learner progress will be stifled.
2. Program planning is done on the basis of anticipated results. Effective planners must also identify alternative actions in terms of results variations. Sudden reactive actions result in a breakdown in continuity in learner progress and direction.
3. Given individuals function best in certain roles and responsibility levels. For them to attain satisfactory performance, their stated results objectives must be within the scope of their role and responsibility levels. Exceeded performance expectations indicate a need for re-assessment of assignment, of objectives, and/or of personal capabilities.
4. Whenever a singular appraisal process is developed and adopted for a given school, the staff should be permitted to work with it on a pilot basis for a time. This will help them become acquainted with the process, the priorities, and the method of implementation before they will officially be subject to it. No one should be appraised through a process with which he is unfamiliar.
5. Realistic self-appraisal is essential to the success of a performance results approach. A person who does not know his own strengths and weaknesses cannot be expected to perform well in a position necessitating his making decisions about the performance of others.

Performance:

1. Learner performance characteristics must be the bases for programming change. These must be delineated before there can be valid changes made in the program structure. Program characteristics need to parallel learner performance characteristics.

2. Performance appraisal must be just as concerned with why a specific objective was reached as with why it was not. The extent of gap between actual performance level attained and desired level indicates a need for additional sequential growth objectives at the problem level.

3. Staff performance appraisal must be developed in terms of learner performance because the teachers are vested with authority that can facilitate or hinder student progress. The ways in which this authority is exercised should be part of the staff's assessment criteria.

4. Performance appraisal actually begins with a person's selection for a specific role. The selection process is based on the assumption that he can perform satisfactorily in the given responsibility area. Once the person agrees to, and accepts, the responsibility, he has entered into a performance contract and is responsible for functioning according to the stated conditions outlined by the program demands.

5. Many times, performance appraisal is concerned with the way a person functions within his own area of responsibility only. The extent to which the individual is a force for total program improvement should also be considered important because of his revealed leadership influence beyond his own area of emphasis.

8

TEACHER FUNCTIONING IN
A PERFORMANCE RESULTS
PROGRAM

Learning behavior is determined by teaching behavior. Teacher functioning must be developed in terms of specific learning objectives. The teacher must focus on continuous learning and curriculum change through an emphasis on the design and management of flexible programming developed on the basis of learner results.

RESOLVING TEACHER-LEARNER CONFLICTS

All students possess a drive to learn. They possess inherent motivation and initiative in terms of their self-identified needs and interests and in terms of their projected desires—objectives. Conflicts between students and school programs materialize because of inconsistency between student emphases and program emphases and teachers as they attempt to implement instructional activities in terms of their own biases and teaching objectives. The obvious result is that students and teachers disagree in various ways as to the methods, procedures, and means used to reach learning objectives which often, both students and teachers agree are important.

The following case history, written and given to the author by the counselor handling the situation, illustrates the gapping between learning and teaching patterns.

Problem Definition:

Mike, an 8th-grade boy, had been causing his three afternoon teachers a lot of problems. During these three periods, Mike seemed to be really "wound up." He was very physical with other students and consistently behaved in a manner which solicited student laughter and teacher reprimands. The three teachers came to me, Mike's counselor, for some ideas on what to do. We aimed at a terminal behavior of no hitting, pushing, or scratching. Reinforcer sampling found fellow student attention to be the reinforcer.

Procedures:

First, a baseline was found of the number of times within a ten-minute period Mike hit, pushed, or scratched other students. All three teachers did the baseline.

Three procedures were used:

Extinguishment:

The teachers were to ignore inappropriate behavior. If necessary, fellow students and parents would be sought for support. (It was not necessary.)

Time out:

Mike was to be sent out of the room to the hall for five minutes each time he hit, pushed, or scratched someone.

Reinforcement of an incompatable behavior:

The teachers were given a list of social reinforcers to be given immediately after an appropriate behavior where he did not hit, push, or scratch. Also, Mike was to be given group leadership jobs within the classroom after he'd made no physical contact with other students. The teachers were also to compliment Mike in front of the whole class. They decided not to tell Mike they were going to try the above procedures.

Discussion:

The procedure was implemented in the middle of the marking period. I asked his other teachers to take a 10-minute pre- and post-baseline to see if Mike would generalize a changed behavior. He did generalize the behavior. He also received, that quarter, the best grades and the fewest poor behavior comments (one) on his report card that he had ever received.

I noted that the teachers doing the procedures were not committed to systemitized record keeping. Their verbal feedback to me that it was working was enough for them. They obviously were very pleased as their problem with Mike was gone. This had been their first concern. Mike's behavior did improve. Next time, I will emphasize more the incompatible behavior reinforcement and a record keeping commitment necessity.

Teachers often encourage students to compensate for their "failure to learn" rather than reinforcing students' innate motivation to learn. The learning is present, but students initiate their own learning to compensate for the roadblocks set up by the program structure and by the teachers' implementation methods. Students will grow, mature, and learn, regardless. To increase the effectiveness of their growing and learning, the school must provide staff-student structures within which the students can function comfortably, and objectives which both teachers and students feel are reasonable to attain.

Again, the desired results relate to human behavior in terms of individual values. Learning is greatly affected by the compatibility of the learning patterns used by the students and the instructional patterns used by the teachers. The student patterns are based, and the instructional patterns must be based, on what the learners are capable of assimilating and applying.

Teacher planning and student planning must be consistent in terms of values, areas of emphasis, and patterns of learning. If they are not, there is a gap between instruction and learning. In order to eliminate this, both teacher and pupil must modify their approaches. The primary responsibility, however, to initiate change for improved coordination between teaching and learning lies with the teacher. If he fails to make the necessary adjustments, his teaching is based only on assumptions.

Learning comes from individualized endeavors. The teacher, before he attempts to do any instructing, must take the necessary time to become familiar with individual student plans and learning patterns. He then must develop techniques, procedures, and activities for instruction which are in harmony with the student characteristics. A teacher cannot manage the unknown or develop instruction in a void. Consequently, the first several days a teacher meets his class should be devoted to activities that help the teacher and his students become acquainted with each other's operational skills, expectations, and objectives. Once these have been clarified, then the more specific academic teaching-learning activities can begin.

The author, having concern for performance results, has spent a considerable amount of time obtaining feedback from middle level students concerning curricular effectiveness since, at the middle level, students' attitudes toward schooling are generally crystallized with reference to learning effectiveness and consequent plans for staying in school. Typical and consistent feedback statements from these middle students from differing geographic sections indicate that:

1. The main problem is that schools are not teaching children to make their own decisions, plan their own time, and to have proportionate outlooks on life.
2. Teaching is not always an aid to learning in class. Learning is not just memorizing facts and figures or covering material. Learning is discovering, developing, and understanding.
3. Better communication is needed between students and teachers. Teachers may talk at students and students may talk at teachers. Nobody really listens to anybody else.
4. School, in general, seems a waste of time because material covered seems irrelevant to later life. Some material is used as filler in all of class time.
5. Too much importance is put on grades.
6. There is a need for students to set priorities—home, school, pressures, keeping conflicts in mind.

BEHAVIOR–A BASIS FOR INSTRUCTIONAL PLANNING

Effective instructional management, then, involves teachers' developing procedures, techniques, and activities that are consistent with such human characteristics as student motivation, patterns, individual student conflicts, motivation forces, and the physical chemistry of learning. This also involves the teachers' developing instructional patterns and styles that dovetail sequential curricular content with the non-sequential moods, attitudes, and other personal characteristics and attributes of each potential learner.

PROMOTING A POSITIVE BEHAVIOR OF LEARNING

Basic to this is the teacher's placing more instructional emphasis on the students' developing a positive behavior of learning as opposed to the development of student reacting behavior. Too often, the teacher is on the offense and the student is on the defense in the typical classroom structure. Consequently, a great deal of time is spent by both on the development of strategies designed to out-maneuver each other. This, in effect, becomes a power struggle of sorts, involving status quo performance patterns, values, and behavior expectancies. Typical, but not always identified by the teacher, are such teaching and learning conflicts as the following:

TEACHER	STUDENT
1. Acceptable teacher-identified behavior	1. Accepted peer-identified behavior
2. Teacher-set performance patterns	2. Extent to which student accepts them
3. Classroom structure based on content	3. Student's need for change and desire for individual recognition
4. Insistence on dominance by authority	4. Desire for interaction and involvement in rules development
5. Program based on learner conformity	5. Program adaptability to student traits and characteristics

To avoid such predicaments, the teacher needs to consider learning behavior as a result to be achieved. Educational skills, techniques, and even the course content itself should be considered as vehicles toward this end. If not, the skills and content, or rather knowledge of facts, become ends in themselves— memorized with little possibility, or thought, of useful application by the learner. Students' opposition to this indicate they are more perceptive than their teachers in various ways.

DEVELOPING POSITIVE MOTIVATING FORCES

In order for the curricular structure and the learning activities to have meaning and value to the students, school staffs must concentrate on the development of positive motivating forces within the students themselves. Teachers must endeavor to create a learning environment that stimulates a desire to grow within the learners; teachers, then, must provide the curricular tools the students can use to satisfy this desire. Basic requisites of effective education, then, are the skills of managing motivation forces and creation and maintenance of an educational micro-ecology within which each student can function in reference to his singular motivational forces.

As the teacher restructures his approaches to increasing learning effectiveness, he must identify the possible motivating forces within his specific course area. These motivating forces, of course, will change or vary in intensity as the student and teacher function within the course spectrum. With this in mind, the following are examples of possible types of motivating forces the teacher must identify within a given course area

1. Most effective learning techniques for each student
2. Relevant performance objectives
3. Teacher-learner interaction techniques
4. Extent to which functioning demands are within the student's functioning level capacity
5. Relationship of course and teacher expectancies to student interest, needs, and daily living activities

These forces must be coordinated with the singular motivational forces of both the teachers and the student. They must be managed by the instructor, but they cannot be set by the teacher. The teacher can manage these effectively only as he has mastered the skills related to his functioning in such terms as:

Human interaction
Self-ego building in teacher and student
Demonstrable application of learning satisfying to the learner
Inherent student competition factors
Student desire for acceptance

The learning program at Dodson Elementary School in Hermitage, Tennessee, provides an example of a school featuring strong motivational forces developed as integral parts of the overall program. Among these are

Individualized learning
Classes in typing, cooking, and sewing
Outdoor learning center with animals and a garden
Learning center laboratories
Weekly student-teacher conferences

In many cases, teachers do not need to instill motivation in students as much as they need to direct student motivation so that it dovetails with both pupil and teacher desires and with curricular operational demands. To accomplish this, staff members must learn to recognize specific, inherent student motivation forces. Teachers need to learn how to stimulate and to provide a motivational environment based on student learning behavior. As their environment becomes a reality, the students' academic learning effectiveness will increase.

Learning cannot be forced, imposed, or created; however it can be stimulated, guided, and reinforced by the teacher—if he knows how to manage the forces that affect or influence it. Since the teacher cannot manage the unknown, he must identify the results he wants to attain, select the knowledge and skills students will need to learn and to use in order to attain the demonstrable results, structure, and then manage the motivational factors. All of this must be done from the standpoint of the learner emphasis, not primarily in terms of subject matter content, curricular structure, or operational convenience.

CURRICULUM DEVELOPMENT AND STUDENT BEHAVIOR

The school staff must develop a productive educational ecology and then manage it. If a purpose of education is to affect or change behavior values and patterns of the learner, then the curricular structure, within which the student is expected or required to function, must provide opportunities and the flexibility for change in pupil behavior in terms of such variables as student maturation, social and human conflicts and value systems. It is obvious that a learning structure cannot be developed that will take into consideration all variables and all possible social and human changes. However, the structure can be designed with adequate flexibility so that a responsive teaching staff can react and adjust to the changes as they occur. There are predictable changes on which the staff can build. Also, through anticipatory planning, a school faculty can structure learning activities in terms of future student needs.

KEYING CHANGE TO OBSERVED BEHAVIOR

Conflicts influence change. Curricular structure and instructional procedures and emphases must change as conflict dominations change. Too often, conflicts are viewed in the negative sense, especially from the standpoint of behavior. Not all conflicting student behavior is negative reaction; it is observable conduct in terms of revealed needs and interests. Consequently, observed student behavior can be utilized as a basis for curriculum and teacher change. Initiative for change here lies with the instructional staff if positive individual and group learning environments are to be maintained. Lack of flexibility and assumption of initiative by the staff can result in the development and strengthening of teacher-student conflicts based on reflexive behavior.

Again, this involves the teacher's utilization of management skills, not only of conflict situations, but also of conflict development. Since learning motivation is directly related to the learner's recognizing a need to learn a given skill or fact, every faculty member should be able to create positive conflict situations to stimulate student initiated learning activities. As the teacher becomes more adept at utilizing such techniques, he becomes more concerned with, and involved in, learning planning—not just lesson planning.

The teacher's use of positive conflict creation techniques, to be effective, must be related to student interests and desires such as in the following cases.

Objective	Conflict
1. Student decision-making	1. Built-in conflict in choice of two desired courses
2. Improvement of reading	2. Assignment of student to his desired job in work-study program with a basic requirement of on-the-job reading responsibilities

| 3. Improvement of overall level of student performance | 3. Student options in selection of appraisal criteria and methods of reporting progress |

This leads to more consistency between the philosophical statements of the school and what actually takes place in the classroom. Emphasis on students as individuals and on planning in terms of learning comes to the fore. After all, this is the primary purpose of curriculum development.

Each individual staff member is continuously involved in his own area of curriculum development. Since learning is directly related to behavior, both teacher and student must build their educational endeavors on existing values and revealed needs, then provide directive outlets in terms of subject matter content that will facilitate progress toward the attainment of mutually desired student performance results. Subject matter then serves as a ways and means vehicle. The curricular aspects are developed and implemented in terms of individual learned behavior. Because present student behavior characteristics are revealed needs, they must serve as a basis for the teachers' and students' planning, if individualized, personalized, relevant teaching and learning are to result.

De Soto Middle School in Arcadia, Florida, utilizes an "employment service" for eighth-grade students which ties together academic courses and on-the-job student behavior.

This school, through its guidance program, places students in part-time jobs with cooperating employers. The students must receive satisfactory reports from their employers before they are assigned to other jobs. Based on these evaluations and the types of jobs available, additional enrichment short courses are incorporated in the curriculum.

CHANGING BEHAVIOR EXPECTATIONS

In order to bring about increased learning effectiveness through individual curriculum development based on student learning behavior, the teacher must, at the outset, change his own behavior-expectations to parallel more closely the present learning behavior levels of the learner. He must set specific anticipated results-oriented behavior objectives for both himself and the student. Once he begins to make progress toward these objectives, he can then look for consequent student progress toward subject matter objectives.

Learning behavior and learning subject content are dovetailing endeavors. Just as each faculty member should begin his instruction "where the child is," he should also recognize the singular behaviorial level of each child, "where he is behaviorally," and "take each child as far as he can go." In other words, the teacher must devote efforts to the development of a positive behavior environment as well as the development of a positive content learning climate. Otherwise, behavior conflicts will block content learning endeavors.

It is essential that all teachers of each student work together in a consistent manner in their efforts to build positive student behavior patterns. They must base their efforts on existing student strengths in the various levels of student interaction, adult-student level, student-peer level, and at each course level. Otherwise, different expectation levels of each teacher working with the individual student in differing situations can result in the development of value conflicts which are confusing to the student and which inhibit his progress toward the development of his own patterns of learning behavior.

SETTING SPECIFIC BEHAVIORAL OBJECTIVES

As the building faculty concentrate on developing a program of studies, they spend considerable attention to scope and sequence, articulation, and coordination of the subject matter at the different levels of study. Considerable attention should also be given to the identification of the learning behaviors expected at the different levels in each course area. These must be identified and developed in connection with the skills and content levels identified for each course level. This can be a relatively difficult task because teachers traditionally have tended to concentrate on content and because their own teaching behavior levels often are not consistent with the skill and content levels identified and listed in their course outlines and lesson plans. Unfortunately, students can more accurately recognize and anticipate teacher conduct patterns than teachers can describe their students' patterns.

Functional Learning Behavior Objectives in a Middle Level English Program

1. The student will participate in group discussions in terms of working to attain group-identified performance results.

2. The student will accept responsibility for appraising his own level of achievement in group activities.
3. The student will demonstrate that he can function with the teacher in developing a learning framework for improving reading skills that is best suited to his functioning patterns.
4. The student will be able to recognize personal conflict situations and identify several courses of action that will lead to a resolution of these conflicts.
5. The student will be able to set realistic performance objectives for improving his composition skills and will develop an estimated time schedule for attainment of these objectives.
6. The student will be able to select and use the methods and techniques which best facilitate his study of poetic forms.

Learning is determined by behavior. How, then, can a teacher really expect to be an effective learning motivator if he has not become proficient in the use of the necessary behavioral skills? How can he learn to identify, develop, and manage behavior patterns? He must start with himself, where he is. He must develop teaching-learning behavior plans for himself. This involves the use of anticipatory planning in terms of his own motivational behavior as he acts and reacts to the change situations presented by his students. This anticipatory planning helps the teacher maintain the necessary positive approach to learning; it helps to eliminate his being placed in a relatively defensive, and consequently authoritarian, position resulting from his having to react to, rather than manage, the teaching-learning situations and their individual demands.

MANAGING A FLEXIBLE LEARNING ENVIRONMENT

Knowing what to do, how to do it, and then doing it are three different things. In actual practice, there are big gaps in understanding, interpretation, and application when a staff member attempts to move from theory to experimentation to implementation, and when he attempts to change his emphasis from subject matter to learning patterns and behavior. If the teacher has problems, then he should not be surprised when the student fails to live up to the learning levels expected by his instructor.

THE TEACHER AS CATALYST

Consequent conflicts arise because the teacher and the student are in two different worlds—one in a teaching environment and the other in a learning environment. To reconcile these, the teacher must be a catalyst who molds these two different emphases into one effective educational structure from the raw materials provided by the student. In order to do this, the teacher must also learn to manage the learning environment, rather than impose it or simply let it evolve, if he is to develop and maintain a learning results-producing environment.

The Roosevelt Elementary School District in Phoenix, Arizona, through a planned program, has introduced career education in grades three through eight. Teachers develop and manage the program in terms of "an emphasis on society's values pertaining to the world of work."

Through this approach, students in grades three through five become aware of the importance of career choice by meeting and talking with workers from various job areas. In grades six through eight, students are encouraged to give consideration to types of jobs in which they may be interested. In this way, teachers are concerned with both present and future student needs.

Too often, the existing school setting is accepted by the teacher as being an adequate educational environment to which the teacher adjusts and within which the student must function. Neither is expected to control it. As a result, teaching-learning situations are the result of a process of evolution. Educational effectiveness, then, is limited because both student and teacher assume the primary role of reacter rather than that of initiator. Teacher and learner potentials are not realized because the learning structure is not planned, developed, and managed in terms of desired results based on teacher and student talents.

Examples of Managing Conditions

1. Initiating and maintaining positive change
2. Structuring for practical student performance
3. Design emphasis on learning
4. Maintenance of a flexible program structure
5. Programming functioning demands on both student and teacher
6. Course development according to need
7. Implementing instructional objectives

If schools are to increase learning effectiveness, the school staffs must devote added effort to the managing of conditions and emphasis and less attention to the almost exclusive efforts to manage the student. Special in-service activities must be utilized to bring about a change in faculty attitudes so that teachers place a primary emphasis on the development of the human aspects of education rather than on the academic aspects. Care must be taken, however, that the two must coincide if the observable results of "education" are to be attained.

BASING CURRICULUM ON BEHAVIOR PERFORMANCE

A primary result to be attained through the educational process is behavior performance. Subject matter, activities, and conditions, then, are selected to facilitate the achievement of this desired result. The extent to which the desired result of behavior performance is achieved relates directly to relevancy and accountability.

In the last analysis, it is the student who determines the value and relevancy of the learning program. He makes this decision on the basis of the success he feels he attains within, and relative to, the educational structure in which he is expected to function. His success affects progress and progress determines results. Through the student's desire for relevancy, he is actually asking for student-oriented accountability. Heretofore, teachers were the ones demanding learning accountability.

Since accountability is determined by the actual observable results coming as a result of learning endeavors, there must be developed within the school attitudes and teaching-learning structures based on mutual accountability of both student and teacher. Specifically identified aspects of relevancy, accountability, and applicable results make it much easier for teachers, students, and parents to recognize learning results, for there is common understanding of the objectives all are working to attain.

Some specific inter-related aspects of relevancy and accountability with which both the teacher and the learner must be concerned are

1. Utilization in everyday living of skills learned
2. Mastery of skills necessary for effective personal decision-making
3. Learning purposes and demands related to student-recognized needs and demands
4. Program performance demands developed in terms of what a student can successfully do now as well as in terms of what he is expected to learn

5. Paralleling sequential instructional demands with existing student learning patterns
6. Providing learner opportunities for input relative to instructional framework, teaching techniques, and learning needs in terms of how the student sees his functioning role and responsibilities
7. Relating learning demands to development of student self-satisfaction in accomplishment
8. Appraisal techniques and emphases paralleling the general program demands, yet individualized in terms of each student's singular learning program
9. Teacher recognition that proof of student learning should not be restricted to the formal school setting
10. Flexibility in standards of achievement according to individual student performance capabilities and characteristics

Often, such aspects as these are difficult for the teacher to identify because they are viewed as "intangibles." However, a primary source of difficulty is that the teacher attempts to limit, isolate, and categorize them instead of developing them in terms of their relationships to each other and to the skills and talents of both teacher and the learner.

It is the responsibility of the student-teacher team to develop learning activities in terms of these aspects as they relate to both the student's and teacher's present desire and achievement and to both of their present and desired improvement application levels. This is necessary if the teaching-learning motivation gap is to be bridged and motivation responsibility is placed where it belongs. Too often, educators complain that students are getting increasingly harder to motivate—placing the blame solely on the learners. Of course, this should not be because difficulty in motivation really occurs when there are conflicts between what and how the students want to learn and the conditions under which the teachers expect them to learn. In many cases, the teacher demands and the students resist, passively or overtly. Consequently, many instructional conditions, demands, and procedures must be changed first. This is logical, since teachers are more mature than students.

Staff members must always keep in mind that the basis of effective learning is a structure, and an approach, which are flexible and expanding in direct relation to the motivation of the learners. If educators continue arbitrarily to define, limit, categorize, and specialize their subject areas, their roles, and their efforts, then they can expect to create conflicts that impede student progress and decrease teacher effectiveness. Teachers must be able to manage their own classroom teaching environments if they honestly expect to help students develop the skills to manage learning environments.

INSTRUCTIONAL STRUCTURING FOR RESULTS

"Education" is personal. In the last analysis, the extent of, the various aspects of, and the results of, "education" are determined by the learner. They cannot be imposed with any lasting effect by another person without the learner losing something. The instructor must accept this limitation imposed on him by the learner. The way the instructor can be effective is to determine the starting role he must assume within the framework established by the student. The teacher then begins to function on the basis of common ground and level.

SETTING INDIVIDUAL PERFORMANCE GOALS

Methods and procedures pertaining to student learning will have to be selected in terms of the student-determined framework, including desired results or what the student hopes to get out of the activities. A follow-up step is to help the student set the level of results he should attain in order for him to be able to function at the desired self-satisfaction level. Planning and implementation here involve the interwoven aspects of goals, behavior, learning, and progressive results levels in terms of the existing learner value system.

The teaching-learning structure needs to be developed in terms of the demonstratable results to be attained. This involves a re-thinking of the teacher and student from the standpoints of priorities and the selection and organization of those priorities. A first step is the identification of the observable results to be attained. Following this, the teacher must work with the individual student in developing a reasonable time line, spelling out the sequential stepping stone performance levels necessary for the student to reach as he works toward the desired results. These intermediate performance levels are more sequential aspects of the end result rather than being part of the traditional emphases on just mastery of content; they do, however, involve content and skills but in a different manner and from a different approach.

The individual student end results and the progressive performance levels must be developed in such a manner that content and
skills are necessary tools that need to be learned in order for the
student to show he has attained the end result through his applied
performance beyond mere oral feedback to the teacher. This same
approach also applies to the testing aspects. The traditional
approach to formal testing at the end of a content unit, the end of
a quarter, or the end of a semester, for example, will have to be
changed. With an emphasis on performance and applicable results,
checking of progress along the time line can be done by the
teacher's observing how well the student performs at each of the
stepping-stone levels.

Following are examples of student-written performance goals
collected by the author.

1. To complete 90 percent of my class assignments to the extent that I
   will receive no grade lower than a "C" on 80 percent of them
2. To improve my research skills to the extent that I can move into an
   independent study group by the end of the first semester
3. To improve my playing skills through practice at home and participation in intramurals so that I can make the varsity basketball team this
   year
4. To learn to use the laboratory equipment well enough to become a
   laboratory assistant in my biology class next year
5. To expand my circle of friends by showing more interest in others
   and starting conversations rather than waiting for people to come to
   me

These goals represent personal desires of the students. They not
only give the teacher some insight about the character and purpose
of each individual writer's immediate educational focus; they also
reveal to the teacher important individual student motivational
factors. These are the bases from which the teacher can develop
relevant student learning experiences. Student performance desire
is established. A primary job of the teacher, now, is to provide the
structure that will facilitate this desire to perform.

Each student has identified specific motivational purposes and
the end result he wants to attain. These are two learning aspects
good teachers try to help students identify. However, too often,
they attempt to attain this result through arbitrary instructional

means rather than through personalized learning related to individual student-identified needs and desires.

Archbishop Ryan Memorial High School in Omaha, Nebraska, has implemented a progressive performance approach through its "self-paced learning" program. This program is operated on the basis that the school "is a large educational resource center" in which the staff's primary jobs are "to create a climate in which students can learn" and "to get the student to learn. All other things are secondary."

According to the latest information available to the author, the Ryan program features

1. The absence of class schedules for staff and students so that students can go to the area in which they need to learn and consult with staff members the learners feel can be of most help in assessing their progress
2. The involvement of students in the teaching procedure. Students are unscheduled so they can teach each other
3. The availability of student options in
   a. learning partners
   b. staff selection
   c. length of school week and year
   d. learning activities
   e. departmental course requirements
   f. study areas

Ryan emphasizes content and process competency rather than arbitrary time limits in determining issuance of student credit. As a result, each student determines when he graduates through his own rates of progress and levels of revealed competency. Though formal graduation exercises are held three times a year, a student can be issued a diploma any time he completes the departmental performance criteria.

PERSONALIZED MEASUREMENT AND SELF-EVALUATION

Since various skills and content aspects are built into each sequential phase, the student's mastery of the required content and skill will be readily apparent to the instructor as he observes the student's performance tasks. Not only does this lead to a more reliable, objective evaluation by the teacher, it also helps the student better understand his progress, his strengths, and his weaknesses. And, it helps eliminate one of the major complaints of teachers—"being snowed under with paperwork." The student must prove his learning through applied action rather than just writing about isolated phases.

Testing also becomes an integral aspect of this type of action curriculum structure rather than an evaluation exercise, which arouses in the student much the same feeling that administrative evaluation arouses in the teacher. This consequent result is the evolving of negative attitudes that can permeate the total spectrum of learning. Obviously, this is inconsistent with the philosophy that advocates the concern for the individual, the development of a functioning, expanding learning environment, and an emphasis on learning.

Through a de-emphasis of the content/testing approach, education becomes more of a student "in-service or on-the-job training" approach. The student can more readily ascertain his own progress through his own performance and develop his own singular patterns and procedures for improvement. What actually evolves, consequently, is that student takes the initiative for developing his own job descriptions in terms of the results to be attained, his progress toward those results, and his revealed performance effectiveness at each checkpoint along his individual time line.

These job descriptions, prepared by the student, should not relate only to the results pertaining to the practical application of the knowledge and skills he has learned. They should also involve his behavior objectives, not only as they relate to a particular area of emphasis, but also to the general student desires and program demands of the total educational environment. As the student progresses, he should be allowed to assume more and more of the responsibility here, not only from the standpoint of his developing self-discipline, but also from the standpoint of his learning how to manage his own time outside of the more formal educational structure. The obvious carryover here is related to his leisure time. Also, a key to motivation is giving the individual learner authority and responsibility in direct relation to his revealed and potential capabilities for handling these.

To develop the instructional structure described here requires that the teacher know each individual student well enough through personalized student-teacher interaction and other prognosis techniques so that he can predict fairly accurately what a given learner should, and could, be able to do at each stage of his time line. Emphasis here is on not only identifying where the student is, and taking him from there, but also helping him develop projected sequential stepping-stone objectives that help him readily identify his progressive end results and how they prepare him for his continued progress to future objectives.

OPPORTUNITIES, ALTERNATIVES, AND DECISION-MAKING

Educators have traditionally taken the negative approach to instruction. They have generally developed programs of study on the basis of what students did not know or were capable of doing rather than taking the opposite or positive approach. Because of this, there have been inconsistencies and gaps between the processes of learning used by students and the patterns and processes demanded by the educational structure within which the students are expected to function. The result is the creation of a negative attitude in the learner and a consequent lack of confidence in the instructional framework.

An Example

Grading is a typical example of the negative approach. Historically, a student begins study in a given course with no credit even though he brings certain skills, attitudes, and knowledge with him. He is not completely lacking in the necessary tools needed for study in the course, assuming his performance level placement was reasonably accurate. Teacher expectation of the student may be high, but there is no observable evidence of this as far as the student is concerned. If instruction is to be developed on a positive approach, the student should be given some type of credit for the learning tools he brings to the course. The extent, then, to which he shows additional progress would determine the amount of additional credit awarded to him. If grades must be given, then they will not be awarded in isolation, or at best, just in terms of how well the learner can express in words ideas and facts deemed important by the instructor. Competence here tends to build the ego of the learner but does not necessarily reveal the benefits he has gained from being with the teacher, except that he has learned how to function effectively in terms of that teacher's ego needs.

The student, in such cases, is developing reacting skills and patterns of learning in terms of an imposed teaching structure. This is not the basic purpose of education. It is the responsibility of the teacher to help the learner develop patterns of learning consistent with the potential, achievement level, present and sequential skills, maturation patterns, and other singular characteristics of the widening and open-ended development of the young individual. As the student develops these patterns, the teacher, and the educational structure, must provide adequate opportunities for the student to utilize them in practical application.

Self-initiated learning comes as a result of an individual's recognized need to know in order to facilitate his achieving a desired objective. The key here, of course, is that the individual is learning for an applicable purpose. This is the basic purpose of education, which has been misinterpreted and misapplied by too many numbers of the traditional educational establishment. The result is a dichotomy between instructor and learner. A consequent primary responsibility of the instructor, then, is to develop a teaching-learning framework which encourages the student to identify his own objectives and then engage in learning activities that will enable him to progress toward his desired results. The role of the teacher, in this respect, is to help the student to identify these objectives and to provide him with a learning framework that initiates positive forces to which the learner must reach in terms of his utilizing learning skills he has already mastered *and* in terms of additional learning skills he must master and apply, if he is to meet the challenge of these imposed forces satisfactorily.

DECISION-MAKING OPPORTUNITIES

Adequate mastery and application of specified learnings do not occur simply through student reactions and self-initiated actions to learning forces that require single-track approaches. If the learner is to develop self-discipline and self-direction, if he is to learn to function in terms of self-management, he must be given opportunities to make decisions. Therefore, the instructional activities in which he is asked to engage must be open-ended; that is, the student must be able to make decisions in terms of objectives and desired results priorities and in terms of changing objectives and alternate learning routes. This approach is essential if education is to increase an individual's level of responsibility for his own actions.

The student should be given opportunities for, and held responsible for, making such decisions related to

1. Identifying the major skills and content he needs to master
2. The extent and levels of progress he expects to achieve in an identified time period related to objective identification
3. Identifying areas of study in which he feels he will need teacher help and areas he feels he is capable of progressing on his own
4. Identifying methods of instruction that are most productive for him
5. Listing of the types of learning responsibilities he feels he is capable of assuming
6. Identifying what his teacher and parent can expect from him in terms of performance

When a learner accepts the opportunity to participate in making decisions directly affecting his individual learning endeavors, he also accepts some responsibility for the results of those decisions. This involves his continued participation as he progresses through the program stages. He cannot be expected to appreciate, and become proficient in, decision-making processes if he is permitted to participate in making decisions only in the initial planning stage of his program. Consistent instructor follow-through is essential here.

Student participation in decision-making processes must be a progressive activity. If it is to be an effective learning activity, the teacher must, as in other learning endeavors, start "where the student is"; that is, not expect the student to participate effectively in decision-making levels beyond his functioning level. These demands must be consistent with his other functioning levels.

To help bring about desired results in this area, the teacher needs to structure his instructional activities, including such specific endeavors as homework and class discussions, so that the learner not only has adequate direction and guidance for the study within the curricular structure, but he is also given opportunity to select options in terms of the specific activities. These activities must be selected and developed so that the learner can select and/or develop differing processes and procedures to reach the identified objectives.

For example, after the teacher and student decide on a particular area of learning such as a study of the use of the figures of speech in literary selections, the learner should be given opportunities to make decisions relative to learning methods, techniques, and experiences. Among the options the student should be afforded are those pertaining to

ACTIVITIES	METHODS	APPRAISAL
1. Study of selected poems	1. Group discussion	1. A-F grading
2. Writing of original poems	2. Independent study	2. Essay reporting
3. Changing poetry to prose form	3. Oral reports	3. Pass/Fail
4. Writing a one-act play	4. Student lesson presentation	4. Assessment of objectives attainment
	5. Student team study	
	6. Individual student conferences with a professional writer	

This approach is consistent with the nature of the learner. It is not consistent, however, with the traditional method of providing instructional activities in which the student follows a rigid prescribed procedure developed by the teacher or found in the basic text, so that the student can eventually come to a conclusion selected by the instructor. No provision is provided or considered for satellite learnings or interests the student may have brought with him to the activity or that he may have developed as he participated in the activity. Because the learner is growing and expanding his horizons, the general school program and specific classroom activities must be structured similarly.

Since it is the learner who ultimately determines the effectiveness of the educational structure and the teacher, it is essential that every faculty member recognize that he cannot determine fully the learning aspects because, basically, learning is a personal thing with the student. The teacher can facilitate or inhibit learning; he can manage learning, but in the last analysis, he cannot dictate learning.

By providing open-ended learning activities, by managing the learning processes, and by maintaining a flexible role as dictated by the needs of student, the teacher, then, can talk realistically about increasing learning effectiveness. By using learning skills and content as educational tools, through the use of which the learner can achieve his identified results, the teacher is serving as an educational facilitator in fact as well as in name.

DETERMINING INSTRUCTIONAL MANAGEMENT OBJECTIVES

Whether or not a teacher realizes it, his students look to him for guidance and direction because they see him as an authority figure. The extent to which he functions in terms of their expectation image determines the basic level of classroom management effectiveness. Because, traditionally, students react in a conditioned manner to, and in, a typical classroom setting, the teacher who expects to use an instructional management approach must help his students rid themselves of the conditioned limitations and replace them with desires to learn for specific reasons and a self-awareness of personal progress. The student's development of these is based on the learner's understanding of "where he is" at any given time on his personal time line.

PERSONALIZING EDUCATION

Effective instructional management is based on the belief that education is a personal force that can bring about change which is unique to each individual. This approach mandates a change not only in areas of emphasis by the teacher, but also by the learner. Both teacher and learner need to develop the attitude that learning is the primary responsibility of the student and that the teacher is his resource person. As both teacher and student become more adept at implementing this concept, the role of the teacher becomes more flexible. The teacher plays a more forceful direct role, from the instructional standpoint, when the student is in the early stages of a learning unit, for example. As he progresses through the unit, he becomes more aware of the specific results expected, of the options he has available to him, and of the skills and areas of knowledge needed to facilitate his progress. As he becomes more familiar with these, the active role of the teacher diminishes in proportion to the learner's familiarity and progress.

**Sample Chart of Progress Through a
Specific Unit of Work.**

Progressive Class Activities Toward Attainment of Specific Results	Increasing Options Available to Student
1. Reading a recipe. Understanding and computing fractions.	1. Decide what he wants to make.
2. Obtaining ingredients and materials from store.	2. Selection of ingredients.
3. Preparation of the product. Accurate measurement.	3. Actual buying.
4. Discussion of how recipe could be changed, decreased or increased.	4. Keep records of the project in order to advise others on their ideas.

Areas of Increasing Competence	Progressive Steps to Self Direction
1. Analyze the recipe.	1. Learned something of the responsibility of meal preparation, budgeting of money, and home management.
2. Becoming a wise buyer.	
3. Making a finished product.	
4. Analysis of cost factors of product in relation to budget.	

Students are creative and innovative. Otherwise, they could not be exposed daily to the pressures of conformity imposed on them by the traditional educational structure and still retain their individuality. Individual learning progress is inhibited when the students' creative and innovative drives come into conflict with the pressures of conformity peculiar to the curricular structure. Again, the effectiveness of the learning endeavor is directly related to both the student's and teacher's management of these opposing forces in terms of each individual. This emphasizes the personalization of education. The extent to which it is personalized for the individual can be directly related to the extent a given student improves his learning level and progress.

DEVELOPING A TEAM RELATIONSHIP

Increases in learning effectiveness come about as the learner and his instructor develop a working relationship that breaks down the traditional operational division between teacher and student. This is not to imply that teacher and student must function in an equal social and professional level so that there is a peer group relationship. It does mean, though, that there must be developed between the two a spirit, an understanding, and an approach to learning based on teamwork, with the student gradually assuming more and more initiative and responsibility for his own learning endeavors. It means that the teacher must be able to recognize how, and when, he must relinquish degrees of his traditional responsibility and authority to the student.

In taking this philosophical and practical approach to learning, the teacher is matching his judgment and competence against possibilities for student success just as he does in the traditional structure. Here, however, he has a greater opportunity for judgment justification and student responsiveness because he is assuming a more positive outlook toward the student and his potential. Because it is a natural tendency for human beings to react favorably to trust, the teacher should not look upon students as "good" or "poor" learning risks, but rather as the teacher's and student's being involved in a mutual investment program. In other words, they will be coordinating opportunities, not just matching wits.

This approach also offers greater educational and human potential for the reduction of discipline problems since it is based on commonality of teacher and student purposes and procedures, rather than structurally promoted differences. The traditional approach is based on the supposition that teachers must control students and that control is an entity apart from the learning process and must, of consequence, come before the student can be taught. This may be a teaching objective, but it is neither an instructional nor a learning objective.

The traditional methods of discipline treat the student as a subordinate in a structure that is by name, and by definition, designed specifically for the student. The "subordinate" cannot be continually controlled by forces outside of him. The determination and selection of instructional objectives, then, must also be made in teams of how progress toward desired results will help the learner develop and practice self-direction and self-discipline. It is true self-direction and self-discipline are goals greatly to be desired, but they cannot be achieved in isolation from the rest of the learning processes and instruction activities. When they are isolated as separate "skills," just as subject matter content is arbitrarily divided, the teacher cannot honestly expect to have much carryover effect. They need to be developed as learning tools just as are other skills the student must use in order to reach his identified results.

Teacher functioning patterns and emphases play an important role in learner objectives attainment. These teacher operational methods must be selected and implemented in a manner that brings about consistency and continuity in learner progress through the school program. This means the school staff must look at themselves as functioning primarily in an action-initiating, management role that stresses student behavioral, as well as academic, progress, continuous curriculum improvement based on learning objectives attainment, and continuous teacher change as learner, and consequent instructional, demands change.

Some Action Guidelines

Program:

1. Individualization is a key to learning performance. The same holds true for teaching performance; therefore, it is essential that the departmental structures, paralleling the overall structure, provide the flexibility, within the limits of departmental consistency, for teachers to function in terms of their own individual strengths. Departmental demands often are primarily content-oriented.

2. With emphasis on performance results, specific courses are skill and content learning stages, not ends in themselves. By and large, the major program emphases should deal with (1) how the student is expected to function after he has completed the program and (2) the development of a program structure that will best facilitate the attainment of this objective.

3. The classroom structure created by the teacher, and in which the student is expected to function, is *also* the structure in which the teacher must function. Conflicts can arise in the classroom as a result of the teacher's inability to function within his own creation. Here, often, pupil-teacher factors are blamed, when, in effect, the teacher-program factors are the primary causes of conflict.

4. In effect, the "program" is not an orderly sequence of courses, requirements, rules, and regulations. Instead, it is the extent of change, of progress, of skills and tools used and gained by both students and teachers, and the attainment of student-teacher results objectives.

Personnel:

1. Effective functioning within the performance results program demands that each staff member redefine his role and responsibilities within the total program and within the classroom, not only in terms of the continuously changing teacher-learner status quo situations, but also, in terms of various projection stages of continuous program development.
2. Generally speaking, staff members are unable to delineate their functioning patterns, consistency in objectives directions, and areas of learning emphasis. They have little, or no, trouble identifying areas of desired preferences. Until staff members can consistently identify all of these in terms of objective priorities and consistency in direction, reacting personality characteristics can continue, too often, to be major determinants of action.
3. In effect, in the performance results concept, the term "learning environment" includes staff as well as students because the teachers must continuously work to gain new information about the learners in new progressive situations. Emphasis on "teaching environment" must be controlled; otherwise, it can, through attrition, become the staff focal point.
4. Traditionally, teachers are concerned by students' possessing the necessary skill and content tools to do "satisfactory work." Within the performance-emphasis framework, they must be just as concerned about identifying, and possessing, the specific skills, design, and management needed for them to function effectively in terms of the program and the learners. This involves staff members continuously analyzing each learning situation in terms of what functioning patterns, skills, approaches, and talents are demanded from the teacher.

Performance:

1. After the teacher has developed learner-oriented objectives, he must be aware that his selection of teacher-oriented instructional activities can negate the desired objectives by creating situations that put a priority emphasis, again, on teaching objectives.
2. Performance effectiveness on the part of the teacher is influenced

more by his leadership than by his authority. Too often, staff members spend time looking for games and gimmicks to increase student interest. Again, they forget they are dealing with people and that positive human inter-action, through identified learner and teacher roles and responsibilities, is a major force for motivation.

3. Effective decision-making is a skill that must be mastered by each person working within a performance-oriented framework because change and progress dictate that teacher-learner direction and emphases be determined more in terms of existing needs and circumstances than in terms of arbitrary rules and regulations. Rules and regulations must serve as reference points, not as reasons for lack of positive action.

4. As a program is developed, at each stage or point of action demand, the staff involved should come to agreement on the primary type of staff-student functioning that is needed, staff skills needed, and general performance characteristics that should be expected of the students as they complete the stage.

9

PERFORMANCE CONTRACTING
AND PERFORMANCE RESULTS

Performance results emphasize the identification by the teacher of specific results objectives he expects to accomplish and the specific ways he expects to bring them about. He agrees to be accountable for certain results and, as a consequence, assumes singular identified roles and responsibilities. In effect, then, as a result of this identification, the teacher enters into a type of contractual agreement. He becomes a party to a teaching performance contract, functioning within a clearly delineated phase of the building instructional framework. This is one approach to performance contracting.

In order to bring about the attainment of specific instructional objectives and identified learner performance levels, the performance contracting approach is essential because it identifies the specific objectives to be attained and who is primarily responsible for their attainment. Also, the contractual approach helps to identify more clearly the need and role of support personnel.

The availability and use of support personnel continues to be a pressing need because the building faculty, alone, cannot be expected to possess all the skills and talents needed to meet all the educational demands directed at them by students, by parents, by legislators, and by their own desires for increased operational effectiveness. Though, in general, school faculties recognize the need and value of support personnel, they tend to limit their definition, and acceptance, of resource personnel only to persons holding teaching certificates. Of consequence, they are excluding others who can provide them with valuable assistance.

DEFINING THE ROLE OF COMMERICAL
SUPPORT FIRMS

Business concerns are recognized as valuable adjuncts to the school program in such areas as distributive education, vocational training, and standardized testing. Commercial firms can be utilized effectively by schools in other areas, also, if they are carefully selected and used in clearly-defined support roles. Just as the support personnel employed by the local school district are used in terms of particular needs, commercial organizations can also be used in specialized supportive roles.

In a supportive role, contracting business firms can be used by a building staff in various ways. Based on the identified role of the contracting unit and the resultant anticipated extent of use of the support unit by the staff, the contractual arrangement can be developed, for example, on a retainer basis, on a continuing support partnership basis, or on a specifically pre-determined function basis such as

1. Providing standardized testing services
2. Providing specialized personnel services related to singular learner problems
3. Providing extended time support instruction as outlined by individual staff members

The contracting agency would of necessity have to function within the framework established by the school staff. This framework should include the agency's specified role, responsibilities, areas of functioning, and expected performance results levels. It should also include an organizational flow chart identifying specific staff members given the authority and responsibility for scheduling, coordinating, and supervising the work of the agency personnel.

With this approach, the individual teacher is still the person primarily responsible for the learner, but he has available to him additional specialized resources to use as he sees the need. As a consequence, he is able to devote more time to direct student-teacher relationships. He is also able to concentrate more on student learning performance when he is required to spend less time personally providing specialized support services.

IDENTIFYING THE CONTRACTUAL PERFORMANCE LEVEL

Perhaps, the departmental level would be a most appropriate level at which to utilize the performance contracting approach. At this level, specific functioning needs are more readily identified by staff members. Consequently, performance contract utilization can be more easily applied to specific support areas and staff members can more readily provide the necessary direction, supervision, and coordination deemed basic to the effective use of the commercial support personnel.

This provides for maintenance of staff regulation of the support unit's activities. It also helps to insure that the contracting agency remains in a support role subordinate to the primary staff role and responsibility, rather than evolving as a separate programming system and force functioning in isolation from the school staff. This has been one of the major reasons expressed by teachers for their being opposed to commercial firms contracting to provide instructional services. Their concern about this evolving dichotomy is a legitimate concern, if they have little to say about the identification of the functioning areas of the contracting firm. The school staff, in the last analysis, is still held responsible for the learning performance of the students and the overall effectiveness of the school's program. Accountability, in the eyes of the school patrons, cannot be delegated.

STAFF RESPONSIBILITIES IN PERFORMANCE CONTRACTING

Effective use of support personnel through performance contracting involves careful planning and structuring on the part of the school staff members. The extent to which the support people can attain desired results will be determined by the capability of the school staff to provide a clearly defined functioning framework, consistent operational demands, and coordination that dovetails the staff and support personnel functioning areas. This, to many teachers, is a new functioning area because they have never worked with outside support personnel on a cooperative performance results basis.

As the staff members, especially at the departmental level, work to design the operational framework within which the contracting personnel will function, they need to give primary emphasis to support performance factors that will contribute to the attainment of the staff-identified objectives. Otherwise, a resulting effect will be the support people's working in isolation from the teaching staff with a consequent loss of performance effectiveness.

Some of the major performance factors that must be considered are

1. Specific results to be attained
2. Methods and means of dovetailing support and staff functions
3. Operational assessment
4. Attainment of needed functioning skills by both staff and support personnel

DEVELOPING CONTRACTUAL OBJECTIVES

The participating staff members must develop specific performance demands and identify satisfactory performance levels for the contracting personnel. These must be in accord with the departmental and individual staff member objectives and expected performance levels. The support objectives, however, should be more limited in scope because they pertain only to a phase of the departmental program. Because of this limitation, most likely, the support objectives would deal primarily with the more mechanical operational functions related to instructional-learning endeavors. They could fall into such areas as

1. Improving remedial reading levels
2. Standardized test administration and scoring
3. Development of programmed materials
4. Development of program structures for learners with special needs—
   learning disabilities
   homebound
   hospitalized
   adjudicated

These performance objectives would be sequential to the broader teaching results objectives but should be directly aimed at the sub-system functioning level. This provides concern for process and output. Also, it helps insure that the staff maintains control of the program and primary responsibility for instructional-learning endeavors.

DOVETAILING STAFF AND SUPPORT AGENCY FUNCTIONS

The functioning of the contracting support agency cannot be allowed to become a functioning force separate from the faculty, as a whole, and the involved departmental staff, in particular. The secondary functioning of the support personnel must be a direct outgrowth of the primary functioning of the teaching staff. In effect, the support agency functions are extensions of the staff functions. Singular methods used, support staff operational patterns, and emphasis priorities will vary somewhat, however, because the programmatic spectrum of functioning concentration will be narrower. The support staff will be operating more in terms of specific performance tasks identified and delegated to them by various cooperating members of the departmental staff.

It is the departmental staff's responsibility to identify and to delineate these tasks. It is the contracting staff's responsibility to produce the specified results in terms of task definitions. Coordination of support and teaching staff functions at this stage is facilitated, then, through the articulated development of performance objectives and the integrated functioning frameworks. In addition, dovetailing of the two functioning areas will be facilitated by the consequent team approach that results from this structural emphasis.

Examples of Functioning Area Coordination

1. Individualized instruction

2. Special learner needs scheduling

1. Development of staff prescribed programmed materials

2. Special instruction for students below designed program continuum

3. Use of multi-media approach

3. Manufacture of films, slides, and tapes according to staff criteria

4. Use of community business technology

4. Business supplied specialized resource personnel, equipment

5. Implementation of new program aspects

5. Provision for on site staff familiarization and use of company equipment

DETERMINING OPERATIONAL EFFECTIVENESS

Assessment of operational effectiveness here involves the school staff's determining the attained results levels of the contracting unit, of the participating staff unit, of the affected learners, and of the individual faculty members functioning within the contractual framework. Though these need to be appraised separately to ascertain individual component functioning effectiveness, it is the composite operational analysis related to learner performance in the overall program that is most important.

The participating staff members are primarily responsible for the development of the assessment criteria and for the carrying out of the appraisal activity, since they carry the responsibility of integrating the specific functions and attained results of the contracting unit into the students' total program of learning. They must also assume the responsibility for bringing about in the broader program structure any change that is deemed desirable as a result of the contractual approach.

The type of appraisal criteria developed will depend upon the stated objectives, the type of operational framework, the consequent functioning demands, and the expected performance levels to be attained by the individuals involved. Though there will be differing criteria developed for each unit, there will be basic criteria common to all units because they are all functioning in terms of the same overall performance objectives.

Common Contractual Unit Assessment Criteria Areas

1. Extent of performance effectiveness within the same specific results area
2. Contribution of each sub-unit to the revealed performance of a common group of students

3. Contribution of sub-unit organization to the attainment of overall program objectives
4. Contribution of endeavors of each sub-unit to reinforcement of effectiveness of other sub-units
5. Consistency in concern for functioning demands of existing program structure
6. Dovetailing of results priorities
7. Related results emphases in individual unit feedback methods
8. Development of a contractual structure that facilitates student functioning and progress
9. Concern for process as well as with results
10. Extent of functioning effectiveness within the same management structure
11. Integrated unit planning and design
12. Emphasis on learner performance results application

DEVELOPING NEW TEACHER OPERATIONAL SKILLS

Implementing a performance contracting approach demands that the involved faculty members develop a variation in their operational patterns. This change necessitates their identifying and using differing functioning skills because they are working within an expanded instructional framework that includes non-district personnel, that demands increased inter-unit planning, and that requires staff coordination and articulation beyond the traditional departmental limitations.

These skill needs are by no means imposed on the staff by the performance contracting approach. Rather, they are selected by the staff as the teachers develop the contractual framework and as they plan and design the working details and operational patterns within which the participating teachers will function. Because of this, teachers selected to work within the contractual structure must be carefully screened for performance capabilities. Above average staff members must be chosen because the efficiency of program design and operation and the consequent level of unit performance effectiveness depend on their proven abilities. Mediocre teachers develop mediocre programs within which they do not have to master new methods and techniques.

In addition to the new skills identified as being essential to the program, the participating staff members must possess the capability of developing still more techniques and approaches which will facilitate operational effectiveness as new situations, un-expected or deliberately created, arise. Surely, this does not imply that the performance contracting approach demands a radically different mode of teacher functioning. It does mean, however, that the teacher must be able to alter his performance patterns in terms of learner change and in terms of the revealed results of other sub-unit personnel.

Staff members participating in performance contracting will need to master functioning skills related to

1. Working in a multi-unit team structure
2. Correlating commerical-educational personnel activities
3. Developing and using performance appraisal criteria for program and personnel
4. Developing program justifications related to accountability
5. Working within specialized sub-contract requirements
6. Functioning in a team management position
7. Participating in the development of performance contract specifications
8. Developing sub-program guidelines for use by other sub-unit team members

Performance contracting can serve as an effective in-service vehicle because of its singular overall functioning demands. A teacher must work in terms of specific results, his and others, in terms of program and personnel development and assessment, and in terms of responsibility for another person's performance effectiveness. Learning to perform effectively in these areas can help him to improve his overall professional competence.

EXAMPLES OF DEPARTMENTAL PERFORMANCE CONTRACTING

The performance contracting approach can be used in any area of the school program where singular student needs demand particular instructional programming, skills, and time allotments beyond those the school staff can provide, either because of capability limitations or because of lack of available teacher time. The particular contractual structure, areas of emphasis, and operational procedures developed will depend upon the unique situation of each school. Consequently, no attempt will be made to describe ready-made programming approaches. Instead, only examples of ways the performance contracting approach can be utilized at the departmental level will be included here. Though these examples are identified by specific subject area, the approaches can be utilized in the other areas of a school's program.

Language Arts

OBJECTIVE:

To expand the individualized program structure by contracting for additional support staff to work with students requiring a specialized reading program

FUNCTIONS:

Staff Unit	Contracting Unit
1. Identify potential students and provide performance history	1. Administer diagnostic tests
2. Identify diagnostic approaches to be used	2. Meet with staff to discuss results a. specific student needs b. student grouping according t skills and weaknesses c. student functioning levels
3. Develop contracting unit functioning guidelines, objectives and performance expectations	3. Work with students in terms of guidelines, providing needed materials and equipment a. programmed material b. tachistiscope c. interdisciplinary study exercises
4. Analyze progress reports and gear demands of students' other classes to the reported progress	4. Provide progress reports to staff team members a. skill development b. change in learning patterns and levels c. recommendations to other teachers
5. Analyze final progress report and develop new student learning schedules	5. Provide final progress report with followup recommendations
6. Staff unit self-evaluation	6. Unit self-evaluation
7. Contracting unit evaluation and consequent recommendation for continued use	7. Recommendations for continued use of contracting unit

APPRAISAL:

Staff Unit	Contracting Unit
1. Increased level of learner reading skill application	1. Reading level attainment
2. Extent of improved learner performance in other subjects	2. Program design and implementation in terms of individual learner needs and functioning patterns
3. Satellite effects of contracting unit	3. Student-staff relationships
4. Cost-results correlation	4. Possible subsequent value of sub-unit functioning

Social Studies

OBJECTIVE:

To provide a continuous progress structure by developing programmed learning materials related to selected module courses offered by the Social Studies Department

FUNCTIONS:

Staff Unit	Contracting Unit
1. Develop module course outlines and leveling sequences for ninth grade Social Studies a. conservation b. ecology c. communication	1. Meet with staff unit to discuss job description, demands, and expectations
2. Develop procedures for student functioning in the continuous progress structure	2. Develop material development guidelines, cost factors, target completion dates, and feedback procedures for staff
3. Develop programmed material objectives, specifications, and application procedures a. problem identification b. knowledge value relationship	3. Meet with staff unit on a regular basis to review and appraise development of programmed material

c. determine course of personal action

4. Identify primary staff-student functioning skills and patterns for which the material is to be developed
   a. problem solving
   b. value judgment
   c. self-evaluation
   d. option approach

5. Identify equipment with which the material is to be used and related support material

6. Outline contracting unit functioning guidelines, objectives, and performance expectations

7. Develop and use quality control measures for material development and use

8. Staff use evaluation

9. Contracting unit appraisal for possible continued use

4. Work with teachers in using and appraising developed material

5. Implement necessary developmental processes identified by review and assessment procedure

6. Unit self-evaluation

7. Recommendations for possible continued staff use of contraction unit

APPRAISAL:

Staff Unit

1. Improvement of student performance as a result of using programmed material

2. Satellite effectiveness in other subject areas

3. Cost-results correlation

4. Contributing effect to continued development of module courses

Contracting Unit

1. Extent of objectives attainment

2. Applicability of material design to other program areas

3. Learner performance assessment

4. Possible subsequent value contracting unit utilization

Mathematics

OBJECTIVE:

To implement a pilot program in basic mathematics that will involve a teacher team working with a selected number of 12-15 year-old students in an ungraded, continuous progress structure

FUNCTIONS:

Staff Unit	Contracting Unit
1. Develop an individualized structure using a teacher-student-developed math skills continuum, continuous performance appraisal, and student regrouping	1. Correlation of contracting university personnel skills, functioning patterns and philosophy with those of staff unit
2. Develop performance objectives, operational framework, and functioning demands for staff and students	2. Serve as pilot team members a. development of pilot mathematics structure b. development of goals and objectives c. working with students in team structure
3. Identify sequential programming needs for students as they move beyond pilot continuum stage	3. Serve as observers a. relationship of instructional application to program design b. progressive design needs
4. Define roles, responsibilities, and involvement stages of contracting unit	4. Serve in research function pertaining to developing change, needs, and team functioning patterns and emphases
5. Identify contracting personnel qualifications and desired resource institutions	5. Work with staff in progress and effectiveness analysis
6. Continuous self-appraisal student appraisal and contracting personnel appraisal	6. Unit self-evaluation

7. Assess pilot program effectiveness and identify ways of integrating pilot program in overall program
8. Contracting unit recommendation for subsequent use

7. Recommendation for continued functioning of contracting unit

APPRAISAL:

Staff Unit	**Contracting Unit**
1. Increased student performance levels	1. Contribution of unit to team efforts
2. Extent of student application in other functioning demand areas	2. Contribution of pilot program to teacher preparation programs
3. Adaptability of pilot program to other program areas	3. Assessment of pilot program effectiveness
4. Cost-results correlation	4. Unit self-evaluation
5. Effectiveness of contracting unit	

Science

OBJECTIVE:

To improve science departmental staff organizational and functioning effectiveness in new program design and development

FUNCTIONS:

Staff Unit	**Contracting Unit**
1. Identify need for new program and anticipated staff skill demands	1. Identify role and responsibilities of consultants
2. Identify learning results to be attained through implementation of the new program concepts a. laboratory skills b. cover education in science	2. Work with staff unit in the development of each stage f the program

c. application to ecology and conservation

3. Develop new program structure in terms of its placement in the science curriculum

4. Identify expected levels of teacher and student performance in terms of that expected of the career scientist in the same area of emphasis

5. Identify areas of consultant need

6. Develop appraisal procedures

7. Schedule appropriate staff in-service activities

8. Implement new program

9. Determine effectiveness of contracting unit

3. Serve as resource persons and appraisers in terms of program design and management

4. Serve as quality control persons in terms of staff's program development

5. Serve as science specialists related to the singular components of the program

6. Help staff unit use effective design and management techniques

7. Serve as in-service training leaders in the development of the program

8. Appraise contracting unit effectiveness in contributing to staff

APPRAISAL:

Staff Unit

1. Contribution of new program approach to increasing learner performance

2. Improvement of staff skill levels as a result of developing the new program

3. Extent of science curriculum improvement as a result of implementing the new program structure

Contracting Unit

1. Work with staff unit in appraising the results attained as a consequence of the implementation of the new program

2. Work with teachers in identifying improvement of functioning levels of staff unit members

3. Recommendations for subsequent staff unit work in terms of the new program management

4. Assessment of contracting unit contributions	4. Assess contracting unit effectiveness

PERFORMANCE CONTRACTING
AND CURRICULUM IMPROVEMENT

The school staff is responsible for curriculum development and consequent learner performance. Performance contracting, as discussed in this chapter, can be an effective method the staff can use to increase student, teacher, and program effectiveness. To be effective, however, contracting personnel must be used by the staff; they must not be used in place of individual staff members.

Effective use of performance contracting units not only provides the school staff with resource personnel who are specialists in their fields; it also provides opportunities for staff members to improve their own levels of performance because of their working closely with selected experts in areas of mutual professional interest, with the staff members serving as team leaders. In effect, performance contracting can result in improvement of both teacher and learner performance. Improved performance means more effective education. This is accountability, keyed to specific needs, objectives, and results.

Some Action Guidelines

Program:

1. A flexible program structure makes provision for the inclusion of lay persons. Care must be taken by the appropriate staff members to define the roles and responsibilities of the lay people so that their functioning has a direct relationship to specific building objectives.
2. Selection of a commercial contracting firm should be done on the bases of the company personnel's capability to function in terms of the school objectives and the extent of harmony existing between firm and school staffs' operational methods and philosophies within the proposed contractual purposes.
3. Performance contracts should not be developed in isolation from the overall school program. Correlation should be such that positive aspects resulting from the contracting structure can be readily used in other areas of the program by other staff members.
4. Staff members cannot expect to develop an effective contractual structure at any level unless overall school program objectives and

performance demands are identified to serve as contracting reference guides.

Personnel:

1. The utilization of a form of performance contracting with district support personnel often can be an informal arrangement whereby the in-building staff members and the support people agree on a specific objective and the cooperative means of attaining it. Within this informal structure, individual participant accountability must continue to receive priority emphasis or the informal structure can contribute to inconsistency in individual functioning.
2. Staff members responsible for working closely with representatives of a commercial firm need to keep in mind that it is the school personnel's responsibility to recognize and reconcile any evolving operational differences between the two groups. Otherwise, personal and operational conflict can destroy the team concept.
3. Within a given departmental contractual structure, it is often advantageous to include a member of another department. In this way, the contracting structure provides an in-service vehicle for preparing other department members for functioning within this type of framework.
4. Personnel anticipating working within a contracting structure at the building level should gain experience at the student-teacher and departmental contracting levels first. In this way, they can become progressively more capable at functioning within the contractual framework at a graduated pace.

Performance:

1. Performance results will be determined by the effectiveness of the contractual team cooperation. Participants, staff-support personnel, student-teacher, school-company, cannot work in isolation from one another.
2. Selection of contracting personnel must be done in terms of their capabilities for working at the performance levels specified by the identified objectives. Objectives and performance level demands are basic personnel selection criteria.
3. In effect, the performance results curriculum is a performance contracting structure because staff members are agreeing to attain certain objectives. Any more formalized contractual structure is a sub-stage of this overall program.
4. In general, most teachers are experienced only in assessing student work. Special in-service activities must be provided for them to gain skills in appraising other adults' performance when a school enters into a contracting framework.

APPENDIX I

Following are detailed steps a departmental staff can follow to develop the basic structure and procedures for implementing the performance results curriculum within the classroom. As they work through these basic illustrated steps, the staff members, within their own singular situational demands, will be developing skills, methods, and materials necessary for converting the entire departmental, and overall school, program to the performance results structure.

Though this example is related to Social Studies, the steps are applicable to all areas of the school program.

PHILOSOPHY OF SOCIAL STUDIES

1. That man possesses an awareness of the universal through his very nature.
2. That students have the inherent ability and responsibility to be useful citizens in a democratic society; and that they must be schooled to their commitment in the ever-developing processes of preserving and promoting a democratic way of life.
3. That in the inevitable process of change, it is necessary for the student to understand and cope with the complexities which involve man's behavior as a social entity.
4. That the search for truth necessitates the scientific scrutiny of an unlimited diversity of knowledge.
5. That the Social Studies have as their underlying principles—the development of conceptual understandings, the development of attitudes and appreciation, and the development of skills and competencies in the various disciplines.

247

6. That it is the teacher who holds the strategic position in guiding the learning experiences of the student.

OBJECTIVES

It is our purpose to develop within the student through the acquisition of knowledge in the social studies the following attributes:

1. A respect for the rights and opinions of others.
2. The ability to work in group situations as well as working individually.
3. Capacities for effective participation in the social groups of which the student is a member—home, school, and community.
4. A commitment to well-informed, alert, and responsible citizenship.
5. A realization of the value of the quest for excellence both for self-realization and social usefulness.
6. The ability to think critically and creatively and use problem solving skills in situations involving human relationships; to locate, evaluate, select, organize, and present information effectively; and to base action on sound conclusions.
7. An understanding of the major concepts present within the Social Studies.

STUDENT/TEACHER FUNCTIONS PLANNING

As the class is organized, the teacher and students should work together in selecting operational procedures related to such areas as the following:

1. Areas of Functioning Emphases
   a. Individual and group needs
   b. Student and teacher roles
   c. Development of a specific action plan

2. Instructional/Learning Techniques
   a. Method Options

Lecture	Out-of-class activities
Small group work	Student and Teacher teams
Independent study	Resource person roles

   b. Skill and Content Emphases
   Identification of skills and knowledge to be used for satisfactory class functioning
   Present student functioning levels
      Skill   Content
   Needed skill and content competency levels

3. Performance Appraisal
   a. Appraisal Procedures and Options
      Attainment of performance objectives
      Anecdotal reports
      Descriptive analysis
      Letter grades
   b. Feedback to Students
      Student-teacher conference schedules
      Student-teacher-parent conference schedules
      Student record keeping
         Objectives attained
         Need met—skills, content, personal
      Performance graphing
      Individual progress charts
4. Organizational Effectiveness Assessment

This form can also be used effectively on a weekly and/or a module course basis.

FUNCTIONS AND MODULE COURSES

STAGES	I	II	III	IV
FUNCTION LEVEL DEMANDS	1. Participation in Group Discussing 2. Use of Inquiry Method 3. Identification of own function- ing levels 4. Use of maps and globes	1. Use of options in decision- making 2. Applying learning to own living 3. Recognizing social change	1. Problem solving 2. Value judgements 3. Recognizing cultural differences	1. Research skills 2. Independent study 3. Verbalize thinking with supportive evidence
MODULE COURSES AND LEVELS	I	1. Social Studies study skills 2. Map skills 3. History through music 4. History through short stories	1. You and your environment 2. Great men in U.S. History 3. Life styles – Today and Yesterday	1. American Indian in U.S. History 2. Major battles of World War II 3. Geographic Influences	
	II	1. Current topics 2. American Customs 3. Decision- making and you	1. Dissent and Revolution 2. The Common Market 3. Major Military Dicussion in World War I 4. Local Community Changes	1. U.S. Constitution 2. Values and Value conflicts 3. State Government 4. U.S. Political System 5. Immigration and Minority Influences	1. Contemporary Issues 2. Problems of Urban Geography 3. International Relations 4. Independent Study 5. Nationalism and World Power 6. Technology and Economic Trends 7. Civil Rights Movement

LEVEL I - Emphasis on learning identified functioning skills of each stage.

LEVEL II - Emphasis on using identified functioning skills of each stage.

STAFF/STUDENT SCHEDULE SELECTION

Student Needs/Strengths   Learning Objectives

1. Does not like to express   1. To gain confidence in
   himself as a group member   expressing own opinions
2. Likes to read   2. To expand needing into
3. Feels history "is a bore"   non-fiction areas
                                                 3. To relate past happenings
                                                    to own present living

FIRST SESSION COURSE SELECTION OPTIONS

Course Title   Stage   Level

1. History through
   short Stories   1   1
2. American Customs   1   2

COURSE OPERATIONAL STRUCTURE NEEDS

1. Small group discussions
2. Writing stories based on selected past or current events
3. Student/teacher performance contracting
4. Study focus; factors enfluencing man's behavior

TEACHER SELECTION BASES

1. Can identify student needs and objectives
2. Can develop and implement student self-directed activities
3. Can foster human interaction between students and
   between students and teacher
4. Can develop activities based on individual student
5. Knowledgeable inselected course content

Each individual teacher's and student's, full schedule is developed following
this procedure. The schedule is subject to change as learning priority
needs change.

This same procedure can be followed in terms of group of students revealing
common selection characteristics.

PRESENT SITUATION Limited student understanding of group and individual value structure development process

WHAT STUDENT WILL DO
Reading - Changes in American Customs
Identify major custom changes and reasons for 50% of time be self-directed. Identify class habits and related values

PROGRESS CHECKPOINTS
Student use of skills needed for gathering information
Student organization - time and materials
Weekly check of progress rate objective attainment
DATE 1-8-XX

AGREED UPON DESIRED SITUATION
(OBJECTIVE) To identify specific ways customs
Determine or influence values

WHAT TEACHER WILL DO
Provide resource guidelines offer individual help
Help students identify and use needed functioning skills
Help student analyze data

DATE OF OBJECTIVE ATTAINMENT
2-5-XX

STUDENT J. Arnold

TEACHER Mr. Evans

PARENT R. Arnold

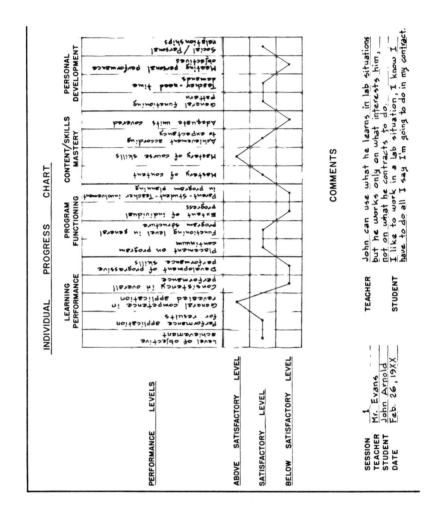

TIME MANAGEMENT ANALYSIS

STUDENT TIME DEMANDS

PERIOD 1 American Customs

ANTICIPATED TEACHER-NEED TIME 50%

OBJECTIVE (S) To identify specific ways customs determine values

ACTIVITIES	MINUTES
	Out-of-Class
Research	30
Discussion	30
Writing	

DOMINANT TEACHER ROLE

Provided resource guidelines served in resource capacity

METHODS / TECHNIQUES USED

Small group discussions individual help conferences Student writing on Reports

MINUTES DEMANDED BY STUDENTS

40

WHAT WAS ACTUALLY ACCOMPLISHED

Some writing progress Limited progress in group analysis of data

REVISED ANTICIPATED TEACHER

NEED TIME 50%

WHAT WAS EFFECTIVE?

Student use of individual help and report writing

WHAT WAS INEFFECTIVE?

Group self-direction in discussions

CHANGES TO BE MADE IN

TEACHER OPERATIONAL METHODS

Devote more time participating in group discussions in guidance role

APPENDIX II

Following are detailed specific school situations and suggested starting points for the implementation of the performance results curriculum in terms of the facilitating and restricting forces inherent within each of the delineated program structures. No attempt has been made to identify any specific school or its program. The specific characteristics used can be found in many schools across the country.

The specific examples given represent characteristics of small and large schools, middle, senior, and elementary levels, stable and rapidly growing communities, and traditional and innovative faculties. Though specific implementation details and procedures may vary in accordance with individual school situational demands, the aspects presented here can, in one way or another, serve as basic guidelines for staff development and implementation of a performance results curricular structure.

SCHOOL A

Size—1100 students—grades 5-9

Basic Program—academic, college preparatory-oriented, some career education, primarily departmentalized

Special Features—open-ended programming in electives, mini-course based, performance results emphasis, teaming, variable student grouping, multi-level teaching assignments

Staff Traits—innovative, capable of designing, implementing, and evaluating programs, performance-oriented, strong leadership at administrative, departmental, and team levels, develops program in terms of "change" as a basic function of school

Community—middle and upper middle socio-economic level, college preparatory-oriented, interested in participating in program development, experiencing rapid growth with a consequent force working on community value
structure

This school has the basic structure and staff to implement a
performance results structure. A limited amount of time would
have to be devoted to preparational in-service endeavors. Instead,
emphasis could be placed on developing a plan of action based on
the existing program structure and staff skills.

Specific planning would be necessary in terms of broadening the
emphasis from college preparatory programming only to programming in terms of present and future learner needs, and
maintaining a balance related to community concerns. Of particular emphasis, would be departmental-level activities focused on
using the open-ended mini-course structure as a basis for developing the overall program structure.

This school staff, in preparation for full implementation of a
performance results structure, would concentrate on such major
areas as

1. Developing a needs and demand assessment procedure
2. Reassessing the school objectives more in terms of applied performance rather than primarily in terms of future collegiate needs
3. Initiating an in-service program geared to the development of total
   staff proficiency in program design, development, and assessment in
   terms of needs projection
4. Defining job demands and delineating staff assignments in terms of
   the consequent roles and responsibilities
5. Restructuring the overall program and departmental sub-programs in
   terms of progressive stages and sequent performance objectives
6. Incorporating the short course structure in all departmental areas
7. Instituting a learning management approach at the individual teacher,
   team, departmental, and building levels
8. Capitalizing on community support of the existing program and
   work for their support of desired performance changes

SCHOOL B

Size—1500 students—grades 10-12

Basic Program—comprehensive high school, departmentalized, primarily
academic, but with some vocational offerings, primarily a traditional

approach to programming of instruction, progressively fewer graduated attending college

Special Features—implementation of a variable scheduling structure, nine-week and 18-week elective courses

Staff Traits—primarily traditional operational patterns, some staff members want to implement new programming approaches; others changing as a result of program structure forces, strong administrative leadership, limited strength at departmental level

Community—low-to-upper middle socio-economic level, above average school enrollment turnover, rapidly growing area, but trend to non-college student influx, some expressed concern for more practical education

This high school is experiencing forced change. In the past, the community was college-oriented. The school, basically, still reflects this emphasis. All staff members are concerned about this change. A number of them, however, have made little, or no, effort to adjust their classroom structures or demands to meet the changing learner and community needs.

There can develop in this school a gap between various faculty groups and between the school and the changing community. Though, through the efforts of the school administration, some department chairmen, and a number of teachers, some change in program structure has been implemented, the total staff must make a concerted effort to be more responsive to the students and to the changing community in terms of more emphasis on applied performance.

To implement a performance results curricular structure, this school needs to place special emphasis on such areas as

1. Determining the changing demands and patterns of the community and the consequent role and responsibilities of the school
2. Identifying the needs of the students and the program structure that best facilitates the school's helping to meet these needs
3. Developing objectives at the building and departmental levels that are cohesive enough to facilitate the development of a total staff commitment to a common effort toward attaining learner objectives
4. Implementing a continuous in-service programming approach that will provide staff members with the skills to develop the program in terms of performance results, beyond the variable scheduling and shorter elective course time demands

5. Developing a procedure that will facilitate the expansion of the shorter course approach into all departments
6. Developing total program stages, learning and teaching operational demands, and sequent program objectives that reflect application of learned skills and content
7. Implementing a staff self-appraisal practice that stresses student action and application as well as teaching attributes
8. Developing a time line detailing needed program changes, staff demand and operational changes, expected performance results, both learner and teacher, and sequent stage development, and expected implementation dates

SCHOOL C
(first year of operation)

Size—250 students—grades 5-8

Basic Program—traditional academic emphasis as determined by district guidelines for required courses

Special Features—short courses as part of the activity period, rotation of periods on a quarter basis

Staff Traits—experienced in traditional self-contained or departmental structure (depending on their previous assignments), staff selected because of their interest in middle school program development, initiated in-service activities to provide themselves with stronger program design backgrounds

Community—small town tradition, low-to-middle socio-economic level, stable, but growing slowly, limited interest in schools but want education to be useful, feels influence of large metropolis close by

This is the first year this school has been in operation. The staff, in this first year, is attempting to develop and implement a more open program structure that is more responsive to the expanding needs and interests of the students than were the programs within which the individual staff members functioned previously. They have been given adequate latitude, and strong support, from the central office to develop this program.

The school staff, as a whole, is inexperienced in total program design and implementation. Consequently, as the school year progresses, the staff members will function as they did in their previous assignments, but at the same time, they will be attempting to develop a curricular structure that will change their operational emphases in terms of performance results.

In terms of staff experience in opening a new school and in developing new programs, these staff members need to concentrate on such areas as

1. Identifying present program effectiveness and improvement methods that reflect staff, student, and community thinking
2. Developing in-service activities that will help staff members gain the skills needed for effective program development
3. Identifying the desired program characteristics, the consequent staff/student functioning demands, and existing staff talents in terms of these demands
4. Developing procedures for restructuring and implementing the traditional course guidelines into the shorter time spans desired by the staff
5. Concentrating on individual performance effectiveness as the staff develops the various functioning stages of the program. Unless staff members can function effectively at each stage level, they will not be able to function satisfactorily within the total program demands
6. Identifying desired skill, content, and functioning capabilities the learners will have when they have completed the three-year program
7. Developing an implementation time line identifying sequent program stage implementation, staff skills to be gained, operational pattern changes, and student/staff progress checkpoints

SCHOOL D

Size—2600 students—grades 10-12

Basic Program—traditional departmentalized structure with required subjects designed in terms of nine-month constant time demands, strong academic emphasis for 55 percent of students who are planning to go to college

Special Features—strong vocational and building trades program, time available for student option use

Staff Traits—subject matter-oriented, emphasize traditional content approaches in classes, limited interest in inter-departmental program development, yet, forward-looking in terms of improving own areas of interest, a number of staff members can be considered as change agents

Community—industrial, low-to-upper middle socio-economic levels, strong emphasis on both vocational and academic school programming, confidence in schools, but want input in planning for change

This school possesses characteristics common to many large high schools throughout the country. There has been competent administrative leadership at the building level and, in some areas, at the departmental level. There is desire for change on the parts of some faculty members, but the existing operational demands, of program and other staff members, tend to limit their effectiveness as change agents beyond their individual assignments.

Because of the singular emphases of the school, academic and vocational, it is important that individual staff members be responsive to the interest of the community and students in applied performance. In order to be responsive to student performance demands, staff members need to design the school program and faculty operational patterns to coincide with the functioning needs of the students. Since students in both the college preparatory and vocational programs identify specific results objectives, the staff must develop a program structure that facilitates student attainment of these objectives.

To implement the performance-oriented framework, the staff needs to concentrate on such areas as

1. Identifying common and differing areas of emphasis of the college preparatory and vocational programs
2. Developing an in-service program designed to bring the staff into agreement on major purposes and results objectives of the school
3. Identifying student needs, staff talents, and programming structures that will best facilitate the matching of needs and talents
4. Expanding the student options approach to all areas of the curriculum. This entails the development of performance objectives for each subject area
5. Developing a program structure that uses time as a variable, and changing student needs as a basis for continuous program development
6. Taking advantage of existing desires for change of some faculty members, and using them as a cadre of change agents to bring about performance and structural change in other areas and other people
7. Implementing the module course structure in all areas of the instructional program

BIBLIOGRAPHY

BOOKS

1. Bruner, Jerome, *The Process of Education.* Cambridge, Mass., Harvard University Press, 1966.
2. Paulson, Robert, *American Education: Challenges and Images.* Tucson, Arizona, The University of Arizona Press, 1967.
3. Redfern, George B., *How to Appraise Teaching Performance.* Columbus, Ohio, School Management Institute, 1963.
4. Rogers, Carl, *Freedom to Learn.* Columbus, Ohio, Charles E. Merrill, 1969.
5. Stradley, William E., *A Practical Guide to the Middle School.* New York, The Center for Applied Research in Education, Inc., 1971.
6. Stroin, Robert, *Teachers and the Learning Process.* Englewood Cliffs, New Jersey, Prentice-Hall, Inc., 1970.
7. Umans, Shelly, *The Management of Education.* New York, Doubleday and Company, 1970.
8. Weber, Lillian, *The English Infant School and Informal Education.* Englewood Cliffs, New Jersey, Prentice-Hall, Inc., 1971.
9. Wiley, W. Deane, and Bishop, Lloyd, *The Flexibly Scheduled High School.* West Nyack, New York, Parker Publishing Company, Inc., 1968.

ARTICLES

1. Cereghino, Edward, "Administrator: Target for Today," *The Clearing House* (May, 1971)
2. Fox, A.M., and Hein, D.D., "Teacher Perceptions in Effective Teaching," *Colorado Journal of Education Research,* (Spring, 1971)

3. Frazier, William, and Bedley, Gene, "Administrator Support System—A Strategy To Develop Performance Evaluation," *THRUST for Education Leadership,* (November, 1972)

4. Glasser, William, "Roles, Goals, and Failure," *Today's Education,* (October, 1971)

5. Gonzalez, Michael, "Humanistic Learning," *Science Teacher,* (February, 1972)

6. Grayboff, Marilyn, "Tool for Building Accountability: The Performance Contract," *Journal of Secondary Education,* (December, 1970)

7. James, Loren, and James, Virginia, "Creating Opportunities for Individual Growth," *Bulletin of National Association of Secondary School Principals,* (February, 1972)

8. Mattas, Frank, "Problem Solving: A Decision-Making Process—Component 2," *ACSA Project Leadership, Association of California School Administrators,* (December/January, 1972)

9. Ojemann, Ralph, "Self-Guidance as an Education Goal and the Selection of Objectives," *The Elementary School Journal,* (February, 1972)

10. Rogers, Carl, "Forget You Are a Teacher," *Instructor,* (August/-September, 1971)

11. Stowe, Richard, "Instructional Development's the Thing," *Audiovisual Instruction,* (April, 1971)

INDEX

Accountability, 99, 101, 106, 112, 113, 119
Achievement, 61, 88, 197-199
Achievement application, 36, 61
Action guidelines, 43-44, 56-57, 58, 89, 91, 245-246
Adding and deleting courses, 75, 147
Administrative leadership, 63, 101, 141, 192-199
Administrative skills, 100-102
Administrator planning, 84, 99, 102, 141, 192-199
Administrator-teacher team, 50, 192-199
Adult courses, 84

Advisors groups, 99
Advisors, teachers, 108, 114, 116, 185-186, 215, 228
Affective domain, 24
Anecdotal records, 54
Anticipated learner needs, 27, 49, 62, 68, 70, 88, 119, 148
Anticipating learner changes, 63, 102, 122, 124, 132, 209, 219-220
Anticipating learner stages, 45, 61, 69, 97, 111, 131, 189, 318
Application of learning, 67, 75, 78, 114
Applied Performance progress, 27, 54, 114, 154, 168, 182
Appraisal options, 87-88, 105, 169, 221, 227, 253
Appraisal techniques, 41, 64, 75, 249
Appraising student progress, 52, 54, 64, 169, 170, 182, 221, 249

Arapahoe County School District Six, 27, 141
Areas of Teacher specialization, 47, 101, 114, 145, 168, 180, 192
Areas, open need, 76

Articulation and coordination of sub-programs, 61, 65
Articulation of learning units, 29, 41, 54, 98, 143, 166
Assessment check points, 69, 70, 88, 169, 170, 192-199, 239, 243
Assumptive criteria, 27, 181
Atlanta, Georgia Public Schools, 61, 81
Attitudes, learner, 11, 37, 102, 107, 124
Authority, 112-114, 192, 199
Avoiding learner conflicts, 53, 60, 77, 112, 203, 205, 210-211
Awarding credit, 77, 112, 169, 175, 182, 203-205

Basic determiners of functioning patterns, 30, 54, 67, 108, 123
Basic learning skills, 25, 41, 71-72, 75, 123, 126
Basic planning keys, staff, 27, 181
Basic skills classes, 25, 41, 66, 72-75, 109
Behaviors of learning, 207, 213, 215
Broad objectives, 32, 108, 138-141, 217-218
Budgets, building, 86-87, 145, 241, 243
Building administrators, 100-101, 231-232
Building contracting form, 139
Building leadership effectiveness, 63, 84, 100, 163
Building intern activities, 71, 187-188, 243
Building level programs, 76, 114, 154, 168, 255-256

Calendar, instructional, 80
California, State of, 185
Capabilities of staff, 30
Career counseling, 25
Challenge courses, 76-77

Change, 62, 72, 92, 111, 145, 175, 176, 185, 210-212, 247
Change agents, 51, 175-176, 185, 247, 255-256
Change-oriented approaches, 62, 175-176, 178, 247, 255-256
Changing learner needs, 41, 111, 176, 247, 255-256
Changing learning endeavors, 92, 123, 176, 247
Changing needs, 92, 111, 131, 175-176, 255-256
Changing program demands, 59, 175, 247, 256
Characteristics, learning structure, 107'
Charting individual progress, 54, 123
Check lists, 54
Chronometry and demand, 48
Class attendance requirements, 77
Class discussions, 66
Class size, 146-147
Class scheduling, 45, 126, 127, 131, 183
Classroom demands, 37, 60, 67, 77, 123, 259
Classroom operations, 49, 123, 141, 183, 244
Clerical pools, 99
Closed space ideas, 92-93
Cognitive domain, 24, 53, 175
Colorado Department of Institutions, 176-177
Common learning, 61
Communications and electricity, 37
Communications, parent-teacher, 87, 108, 111, 145, 187
Community-student program, 79, 182, 258
Conferences, 60, 87, 126, 127, 128
Conflicts, 60, 77, 112, 169, 175, 182, 203, 205, 210-211, 213-214
Content pre-requisites, 61
Continua, 102, 106, 178
Continuous Objective attainment record, 71, 240
Continuous progress, 63, 70, 84, 111, 131, 166, 185
Continuous stage locations, 41, 63, 84, 111, 131, 166, 178
Continuum, 69, 102, 111, 169, 178
Continuum subject matter sequence, 95, 178
Contracting, 238-239, 245
Controversial topics, 32
Correspondence courses, 78
Counselors, 50, 76, 100, 108-109, 127, 139, 183

Course content development, 84, 124, 147
Course experiences, 53, 147, 183
Course, unit adaptability, 41, 141, 147, 183
Creating sequential module units, 29, 35, 41, 45, 54, 209, 240-241, 248-250
Credit for achievement, 70, 176
Crises levels, 51
Curriculum, 240, 244, 245, 248, 254, 255
Cycling of courses, 29, 41, 54, 64, 166

Daily time schedule, 29, 77, 124, 209, 212, 240-241, 250
Decision-making, 67, 221, 224
Decision-making and performance attainment, 50, 221-224
Defensive teaching, 49
Delegating responsibility, 50, 61, 67, 124, 186, 195
Delegation of activities, 49-50
Delegating teacher functioning demands, 47, 147
Department chairmen, 63, 84, 163
Departmental objectives, 41, 163, 247
Designing program structures, 60, 94, 101, 226, 235, 249
Determining instructional stopping points, 70-73
Determining performance results levels, 65, 68-70, 123, 183, 244
Developing broad course frameworks, 32, 141, 183, 240-241, 248-249
Developing individualized progress chart, 53
Developing the instructional environment, 41, 59, 134, 224-225
Developing learning conditions, 69, 147, 240, 244, 245
Developing progress criteria, 68-70, 148, 168, 188, 253
Developing teacher assignments, 45-46, 61, 114, 124
Developing teacher functioning patterns, 67, 93, 99, 124, 168, 188, 215
Developing teacher need time, 47, 49, 61, 186, 195, 227-228
Development of course content, 24, 33, 41, 147, 183
Diagnostic methods, 37, 53, 60, 68, 70, 88, 148, 183
Diagnostic needs, 54, 83, 98, 148, 168
Differentiated staffing, 107, 121, 131-132, 183, 256
Direction, learning endeavors, 59, 123, 141, 145, 183, 212-213

Distribution of instructional time, 50, 61, 124, 181, 186, 195
District staffing structure, 107, 132
District testing program, 82-83, 135, 136
Dress codes, 60

Educational literature, 100
Effective change procedures, 63, 148, 247, 255-256
Effective learner programming, 45, 111, 176, 247
Elective courses, 31, 75, 166, 183
Elementary electricity, 36-37
Environment of learning, 67, 76, 103-104, 124, 130, 154
Establishing individual objectives, 37, 68, 103-104, 111
Evaluating curricular aspects, 49, 62, 64, 68, 70, 148
Evaluation, 98-99, 119, 148, 168, 182, 253
Evaluation processes, 51, 64, 83, 88, 119, 148, 168, 182
Evaluative and diagnostic methods, 53, 60, 64, 68, 70, 88, 119, 148, 182, 253
Evaluative criteria framework, 69-70, 88, 119, 148, 182, 248, 253
Example, Educational environment, 76
Example,Individualized progress chart, 54
Example,Teacher-learning performance objectives, 24, 61
Example,Teacher scheduling, 93
Example,Time management analysis, 52
Example,Staff operational skills, 90
Excessive student dependence, 49, 68, 104, 124
Expanding the program structure, 65, 75, 147
Expectancy of teachers, 50, 93, 99, 224-225
Extended days, 78
Extending results approaches beyond the building level, 50, 86, 97, 109-110
Extension classes, 77

Facilities, 37
Faculty advisor, 38
Faculty operational patterns, 93, 101, 131, 181, 183, 235, 248
Federal accountability, 99
Feedback, individual, 102, 168, 171, 237, 249, 253
Financing, 37
Flexibility, 27, 75, 82, 87, 141, 143, 164, 166, 213

Flexible teacher assignments, 47, 75, 131, 141, 143, 164, 166, 213
Flexible use of time, 47, 75, 143, 164, 166
Flow chart, organizational, 116-117, 179
Focus on planning, 48, 98, 108, 181, 186, 195, 225-228
Forcasting learner need, 37, 41, 49, 124, 130, 154
Formal content, 67, 77, 87, 126, 147, 183
Formal student observation, 64, 68, 70, 148, 168, 182, 253
Formulating action techniques, 124, 179, 225, 228, 244
Forty-five fifteen plan, 81
Framework, action, 29, 122, 179, 209, 240
Functioning characteristics, staff, 93, 101, 106, 141, 192, 195
Functioning demands of progress, 148-150, 154, 168
Functioning need changes of learners, 42, 131, 168, 188, 255-256

Gapping between learning levels and teacher demands, 41, 64, 72, 107, 180, 187
Gapping of objectives, 41, 63, 180, 187
Goals, operational, 65, 76, 84, 163
Goddard Middle School, 22, 35, 39, 79, 129, 155, 189
Grading, 88, 130, 145, 150, 169, 221, 222, 249
Group guidance, 25, 84, 127, 139, 183
Group objectives, 103, 106, 108, 138
Group personalities, 108, 183
Group value conflicts, 31, 65, 85, 183
Grouping and sequencing of courses, 24, 147, 183
Groups, building administrators, 99, 101, 104, 106, 147, 197-199
Guidance and counseling, 30, 50, 76-77, 108-109, 127, 139, 183
Guidance team structure, 39
Guide to faculty objectives, 99, 103, 106, 148-150, 215
Guidelines, 239

Help, clerical, 99
Homework, 48
"How to" approaches, 72, 98
How to modify the closed program structure, 25-26, 29, 72, 114, 129
Human aspects of learning, 66-67, 208-209
"Human error" problems, 104

Human relations, 108, 208

Idea creation, 78, 181, 186, 199, 227-228
Identified learning priorities, 40, 42, 64, 205-206
Identifying learning levels, 35, 69, 97-98, 102, 180, 183, 244
Identifying specific objectives, 27, 42, 64, 87, 124, 132, 183
Implementing curricula aspects, 48, 147, 240, 244, 248
Improving teacher effectiveness, 52, 114-116, 148-150, 185-186, 215
Increasing learner performance, 54, 59, 70, 72, 75, 99, 227, 235
Independent study, 25
Individual adjustment, 25, 46, 62, 75
Individualized appraisal, 53, 61-62, 82, 136, 205-206, 239, 258
Individualized need scheduling, 27, 42, 46, 62, 64, 137, 205-206
Individualized support programs, 51, 205-206
Inflexible teachers, 26, 75
Influences of program on performance patterns, 65, 69, 99, 154, 168, 188, 217
Indicators of performance, 66-70, 77, 119, 148, 168, 182, 253
Initiating change, 62, 72, 92, 111, 125, 176, 185, 210-212, 247
Innovative techniques, 45, 48, 98, 181, 186, 195, 209, 240-241
Innovators, 51, 103, 135, 254
In-service programs, 63, 102, 108, 120-122, 137, 151-152, 155, 157, 200-202, 228-230, 244-246, 254, 256-259
Instructional attitudes, 46-47, 72, 136-137
Instructional attrition, 41, 189-196, 248
Instructional calendar, 80
Instructional-learning teams, 41, 50, 66-67, 69, 150, 227-228
Instructional variables, 50, 61, 114, 123, 141, 255-256
Instructor-learner cooperation, 69, 75, 123, 141, 150, 224, 227-228
Interdepartmental planning, 41, 75, 139, 141, 166
Interest-time-pressure conflicts, 49, 61, 72, 75, 124
Inter-disciplinary courses, 35, 101, 139, 141, 166
Inter-division sequences, 35, 101, 106, 139

Inter-level interaction, 83, 114, 141, 145, 183
Intra-division emphases, 35, 101, 131, 139, 141

Job delineation, 106, 120-122
Job functioning patterns, 108, 220
Job realities, 112

Keying to student strengths, 53, 62, 66-70, 137, 205-206

Leadership, staff, 99, 127, 132, 145, 250 255
Learner attitudes, 37, 102, 107, 124
Learner function emphases, 65, 102, 122, 179, 225
Learner-oriented structure, 37, 87, 124, 181, 209, 244
Learner progress and expectations, 103-104, 123, 132, 141
Learner reaction to instructional techniques, 68-70, 123, 187-188
Learner self-diagnosis approaches, 49, 77, 189, 209, 244, 248-250
Learner self-evaluation, 69-70, 123, 132, 189, 219-220
Learning achievement, 51-64, 70, 83, 218, 244
Learning activities, 41, 68-69, 84, 111, 131, 211, 257
Learning continua, 24, 41, 54, 61, 62, 69, 103, 126
Learning priorities needs, 23, 97-98, 106, 124, 154, 168, 188
Learning reasons, 22, 35, 180, 247, 255
Learning role, 54, 111, 115-116, 148-150, 168
Learning satisfaction point, 69
Learning skills, 25, 41, 63, 72-75, 126
Learning tasks, 69, 102, 178, 224-225, 248
Learning unit selection, 41, 114, 147, 186, 225-229
Lesson planning, 50-51, 130, 154, 160, 162
Leveled course selection, 27, 141, 147, 183, 209
Littleton, Colorado, Public Schools, 61, 141
Littleton High School, 72
Local budgeting, 86-87
Localized evaluation, 83
Locked-in Teacher assignments, 46, 93, 111, 130, 183
Louisville, Colorado, Middle School, 108

Maintaining on-going programs, 47, 114, 225-226, 235-237
Management systems, personal, 114, 145, 155, 214, 225, 238
Managerial structure, 100, 145, 155, 214, 225, 238
Managing and organization, 51, 145, 238
Managing time, 151, 155, 238
Master schedules, 26-28, 143
Measuring achievement, 27, 53, 83, 148-150, 188, 215
Methods of evaluation, 51, 64, 70
Methods of using support personnel, 50, 86, 97
Middle level English program, 212-213
Middle school, 22, 62, 108, 129, 211, 257
Modular framework, 29, 41, 45, 53, 166, 212
Module courses, 209, 240-241, 248-250
Module courses blocks, 41, 54
Moline, Illinois, High School, 154
Motivation, 28, 122, 131, 136, 141, 143, 145-146, 149, 192, 199, 208-209, 220
Motivational change, 98, 208-209, 220
Multiple curricular resources, 42, 54, 238-239, 245
Multiple-level staffing, 88-89, 94, 99

Necessary instructional time, 47, 53, 59, 123-124, 132, 186, 195
Need emphases, 35, 67, 180, 209, 218, 259
Needs assessment indicators, 88, 124, 147
Needs, changing learner, 41, 111, 176-177, 247, 255, 256
Needs for knowing, student, 60, 77, 87, 123, 141, 155, 244
Negative approaches to learning, 53, 67, 93, 143
New program development, 29, 45, 104, 114, 141, 181, 186, 192, 259
New students, 125
Ninth grade mathematics, 37
Ninth grade social studies, 37

Objectives, building, 101, 103, 106, 138, 248
Off campus classes, 73
On-the-job training, 79, 98, 187
Open choice selections, classes, 75, 224-225
Open-ended methods, 92, 224-225
Open-ended program, 34, 75, 134, 224-225
Open need classes, 76, 134, 224-225

Open personal needs classes, 29, 67, 123, 141
Open staff roles and responsibilities, 93, 99
Open staffing, 88-89, 94, 99
Operation, intra-building, 100, 236, 237
Operational learning structure, 95, 114, 134, 195, 249
Operational tool selection system, 50, 54, 123, 141, 183
Optional grading systems, 88
Options and alternatives, 70, 87-88, 134, 221-222, 226, 248, 251
Oral reviews, 68
Organizational chart, programs, 116-118, 249
Organizational framework, 41, 94, 101, 222, 228, 249
Organizational management, 49, 51, 61, 124, 186, 195, 249
Organizational patterns, 106, 108, 118, 134
Organizational proficiency, improving, 129, 134, 249
Orientation sessions, 156, 187
Out-of-class time for learners, 48
Out-of-school activities, 78
Overall program balance, 37, 95, 99, 114, 168, 243
Overlapping of division emphases, 34, 139, 161, 166

Paper work, 66
Parent involvement, 38, 54, 86, 111, 116, 124
Parental images, 54, 116, 124
Parental influences, 65, 84, 116, 124
Peer pressure, 65
Planning time allotments, 49
Performance appraisal, 50, 68, 77, 83, 87, 92, 110, 135, 138-141, 154
Performance data file, 130-131, 233-236
Performance expectations, 35, 83, 106, 138-141, 154, 188
Performance graphing, 54, 184-185, 188
Performance levels, 66-67, 69-70, 102, 112, 138-141, 154
Performance objectives, 22, 104-105, 135, 138-141, 154, 217-218, 231, 257
Performance results curriculum, 42, 64, 83, 87, 92, 102, 135, 141, 154, 257
Personal and change continua, 26, 38, 46, 76, 88
Personalized programming, 188, 192-197, 219-220, 231
Philosophy of learning, 22, 65, 67, 76, 93, 103, 106, 114, 158

Plan books, 51, 102, 130
Plug-in course characteristics, 53
Pop quizzes, 68
Power structure, classroom, 107, 123, 259
Practical learning approaches, 67, 75, 114
Primary teacher functions, 47, 95, 106
Principal's role in program development, 99, 102
Priority development, 98, 106, 124, 126, 235, 237
Program flexibility, 25-26, 114, 255-256
Program forces and demands, 69, 99, 154, 168, 188
Program restrictions, 5, 37, 114, 243
Program specialization, 93, 115-116, 168
Program staffing demands, 95, 99
Progress assessment, 53, 83, 111, 122, 148-150, 154, 168, 188, 217-218
Progressive performance demands, 59, 106, 115-116, 168
Projecting time allottments, 29, 225-226
Projecting student needs, 29, 225-226, 256
Psycho-motor domain, 24
Public education seminars, 85-87
Public relations, 38, 86, 116, 124, 168

Quality control, 99
Quizzes, 68

Reacting change agents, 51, 63, 175-176, 185, 247, 255
Readiness levels, 124
Recognizing needed staff talents, 37, 66, 96, 127, 256
Re-inforcing instruction, 29, 82, 87, 211, 218-220, 241
Relating process to achievement, 71, 123, 141, 183, 209, 244, 248, 256
Relationships, learning activities and objectives, 69, 123, 132, 141, 209, 259
Relevant learning, 25, 51, 71, 75, 114, 127, 240-250
Required courses, 30, 61, 62, 75, 183
Reporting student progress, 87-88, 126-127, 130, 145, 150, 169
Resource persons, 46, 50, 86, 97, 109-110, 119
Responsibility levels, 102, 110, 181, 186, 231-232, 255-256
Results objectives, 69, 104, 106, 130, 231-232
Results-oriented program, 59, 154, 168, 188, 211-213
Results-oriented teacher, 70, 104, 131-132, 211, 214, 255-256

Re-training and change, 98, 175-176, 178, 247, 256
Rigidity of program demands, 63, 143, 222, 256, 257-258
Roosevelt Elementary School District, 214
Ryan Memorial High School, 219

Sample middle level science series, 35
Sample module units, 28
School industry relationships, 78, 132
Self-evaluation, 38, 72, 83, 103, 189-196, 219-220, 239, 241, 243
Self-satisfying learning, 31, 65, 189, 219, 220
Sequential instruction, 79, 105, 242
Sequential performance demands, 59-71
Sequential skill classes, 27, 41, 123, 126, 167
Shifting to personal interaction emphasis, 25, 108, 208
Short term student needs, 41, 127, 131-132
Short-course structure, 26, 75, 97, 109-110, 141
Short-course term scheduling, 46, 109-110, 132, 141-143, 145-146
Short-term units, 51, 109, 110, 174
Skills courses, 25, 41, 72-75, 126
Skill use levels, 19, 41, 123, 126
Small appliance repair, 68
Social interaction, 25, 66-67, 108, 208-209
Special needs courses, 25
Special programs and facilities, 75, 104, 141
Special projects, 71
Specific course structuring, 29, 45, 53, 212, 240, 241, 248-250
Staff functioning patterns, 25, 250, 255
Staff talents, 37, 127, 256
Staff offerings as learner tools, 42, 132, 208, 251, 256
Staff patterns, 93, 102, 131, 132
Staff scheduling, 25, 46, 93, 113, 141-143, 183, 256
Staffing, multi-levels, 89, 102, 131-132, 145
Staffing effectiveness, 88-89, 102, 131-132, 145
Staffing variations, 46, 141-143, 146
Standardized appraisal system, 23, 66, 82
State of Colorado, 72
Status quo conditions, 48, 112, 159, 160, 162

Structuring the curricular framework, 23, 41, 54, 248-250
Student assistants, 51
Student conflicts, 46, 123, 132, 218
Student-counselor-advisor conferences, 38, 60, 87, 126-128
Student evaluation, 53, 60, 68-70, 83
Student help requests, 48, 54, 69, 70, 123, 132, 218
Student functioning problems, 30, 54, 67, 123
Student interest demands, 41, 54, 67, 123
Student module scheduling, 31, 141, 183
Student needs, 49, 69-70, 209, 259
Student objectives, 38, 77, 123
Student performance usage, 70, 132, 141, 244
Student progress appraisal, 27, 67, 123
Student-teacher interviews, 66, 187-188
Student time allottments, 49, 75, 124, 132
Sub-course units, 35, 51, 174, 180
Sub-objectives, 29, 174, 180
Sub-program articulation, 61, 174, 180
Support courses, 46, 109-110
Support personnel, 50, 86, 97

Teacher action areas, 114, 115, 116
Teacher functioning skills, 63, 101
Teacher functioning patterns, 47, 101, 186, 187, 188
Teacher input, 54, 99, 186, 195
Teacher-learner objectives, 23, 185, 186
Teacher need time, 49, 50, 51, 109, 181
Teacher objectives, 40, 95, 99, 114, 168, 188
Teacher preplanning, 99, 148-150, 215
Teacher self studies, 47, 189-196, 219-220
Teacher scheduling, 93, 141, 180, 183, 259
Teacher skill use levels, 49, 72, 75, 123, 126
Teacher-student-parent team, 54, 61, 69, 227, 228, 242, 248
Teacher-student expectations, 13, 99, 227-228, 242, 248
Teaching-emphasis positions, 65, 181, 183, 244
Teaching-learning processes, 99, 123, 141, 183, 248-250
Teaching-learning sequences, 51, 181
Teaching operational effectiveness, 94, 101
Teaching roles and responsibilities, 48, 181, 186, 192, 222, 228
Teaching priorities and functioning patterns, 48, 98, 106, 126, 235

Teachers as managers, 48, 181, 186, 195, 225, 227, 228
Team leaders, 66, 69, 150, 224
Team student-counselor-parent advisor, 38, 61-67, 227, 228
Testing, standardized, 82, 220
Time allottment, 75, 124
Time and conflict areas, 49, 61, 124
Time and management effectiveness, 51, 61, 124, 186, 195
Time as a variable, 27, 61
Time expenditure, 50, 61, 124, 181, 227, 228
Time-interest-pressure-conflicts, 49, 61, 72, 75, 124
Time scheduling, 45, 61, 114
Total program functioning, 54, 186
Total staff objectives, 93, 99, 102, 106, 138, 152
Traditional course divisions, 26, 143, 222, 256, 257, 258
Traditional grading methods, 54, 88, 130
Traditional program structure, 93, 94
Traditional schedule sample, 28, 143, 222
Transitional program structure, 59, 181
Tutor, 50, 76
Typical continual characteristics, 25, 102, 106, 148
Typing, 46

Unit adaptability, 114, 141, 168, 225-229, 188
Unit tests, 66, 168, 220
Units, course time, 28, 61, 124, 186, 227
Units of study, 147, 168, 209, 212
Units, learning, continuity, 41, 54, 185, 209
Updating of time line, 63
Updating courses, 147
Use of supervisors, 46, 86, 109-110
Using a module structure, 26, 29, 41, 54, 64, 166, 209, 240
Utilizing performance contracting, 138-141
Utilizing teacher time, 47, 49, 51, 61, 124, 186, 195
Utilizing unit series, 41, 42, 54, 209, 240-241

Value system of learner, 65, 85
Variable grouping, 45, 61, 63, 114, 123, 141, 183
Variable scheduling framework, 27, 255, 256
Variations in performance levels, 67, 68, 123, 132, 141

Various performance needs, 30, 54, 67, 122, 132, 244
Varying demand forces, 55, 122, 141, 183
Varying teacher assignments, 46, 122, 180-183, 244
Varying teaching learning condition, 66, 94, 101, 195, 227
Viable areas of evaluation, 148
Vocational needs, 72, 259
Volunteer lay aides, 50, 99

Ways and means committee, 99

Work experience, 67, 75, 78, 114, 132
Work program assignments, 25
Working methods, 29, 78, 132, 167
Writing learning objectives, 22, 41, 101, 103, 130, 154, 176, 217-218, 231
Written test performance, 47, 53, 72, 82, 88, 220

Yearly Objectives, 29, 101, 103, 106, 138, 248
Year-round quarter plan, 81